The Search for God
in Ancient Egypt

The Search for God
in Ancient Egypt

JAN ASSMANN

*translated from
the German by
David Lorton*

Cornell University Press
Ithaca & London

German edition, *Ägypten: Theologie und Frömmigkeit einer frühen Hochkultur*, © 1984
by W. Kohlhammer GmbH

First English-language edition, with revisions and additions by the author
English translation copyright © 2001 by Cornell University

The translation of this work was published with the assistance of Inter Nationes.

First published 2001 by Cornell University Press
First printing, Cornell Paperbacks, 2001

Printed in the United States of America

Library of Congress Cataloging-in-Publication Data
Assmann, Jan.
   [Ägypten. English]
   The search for God in ancient Egypt / by Jan Assmann ; translated
from the German by David Lorton.
     p. cm.
   Includes bibliographical references and index.
   ISBN 0-8014-3786-5 (hardcover : alk. paper) — ISBN 0-8014-8729-3
(pbk. : alk. paper)
   1. Egypt—Religion. 2. Mythology, Egyptian. I. Title.
   BL2441.2 .A8713 2001
   292.2'11—dc21
                  00-012577

Cloth printing 10 9 8 7 6 5 4 3 2 1
Paperback printing 10 9 8 7 6 5 4 3 2 1

Aegyptus
deorum in terras suae religionis merito
sola deductio,
sanctitatis et pietatis magistra

Egypt,
the only land that by the strength of its religion
brought the gods down to the earth,
model of holiness and piety

—Asclepius 25

Contents

CONTENTS

Foreword to the German Edition

Culture is memory—so the definition of the Russian semiotician Yuri Lotman. If this is so, then we must admit that even today, 180 years after Champollion's decipherment of the hieroglyphs, the spiritual legacy of the high culture of ancient Egypt has scarcely become a part of our own cultural recollection. It is an object of fascination, but we do not really comprehend it. And yet, sources of great antiquity and variety are at our disposal.

Such a cultural anamnesis propels this book. To this end, two hermeneutic approaches are employed, one historical and the other systematic. A historical approach exists when a chain of tradition serves to connect us to a temporally distant world. The tractate "Asclepius" from the Hermetic corpus, from which the epigraph of this volume is drawn, serves as an *entrée* into this representation of Egyptian religion. Faced with the threat of divine withdrawal and the destruction of the world, as described in detail in the apocalypse of the twenty-fifth chapter, Egypt is conjured up as the "temple of the world," the epitome of perfect divine presence, and handed down into the cultural recollection of the West. And although details were lost to this recollection, a Max Weber could view the history of religion as a process of disenchantment of the world. If this picture is accurate, then we must first of all reach back to ancient Egypt to encounter an image that is the opposite image of a "disenchanted" world.

The second approach is of a systematic nature. It consists of methodical comparisons and seeks to register positive concepts and to distinguish them from negated alternatives. Siegfried Morenz has already taken this route in defining Egyptian religion with the help of contrasting pairs:

traditional—not founded religion
cult—not a religion of the book
national—not universal religion

But these distinctions are all too unspecific. They state only what everyone knows: that Egyptian religion was not one of the few great revealed religions, but rather one of the rest, from which the revealed religions emphatically distinguished themselves. It is a comparison with these others that could be instructive.

In this study, an attempt will therefore be made to develop differentiated parameters for the comparison of religions on the basis of that of Egypt. Starting with the concept of divine presence so emphatically stressed in the "Asclepius," religion is characterized as a dialectic between divine presence and transcendence. Every contact with the divine entails consciousness of the alterity, the unavailability, the inaccessibility of the sacred, which exceeds the boundaries of its "contactability," although contact is also based on the existence of a sphere of religious communication that I call "divine presence." This sphere has dimensions that are specific to cultures and epochs, but which change and thus determine the distinctive profile of a religion in a given epoch. These "dimensions of divine presence" serve here as the basis of our treatment of Egyptian religion, while at the same time, they should provide a *tertium comparationis* for intercultural comparison.

It is hoped that this book will facilitate such comparative endeavors regarding Egyptian religion and culture, and consequently, the essence of religion and culture more generally. It is thus directed to all who concern themselves with these problems: historians, students and sociologists of religion, theologians, ethnologists, cultural anthropologists—and especially to readers to whom religion and culture mean something, even without immediate professional reasons.

My thanks are due to my publisher, W. Kohlhammer, for having created a forum for this crossdisciplinary dialogue and for allowing my voice to be heard in it.

For many improvements, I am grateful to my students during academic year 1982–1983, and in particular to Heike Guksch, who read the proofs with me.

Heidelberg, July 1984   JAN ASSMANN

Translator's Note

In this book, the following conventions have been followed in the citations from ancient texts:

Square brackets [ ] enclose words that have been restored in a lacuna.

An ellipsis . . . indicates that a word or words in the original text have been omitted in the citation.

An ellipsis in square brackets [. . .] indicates the presence of a lacuna for which no restoration has been attempted.

There is no single set of conventions for the English rendering of ancient Egyptian and modern Arabic personal and place names. Most of the names mentioned in this book occur in a standard reference work, John Baines and Jaromír Málek, *Atlas of Ancient Egypt* (New York, 1980), and the renderings here follow those in that volume. Of the two exceptions, one is the omission of the typographical sign for *ayin*; this consonant does not exist in English, and it was thought that its inclusion would serve only as a distraction to the reader. The other is the divine name Amun-Re, which is more consistent with the form Amun than is the Amon-Re of the *Atlas*.

The citation from Rainer Maria Rilke's nineteenth sonnet to Orpheus in chapter 3 is taken from *Sonnets to Orpheus*, translated by M. D. Herter Norton (New York, 1942), p. 53.

Egyptian religion is a huge and complex topic, and for more than three decades, Jan Assmann has been striving to achieve an understanding of its theological significance. This volume, which is a synthesis of his work, is thus of considerable importance, and it very much deserves to be put at the disposal of the English-speaking public. I wish to express my thanks to Cornell University Press for asking me to be involved with this project, and to Dr. Eckhard Eichler for his invaluable assistance while it was in progress.

D.L.

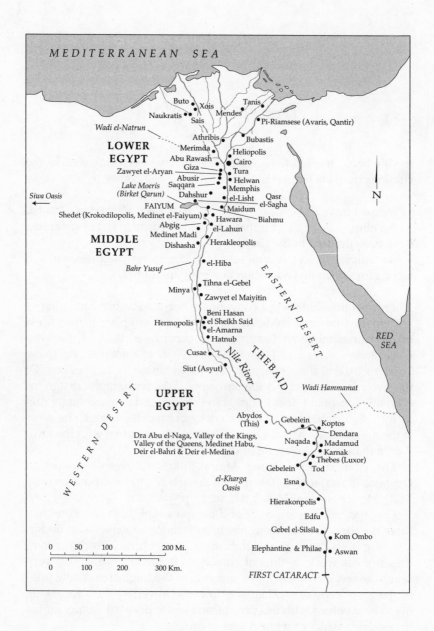

MEDITERRANEAN SEA

Buto
Xois
Tanis
Naukratis
Mendes
Sais
Pi-Riamsese (Avaris, Qantir)

Wadi el-Natrun
Athribis
Bubastis

**LOWER
EGYPT**
Merimda
Heliopolis
Abu Rawash
Cairo
Giza
Tura
Zawyet el-Aryan
Abusir
Helwan
Saqqara
Memphis
Lake Moeris
Dahshur
el-Lisht
Qasr
(Birket Qarun)
el-Sagha
FAIYUM
Maidum
Shedet (Krokodilopolis, Medinet el-Faiyum)
Hawara
Biahmu
Abgig
el-Lahun
Medinet Madi
**MIDDLE
EGYPT**
Dishasha
Herakleopolis

Bahr Yusuf
el-Hiba

Tihna el-Gebel
Minya
Zawyet el Maiyitin

Beni Hasan
el Sheikh Said
Hermopolis
el-Amarna
Hatnub

EASTERN DESERT

Cusae
RED
SEA
Siut (Asyut)

Nile River
THEBAID
**UPPER
EGYPT**

Wadi Hammamat

Abydos
Gebelein
(This)
Koptos
Dra Abu el-Naga, Valley of the Kings,
Dendara
Valley of the Queens, Medinet Habu,
Naqada
Madamud
Deir el-Bahri & Deir el-Medina
Karnak
Thebes (Luxor)
Gebelein
Tod
el-Kharga
Oasis
Esna

Hierakonpolis

WESTERN DESERT
Edfu

Gebel el-Silsila
Kom Ombo
Elephantine & Philae
Aswan

Siwa Oasis

N

0   50   100   200 Mi.

0   100   200   300 Km.

FIRST CATARACT

CHAPTER 1

Religion:
Divine Presence
and Transcendence

The ancient Egyptian language has no word for "religion," but the many treatments of Egyptian religion have encountered no difficulties in determining their subject; the relevant phenomena are clearly distinct within what remains to us of Egyptian culture. Best known is the case of the writing system: when we speak of "hieroglyphs," the picture writing of inscriptions on stone, and "hieratic," the cursive script of papyri and ostraca, we follow the usage of the Greeks, who opposed these sacred (Greek *hierós*, "sacred") writing systems to Demotic, the so-called profane (Greek *dêmos*, "people") writing system. We observe the same phenomenon of distinctiveness in architecture: over the course of time, from the middle of the third millennium B.C.E. on, the rule that sacred buildings were to be erected of stone and domestic structures of mud brick was ever more strictly observed. As in the case of language (and in the later periods, of writing systems), the concept of religion as put into practice in architecture embraced the cults of deities and the dead, that is, temples and tombs.

Indeed, we capture an essential aspect of the Egyptian experience if we think of it as divided into a mundane realm and a sacred realm, on the one hand strictly distinguished from one another, but on the other hand in many ways connected. What could be more appropriate than to orient ourselves to this clearly drawn boundary and to make what the Egyptians themselves distinguished as belonging to the realm of the sacred the theme of a history of Egyptian religion? The fact that this boundary shifted over time should present no difficulty for such an account, provided that it proceeds in a sufficiently historical manner. The problem is rather that the meaning and nature of the boundary changed, at first barely perceptibly, and then ever more distinctly. This process of differentiating religion from the whole of the culture, and of differentiating the profane from a system

1

that was originally religiously determined, appears more clearly on the social level than in language and architecture. In the later phases of Egyptian culture, the priests were a clearly differentiated caste, and priestly descent was a precondition of the sacerdotal vocation. In the New Kingdom, however, it was a common practice to appoint officials of quite different origin and professional training, such as "pensioned" officers, to priestly positions. But even by this time, priesthood was a full-time job, at least in the higher ranks. This was in no way the case in earlier periods. In the Old Kingdom, priesthood was a secondary occupation that was tended to on a rotating basis by officials with rather different primary functions. The only professional priest was the lector priest (the Egyptian title means literally "he who carries the papyrus roll"), for it was he who disposed of the magical power of the "divine words." These sociological facts show clearly that the character of the boundary between the mundane and the sacred experienced a fundamental transformation over the course of the three millennia of the history of Egyptian civilization. The boundary itself is thoroughly problematic, and nothing would be more erroneous than to project late phenomena back into earlier periods.

The problem can be outlined as follows. On the one hand, in an early culture, everything has a religious basis, with the result that it seems inappropriate to take the boundary—however sharply it may be drawn—between the sacred and the profane as a guideline for characterizing the concept of religion or as a thematic boundary for its discussion. In particular, it must be asked to what extent speaking of "the profane" in such an early cultural phase is justified. On the other hand, despite all, the sacred and the forms of dealing with it are conspicuously distinguished from the everyday world. Sacred places (temples and other sanctuaries), sacred time (religious festivals), and sacred activities (rituals) can be unequivocally identified. This clear-cut area of the cultic is too narrow, whereas the area of those matters based on and determined by religion that coincides with the concept of culture is too wide. There is yet another difficulty: the historical process can be described as an increase in the profane—in the course of history, certain areas distinguish themselves as (relatively) profane from the all-encompassing religious basis of cultural manifestations as a whole. This process is designated as "secularization," or perhaps better, "desacralization." But there is also an opposite process of increased religious determination, and in Egypt, we can observe it in the areas of wisdom literature, the concept of history, and the interpretation of everyday experience. Here, we are dealing with a process of "sacralization." In comparison with late Ramesside wisdom literature, such as the Instruction of Amenemope (ca. 1100 B.C.E.), an older wisdom text such as the Instruction of Ptahhotpe (ca. 2000 B.C.E.) seems decidedly secular in outlook. We can speak of a theology of history—in the sense of explaining history as a manifestation of divine will—only beginning with the Ramesside Period (ca. 1300 B.C.E.). To offer just one example from everyday, practical matters, later medical papyri differ from earlier ones in that they contain an increasing number of magical spells.

1.1. *Two Concepts of Religion*

I believe we can get a grip on the problem if we distinguish two concepts of religion: a wider and a narrower one. I shall explain this distinction with the help of an Egyptian text that outlines the role of the king in the world and, in the process, describes in a general manner what the Egyptians understood by religion:

> Re has placed the king
> in the land of the living,
>   forever and ever,
> judging humankind
>   and satisfying the gods,
> realizing Maat and destroying Isfet.
> He (the king) gives offerings to the gods
>   and mortuary offerings to the deceased.[1]

Maat designates the idea of a meaningful, all-pervasive order that embraces the world of humankind, objects, and nature—in short, the meaning óf creation, the form in which it was intended by the creator god. The present condition of the world no longer corresponds to this meaning. The difference manifests itself in the phenomenon of *Isfet*, "lack." Sickness, death, scarcity, injustice, falsehood, theft, violence, war, enmity—all these are manifestations of lack in a world that has fallen into disorder through loss of its original plenitude of meaning. The meaning of creation lies in its plenitude, which yields order and justice. Where all are cared for, no one is oppressed, no one commits deeds of violence against others, no one need suffer. Suffering, scarcity, injustice, crime, rebellion, war, and so forth, had no meaning for the Egyptians. They were symptoms of an emptying or estrangement of meaning from the world, which had distanced itself from its origin in the course of history. The Egyptians "tolerated history only with difficulty," to cite Mircea Eliade's formulation regarding archaic societies. They did not see reality in the contingency of ordinary or extraordinary occurrences and events, but in Maat as the embodiment of an original plenitude of meaning that manifested itself as provisioning and justice. Turning their historical perspective backward, they strove with all their might to keep the original plenitude of meaning in view and to bring it into force through constant activity.

This activity was entrusted to the king. All action was monopolized by his person, but he delegated parts of this comprehensive responsibility to others—priests and officials—with the result that virtually all had a share in the work of realizing Maat. The king realized Maat by dispensing justice and carrying out the cult:

> judging humankind
>   and satisfying the gods.

To do this, he had at his disposal two divine powers that had stood at the side of the creator god himself: *Sia*, "perception," and *Hu*, "utterance." Sia enabled the king to perceive the plenitude of meaning and to keep it in his mind (in Egyptian, "in his heart"), whereas Hu gave his word the power to become a reality immediately.

Plenitude was a matter of abundance and its just distribution. The former was a divine responsibility, and the latter was the king's, a division of labor that was expressed by means of an exchange. In the cult ritual, the king offered Maat to the divine, and especially to the sun god Re. This act symbolized the descriptive hymn of praise that expressed the plenitude of meaning in creation and brought it to fruition by means of authoritative utterance, Hu. One of the meanings of the word *hu* is "abundance, plenitude"; the concepts of plenitude and speech were closely connected. Hu was the creative will of the creator god, directed toward plenitude, that expressed itself in words, while Maat was the plenitude of the well-ordered and tended world of creation that was offered to the divine in cultic praise and was continually restored among humankind by upholding the law in the courts. Maat was a meaning that was perceived by the king with the help of Sia and expressed by him with the assistance of Hu. Through meaningful speech, the king contravened the gravitational pull of history, which tended to alienate meaning.

The sacredness of the original order and the salvation implicit in the notion of plenitude made these concerns with the restoration of this order—both the king's and those of all who shared in this effort—a religious, and not just a restorative, task. Thus, in a very general sense, the Egyptian concept of religion can be defined as the realization of Maat, which can be specified, according to the Egyptian formulation, as the tasks of

> speaking justice for humankind
> satisfying the gods

giving offerings to the gods
and mortuary offerings to the deceased:

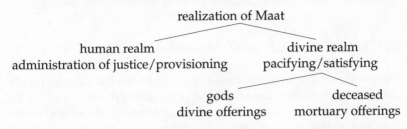

realization of Maat

human realm   divine realm
administration of justice/provisioning pacifying/satisfying

gods   deceased
divine offerings mortuary offerings

In this form, it becomes clear that the comprehensive religious concept of "realizing Maat" includes a narrower concept of religion: pacifying the gods. The two components of the general concept of religion, and at the same time the central functions of kingship, are (1) ethics and the dispensing of justice (the creation of solidarity and abundance in the social sphere through dispensing justice, care, and provisions), and (2) religion in the narrower sense, pacifying the gods and maintaining adequate contact with them, as well as provisioning the dead:

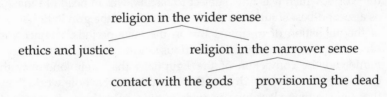

religion in the wider sense

ethics and justice   religion in the narrower sense

contact with the gods provisioning the dead

In light of this distinction between religion in the wider sense (the realization of Maat) and religion in the narrower sense (contact with the divine), which is derived from concepts characteristic of Egyptian culture, we can at least resolve the dilemma posed by the fact that on the one hand, everything was somehow based on and determined by religion, while on the other hand, strict boundaries were drawn between the sacred and the profane, so that contact with the sacred was clearly distinguished from the everyday world. The one refers to the wider and the other to the narrower concept of religion.

We must now decide which of these two concepts should be the object of our treatment. In the framework of what is intended to be an introductory handbook, we can treat only the narrower concept of religion in sufficient detail. A survey of Egyptian religion in the wider sense would be possible only with a wide-angle lens that would take in the larger connections while omitting historical details and problems. From such a perspective, one would have to treat all aspects of the realization of Maat; not only religion in the narrower sense, but also the concepts of kingship, ethics and religious anthropology, and especially the concepts of the Last Judgment and of individual preservation and immortality. I believe I may more easily refrain from such an undertaking in the light of Hellmut Brunner's excellent achievement in this vein in his *Grundzüge der altägyptischen Religion*.

1.2. Divine Presence: Privileged Experience or Cultural Activity?

The treatment that follows is thus concerned with the Egyptian concept of religion in the narrower sense of contact with the divine ("satisfying the gods"). The inquiry is directed less toward the perimeter than toward the center of Egyptian religion, which is designated here as "theology and piety." Both terms refer to the forms in which society and individuals felt close to the divine and conceptualized this closeness. The Egyptian concept of "divine presence" is the theme of this volume. It proceeds from the impression that this divine presence was something special, that is, that the Egyptians felt especially close to their deities. It also proceeds from the fact that the time when the sun god ruled over deities and humankind together, both groups dwelling on earth, was over, and that with the withdrawal of the gods to the sky, the world, which was now subject to history, was in need of kingship as a second-best solution in the struggle against the gravitational pull of the alienation of meaning. But in the later periods, contact with other religions—Neoplatonism, various Gnostic trends, Christianity—reinforced the conviction of the Egyptians that their land was the earthly residence of the divine, the "temple of the whole world," and that only if they slackened in their piety would the gods terminate their terrestrial cohabitation with the Egyptian people and, *dolenda secessio*, withdraw to the sky. Herodotus and others confirm this picture when they call the Egyptians the most pious of all peoples.

Here, I would describe this piety, which neighboring peoples felt to be unique, as a special form of divine presence in its historical specificity. I begin with the assumption that divine presence is not something quantifiable or measurable, as though there were "the holy" on one side and humankind on the other, so that one need only determine a given society's proximity to or distance from the holy in its religion. If we wish to describe the specifics of historical religions, what is far more important is the quality, the internal dimensions, the structure of their experience of divine presence. By "divine presence," I understand a culturally formed and specifically determined area of experience in which specific spheres and roles are ascribed to deities and humans so that they can encounter and communicate with one another—roles such as priest, prophet, shaman, pilgrim, eremite, mystic, magician, oneiromancer, interpreter of omens, sage, and so forth, and spheres such as cult, nature, cosmos, history, myth, state, and the like, as well as forms of the otherworldly (transcendence) and the supernatural (miracles). Of all these possibilities, only certain ones were realized in Egypt, and others were excluded. By selection and negation, this area we call "divine presence" receives its culturally specific form and structure as a semantic universe. Action and experience are possible only through the selection and negation of defined frameworks and within the bounded dimensions of a semantic universe.

Action and experience are the heart and the origin of religion. I take as erroneous the view one often still encounters, which has its roots in phenomenology: that at the beginning stood the religious experience of the individual, from which then developed, with subsequent theological elaboration and conventionalizing, ritual activities and the ideational world that accompanied them. Rather, I assume the primacy of sacred activity and the collective religious experience that was anchored in it. Rituals preceded deities; experience and empirical knowledge were only possible within and beyond the mental horizon of activity: even when they transcended it, they presupposed it. From the phenomenological perspective, religious activity is described as the human *response* to the prior stimulus of the holy, so that we must orient ourselves to the internal standpoint of the actor and refer to the self-understanding of the culture. Without in any way wishing to challenge the legitimacy of this method, I prefer a historico-analytic perspective that occupies an external standpoint vis-à-vis the religion to be described. From this standpoint, the deities and their actions, to whose reality human activity responds, are a cultural creation. Divine presence is not, in the end, an ahistorical and irrational concept, the stuff of the privileged experience of religious spirit and incomprehensible using the means available to scholarship, but rather the historical object of analytic investigation. Because I view the divine realm of the Egyptians as a cultural achievement, as part of the world of meaning within whose framework their religious activity was oriented, I reject a reality outside Egyptian culture while conceding the highest reality within its realm of meaning.

1.3. Dimensions of Divine Presence

What I said about the primacy of activity is also true of the gods. They, too, were sponsors of activities and partners in them, and, as such, they presuppose a meaningfully structured arena of activity. What I call "divine presence" for short is the area of activity and the conceptual horizon of both divine care and human religious activity and experience. Its specific dimensions thus determine both the concept of the divine and the forms of religious experience. Divine presence as an area of activity and a conceptual horizon is presupposed wherever contact with the divine occurs. Because this contact can assume many forms, from priestly rites to mystic contemplation, from magical coercion to self-abnegation, the corresponding area of action has a very different conceptual structure in each case. I call this structure the "dimensions" of contact with the divine. In the case of Egyptian religion, when it is understood as a conceptual horizon of contact with the divine or, put otherwise, of religious activity and experience, I reckon with three dimensions:

1. The *cultic*, which can also be called the "local" or the "political," for these three aspects are inseparably connected: in the cultic dimension, deities are resident in a place in the form of their cult statues and, as local or state gods, are symbols of collective or political identity.
2. The *cosmic*, because to the Egyptians, the cosmos was hierophanic, that is, it was a sphere of divine action and religious experience.
3. The *mythic*, by which is meant sacred tradition, "what is said about the gods," the presence of the divine in the cultural memory as set down in myths, names, genealogies, and other forms of tradition.

The threefold nature of these dimensions can be demonstrated from ancient Egyptian sources. A hymn to Osiris from Dynasty 18 praises the god as

> King of the gods with many *names*,
> with sacred *embodiments* and
> mysterious *cult statues* in the temples.[2]

The concepts "name," "embodiment," and "cult statues" refer to the mythic, cosmic, and cultic dimensions.

A later text interprets the state triad of the Ramesside Period with reference to these three dimensions:

> All gods are three:
> Amun, Re, and Ptah, who have no equal.
> He who hides his *names* as Amun,
> he is Re in *appearance*,
> his *body* is Ptah.[3]

Names, visibility, body: this is the same trio of speech, cosmos, and cult.

There are other such allusions. On the whole, though, this concept of divine presence is less a matter of explicit theological metatexts than of a practiced and thus an implicit theology. The reality of the three dimensions is no more dependent on the existence of such metatexts than is the grammar of a language on the existence of explicit grammatical descriptions. Divine presence as a regularly structured area of action is implicit in all contact with the divine, and the forms of this contact can be deduced, just as the grammar of a language can be deduced from actual usages. Based on practice, one can arrive at a theory of ancient Egyptian religion.

Although our quest for a "theory" of Egyptian religious practice is not dependent on the existence of ancient Egyptian theoretical formulations, when such formulations occasionally occur, they can serve as a welcome confirmation. But there was no explicit and coherent explanation of Egyptian theology on the metalevel of theoretical discourse in ancient Egypt any more than there were theoretical explications in other areas, such as grammar, rhetoric, or historiography. As is well known, the development of theoretical discourse, at least in the Mediterranean world, was an accomplishment of Greek culture. This is also true of theology in the sense of a theory of religious practice. It is surely more than a coincidence, and its consequences have yet to be fully recognized, that the Middle Stoa developed a theological scheme whose tripartite division corresponds exactly to the Egyptian dimensions of divine presence. According to M. Terentius Varro and St. Augustine, theology consists of three modes: *theología politiké* (*civilis*), *physiké* (*naturalis*), and *mythiké* (*fabularis*), corresponding exactly to the cultic, cosmic, and mythic dimensions.[4] For when Varro expresses himself thus concerning "political theology" (we shall not concern ourselves with the correspondence of the other two types), "which state gods each citizen shall worship and what sacred acts and offerings he shall make," the unity of the cultic and the political, as in Egypt, is evident.

In my opinion, this agreement admits of two explanations. One has to do with a universal trichotomy, as also in the Stoic tripartite division of human affairs into *personae*, *loca*, and *tempora* (persons, places, and occasions); in which case, if the same three categories are to be found everywhere, there is no reason for surprise. The other explanation is that in the area of divine affairs, other categories or dimensions exist, in which case the selection and defining of the same three dimensions points to a structural relationship between Egyptian and Greek religion—as is otherwise affirmed by classical authors, especially Herodotus, and always with amazement.

Personally, I incline toward the latter alternative, and I shall say something in support of this view in chapter 6.2; for the rest, I must leave the question, which entails comparison of Greek and other religions to Egyptian religion, to the specialists. It is hoped that the present attempt to describe the concept of divine presence in the context of Egyptian religion in the specifics of its dimensions will prove useful for other religions as well. It seems to me that a comparative study on the level of theory in practice, or (implicit) theology, in the various religions would be both possible and meaningful. The concept of divine presence in the sense of an area of action that is specifically historically dimensioned as a conceptual horizon of divine and human action and experience constitutes a *tertium comparationis*, a context and a deep structure for the phenomena that are to be compared.

1.4. "God" versus "Gods"

The following discussion of Egyptian "theology and piety" is not limited to an attempt to work out the theology implicit in the practice of Egyptian religion. Of the two parts into which the text is divided, only the first, larger part is devoted to the dimensions of divine presence as the theory of Egyptian religious practice. The second part is devoted to the forms of explicit theology, to the unfolding of a theological discourse in the second millennium B.C.E. This might appear to contradict the view expressed earlier, that it was the Greeks who first advanced to a theoretical explanation of religious practice. I must therefore clarify here what is explained in detail in the appropriate places later: namely, that in Egypt, "explicit theology" *never* referred to practice. It was something entirely other than an explanation of traditional implied theology, entirely other than a theory of Egyptian religion. From its beginnings, explicit theology in Egypt ran strictly counter to implicit theology. More precisely put, the opposition can be formulated thus: that explicit theology dealt with "god," in the singular, whereas implicit theology had to do with "the gods." In Egyptology, this distinction has yet to be understood.

It seems contradictory that a language would use one and the same word for two such distinct concepts as "god" as the absolute and at the same time personified embodiment of the divine, and "god" as a member of a polytheistic pantheon, an element of the class "gods," or that in the framework of a polytheistic religion, a concept such as "god" in this comprehensive and even monotheistic sense could arise. I shall not deny the contradiction, or better, the problematic, conflicted nature of this coexistence of concepts. But it would be a mistake to think of the concept "god" in a comprehensive sense over and above "the gods" as the privilege of monotheistic religions, for to do so would hinder our understanding of the complexity of historical polytheisms. When the Greeks used the singular *ho theós*, "god," for the most part they did not mean just any member of the class "gods," but rather their highest god, Zeus, who held the world, humans and gods alike, in his hands. The famous Homeric image of the golden chain with which Zeus could lift the whole world of the gods, if he wished, served the Greeks as a playful visualization of the problem of "god" and "gods." In Egypt, the discourse of explicit theology developed around this problem.

There might well be simple polytheistic religions that have formed no concept of "god" above and beyond their polytheistic world of deities. Erik Hornung has characterized—I believe incorrectly—Egyptian religion as one of these in his book *Conceptions of God: The One and the Many*. But most polytheisms known to the history of religion are complex in the sense that they reckon—or better, live—with a divine realm beyond which there is a "god" or "highest being" who created the world and its deities. This coexistence is always problematic, but therein lies the complexity of genuine, living religions as opposed to scholarly theories that either deprive polytheism of its divine plurality, such as the "original monotheism" of Father Wilhelm Schmidt (represented in Egyptology by Hermann Junker), or go to the opposite extreme and deny a concept of "god" beyond the plurality of deities.

Curiously enough, but understandably in view of the monotheistic stance of Western religion, Egyptology at first saw a "god" and not "gods" in the Egyptian sources. As early as 1839, Champollion wrote enthusiastically of the "pure monotheism" he seemed to encounter in the earliest known sources.[5] This view congealed into a fixation with monotheism in later treatments of Egyptian religion, in particular those of Étienne Drioton and Hermann Junker. The aforementioned book by Hornung is the long-overdue rebuttal of this approach. Hornung has performed the service of emphatically stating the reality of the polytheistic nature of Egyptian religion, and though his discussion suffers from its categorical denial of any concept of "god" beyond the plurality of gods, it nevertheless remains an excellent description of the phenomena we shall summarize here as "implicit theology."

In complex polytheisms that recognize a concept of "god" alongside or beyond a polytheistic assemblage of deities, there is a problem in that the omnipotence of this god undermines the reality of the other deities. The problem is generally solved by having this god abstain from exercising his omnipotence and withdraw to the sky as a *deus otiosus* (inactive god). Even Greek mythology depends on such an abstinence on the part of Zeus, without which it would have nothing to relate about him or the other deities. Homer's image of the golden chain is only an expression of pure potentiality. Zeus could if he wished to, but he refrains, and so the world is not turned upside down, and the reality of the other gods is preserved for the storyteller.

This contradiction cannot be resolved logically. We have here a genuine complementarity, two equally valid but mutually exclusive points of view, like the wave and the particle theories of light. In a polytheistic religion, the reality of the gods rests on the mythic experience of the world as act. In events that escape human disposition and are at the same time existentially significant, the mythic view perceives the workings of the gods, whose plurality and diversity, in this view of the world, are ontologically anchored in two ways: First, reality itself is diverse and varied, in life and death, good and evil, light and darkness, love and strife, order and destruction, height and depth, ecstasy and contemplation, structure and disintegration. Second, reality is interpreted as act, and action always presupposes partners, roles, and a division of labor and power: that which we shall call "constellations" in the framework of our own theory, and which, on the basis of the mythic view of the world and concept of act, constitutes the basic structure of the divine realm of polytheism. To deny the reality of the gods is to deprive the world of its diverse and numinous independent existence, to degrade it into a directly accessible "nature."

1.5. Implicit and Explicit Theology

The plurality of deities is not easy to harmonize with the reality of a single god, which rests on other experiences entirely. It is to the latter that explicit theology was devoted in ancient Egypt. It was sparked by the problem of theodicy, the justification of god (in the singular). It is most decidedly god (and not the gods, or some one of their number) who was made responsible for creation, and also for the transitoriness of order, the fallibility of humankind, and the failure of good. The idea of a *deus otiosus*, of a renunciation of power and a withdrawal from the created world appears in connection with this debate only as a fearful question—"Is he asleep?"—to be emphatically rejected. For the Egyptians, this would have been no solution, but rather the apocalyptic vision of a world robbed of coherent meaning. They held on to both truths, the unity of god and the differentiated plurality of gods, until Akhenaten, who would not tolerate this tension and made an attempt to found a new religion that knew only a single god. That such an attempt could be made, along with its immediate failure, show how indispensably *both* realities were anchored in the complexity of Egyptian polytheism and its experience of the world.

Implicit and explicit theology thus originally had entirely different themes and referred to entirely different horizons of the experience of the world. Implicit theology had nothing to do with the beginning and end of time, or with the justification of the world and of evil; rather, it revolved around sacred activities as they were carried out in the cult, through which it interpreted cosmic reality and in terms of which it made an account of the divine. Implicit theology was necessarily and essentially "constellative," it stood and fell with the differentiated and "constellated" multiplicity of the divine realm. The idea of divine unity was excluded from each of its three dimensions: "god" in the singular had no place in cult, cosmology, or myth. Just as necessarily and essentially, all explicit theology in Egypt was "transconstellative." There was no constellation in which the single god could appear along with the gods. As shown by the example of Zeus and many other polytheistic mythologies, the hierarchic solution of a divine kingship would have been bound up with a renunciation of power or a diminution of the reality of the singular god. The idea of the oneness of god could not be apprehended by means of myth, at least not as an actual, present reality.

The discourse of explicit theology derived the dynamic of its development from this contradiction. Herein lies the problem, which set an unending process of conceptual evolution in motion for centuries, ending with the open conflict of the Amarna Period. Egyptian religion emerged transformed by the presumably painful experience of this conflict, and in the following period, it arrived at a solution that proved workable until the end of Egyptian religion. Beyond the traditional three dimensions of divine presence, as practiced in the implicit theology, the fourth dimension of the transcendent god now became conceivable. The theological discourse of these centuries developed a theology of transcendence, a new sort of concept that made it possible to relate the notions of "god" and "gods" to one another and to mediate the two realities. In this way, under various traditional names, especially Amun (and then Isis in Graeco-Roman antiquity), the single god became an object of popular piety and the protagonist of magical texts, from Ramesside times down to the Greek magical papyri. Via the Corpus Hermeticum and alchemy, the late horizon of this Ramesside pantheism exercised its influence down into our own recent past, down into the Romantic currents with which Champollion sympathized, which spurred him on to his great achievement of deciphering the hieroglyphs and finally to his enthusiastic discovery of a single god in the colorful reflection of the Egyptian world of the divine.

Part One

THE

DIMENSIONS

OF DIVINE

PRESENCE:

THE IMPLICIT

THEOLOGY

OF EGYPTIAN

POLYTHEISM

CHAPTER 2

The Local or Cultic Dimension

2.1. City Gods and Cities of Gods

"Image of heaven" (*imago caeli*), "temple of the whole world" (*mundi totius templum*)[1]—these phrases are invoked in praise of Egypt as the dwelling place of the gods in a rather late Hermetic text handed down in Latin. This beneficent divine presence is jeopardized, however; the text continues with an apocalyptic vision in which the gods abandon Egypt and ascend back into the heavens, leaving Egypt devoid of all divine presence. This astonishing notion is the exact reverse of the widespread mythic picture in which long ago, in the legendary primeval age, the gods dwelled on earth but then withdrew into another realm whose contrast to the this-worldliness of the sphere inhabited by humankind determined reality. In Egypt, this "cohabitation of gods and men" (*consortium hominum deorumque*) characterizes the present, and the thought of a withdrawal of the gods to the heavens resembles a catastrophe! Did the Egyptians really believe that their deities physically dwelled in their earthly temples? Did they confuse cult statue and deity, symbol and reality? Was the distinction between this world and the divine realm foreign to them?

By no means. The Egyptians shared the view held by many archaic societies that the cohabitation of deities and humankind constituted a primordial state that had irretrievably vanished. In chapter 5.2, we shall deal with a myth that narrates how the gods once lived on earth and were ruled, together with humankind, by the sun god. But humans planned a revolt, in consequence of which the sun god finally separated himself and the other deities from humankind by elevating the sky high above the earth and withdrawing to this new celestial abode. He transferred governance of the world to his son Shu, god of the air separating sky and earth, and as such the ideal mediator between what was now divided into the divine and the human, the celestial and the terrestrial spheres. The withdrawal of the divine to the sky entailed (or was compensated for by) the founding of the state.

In a way, this withdrawal of the deities to the sky and their separation from humankind was a reassuring concept. Deities were not to be encountered and experienced in everyday life. In this respect, Egyptian religion differed significantly from both the Greek and the Israelite experience. The absence of deities made room for a specifically human sphere of activity and responsibility: the state, which—despite or because of its being a divine institution—kept the divine at a distance that had to be bridged by "sacred signification." The founding of the state amounted to the same thing as the founding of the cult. The state functioned as a "church" by filling the gap and compensating for the absence of the gods. The state replaced the divine presence that had been withdrawn with a symbolic presence, and it did this so effectively that in the later periods of Egyptian history, the entire land was believed to be symbolically inhabited by the gods.

Quite correctly and in an entirely authentic manner, this late text points emphatically to the immense role played by temples in Egypt. Of all the lands in the ancient world, Egypt was the most densely packed with temples, and thus with deities. The picture of Egypt as a single temple in a profane world, as the terrestrial home of the gods, entailed more than just the fact of an unusual number of temples. The presence of deities in these temples was conceived of as more intense and personal, and less symbolic, than in other religions. What we are dealing with here is the "local" dimension of the Egyptian concept of the divine, which has three central themes:

1. concepts of "autochthony" and divine territorial lordship and their theological expression ("city god theology")
2. the concept of the temple as *imago caeli* and its double function as divine dwelling and economic enterprise
3. the concept of divine residence on earth as conveyed by image and ritual.

I shall treat these three themes in detail in the discussion that follows. It is important to highlight what is characteristic of Egyptian culture as a whole while not losing sight of the historical dimension, for it is only natural that far-reaching changes occurred during a span of more than three millennia. Thus, on the phenomenological level, we stress the astonishing idea of *praesentia numinum* (the presence of divine spirits), a similarity of representation and represented, of symbol and reality, that approached near identity. On the historical level, we must take into account the changes in the specific interpretations of the relationship between symbol and reality within this general framework during the various periods of Egyptian history.

The divine realm of the Egyptians had a local dimension: that is to say, the Egyptians conceived of their deities as resident on earth. How was this residence interpreted?—first and foremost, as *lordship*. The kingdom of the Egyptian gods was emphatically "of this world." They dwelled in their temples like lords of the manor, owners of the temple estates. In Egypt, most of the land belonged to the temples, and it was worked by the temple personnel themselves, or it was rented out. The temples paid no taxes to the state, for they were themselves state agencies. The king favored them with endowments, but he also could dispose of their property: these royal donations did not impoverish the crown, for there was no economic or conceptual separation of church and state. Quite the contrary, the sum of the landowning temples and deities embodied the state. This concept was clearly expressed in the royal rituals of assumption of power (coronation) and its confirmation (jubilee or *sed*-festival). In these rites, the king acted before the assembled deities of the land, and as lords of the land, they recognized him as their representative. They embodied the land as a political unity.

Just as the totality of deities embodied the political concept of "Egypt," the individual landowning local deity embodied the concept of "city." An Egyptian city was always the city of a deity.[2] Paraphrases such as "city of Amun," "city of Thoth," and "city of Ptah" so unequivocally designated Thebes, Hermopolis, and Memphis that the Greeks introduced names of this sort for most Egyptian cities, though they replaced the names of the Egyptian gods and goddesses with their Greek equivalents. "City of Amun" became Diospolis, "city of Min" became Panopolis, "city of Hathor" yielded Aphroditopolis, "city of Thoth" was Hermopolis, "city of Anubis" was Kynopolis (because of the dog form of the god), "city of Wepwawet" was Lykopolis (on account of the wolf form of Wepwawet), and on the same principle, "city of Sobek" became Krokodilopolis. The actual Egyptian names of all these cities were quite different, but the Greek nomenclature captured the concept of an Egyptian city as the territory of a deity. This was a symmetrical relationship. Just as the concept of city was characterized by the rulership that a deity exercised in and over it, so the concept of a deity was characterized by the city he or she ruled. As unambiguously as the "city of Amun" was Thebes, the "lord of Thebes" was Amun, the "lord of Hermopolis" was Thoth, the "mistress of Dendara" was Hathor, and so forth. In the local dimension of the divine realm, the gods were city gods and the cities were cities of gods. Not only the concept but also the practical aspect of a city was determined by its function as residence of the deity who ruled it. As a rule, Egyptian cities were not surrounded by walls. Only the temple enclosures, which contained the divine dwellings and the temple workshops, were walled and fortified. With their walls and bastions, they towered over the flat land like castles, visibly constituting the centers of the settlements that crystallized around them.

For the ancient Egyptians, the concept of the city was thus first and foremost determined by religion. To live in a city meant to be in the proximity of the deity who had dominion there. To belong to a city meant to be in the jurisdiction of that city's deity. In Egypt, everyone had "his" city and "his" deity, whom he "followed" and who cared for him. Feelings of citizenship and home were religious ties, ties between the divine and the human. Evidence indicates that during the course of Egyptian history, the religious aspect of the individual's tie to a city grew ever stronger. Our chiefly phenomenological analysis of this relationship is therefore oriented mainly to sources from the New Kingdom and later and applies principally to these epochs of Egyptian history. But already in tomb inscriptions of the third millennium B.C.E., we read

> I have come out of my city
> and descended from my nome, . . .
> having done right therein.[3]

In the Book of the Dead of the New Kingdom, we find

> I have come today from the city of my god: Memphis.
> It is truly the most beautiful of all the nomes in this land.
> Its god is the lord of Maat,
> the lord of food, rich in costly things.
>
> All lands come to it,
> Upper Egypt sails downstream to it,
> Lower Egypt with sail and oar,
> to make it festive every day,
> as its god has commanded.
>
> No one who dwells in it
> says, "Would that I had!"
> Blessed is he who does right for the god therein!
> He grants an old age to the one who acts for him,
> becoming a worthy,
> and reaching here in a beautiful burial,
> an interment in the Sacred Place.[4]

Coming from Memphis means having served Ptah and having been granted a "beautiful burial" by that god.

By serving as home to deities, Egyptian cities also made humans at home on earth. They held out the promise of divine presence and thus of immortality, for the one who served the divine on earth would be rewarded in the next life. But one could follow only the deity of one's own city, and such divine service was reserved only for city-dwellers. Praise was thus heaped on the inhabitant of a "city of god" who lived his life as a loyal servant of his city god:

Happy is he who lives in Thebes!
He goes to rest in the Sacred Place as a living *ba*
who will hear the call of the offering service,
a perfect transfigured one, who will enter among
[the praised ones . . .] in the Festival of the Valley.
Grant that I rest like them.
He who is buried in the cemetery of *Khefethernebes*
will receive water in Thebes,
will see the beauty of Amun each time he rises,
his shadow will be secure in the netherworld,
his *ba* will be in the sky like [the sun's].[5]

May he reach old age in his city Thebes,
free of what his god abominates.
May he receive favor in Karnak,
with food from the house of his god.
May he receive honor in [Shedebu (?)],
being like a praised one in his essence.[6]

You were born in the city of Thebes
as one who belonged to the following of Osiris.
Its (i.e., Thebes's) homes nourished you as a child,
its walls received your old age.
It will not be devoid of your progeny,
a high priest of Karnak.
Your heart has been found to be right
on the scale of truth.
Your image moves about in the courtyard [of the temple].
Lift your head! Receive the offerings!
See, your son resembles your excellence.
It is he who has assumed leadership in your city,
So that its four sides are as though you were still on earth.[7]

One lands as a praised one in Thebes,
the nome of truth, the land of silence.
Those who do evil do not enter you,
the Place of Truth;
the ferry that conveys the doers of right,
its ferryman does not convey sinners.
Happy is he who lands there!
He will be a divine *ba* like the Ennead.[8]

It is good to tread the way of the god.
Much will be granted to him who places him in his heart.
His monument is on earth.
He who places his (i.e., the god's) way in his heart flourishes
    on it,

completes his life in sweetness of heart,
and is more illustrious than his like.
He grows old in his city
as a worthy of his nome.
All his limbs are rejuvenated like a child's,
And his children are numerous before him,
distinguished in their city,
son after son.

. . .

He arrives at the Sacred Place in sweetness of heart,
in a beautiful embalming, in the work of Anubis.
The children of his children lift him up,
they say to him, the inhabitants of his city,
when he strides off to life:
"This is a follower of Foremost-of-the-Westerners,
no divine reproach is upon him."[9]

Homesickness was one of the favorite themes of Ramesside lyric.[10]
For the most part, these brief poems have an expressly religious tone,
for longing for one's city was at the same time longing for the presence of its deity:

Lo, my heart has slipped away,
it is hurrying to the place it knows,
it is traveling upstream to see Memphis.
But I sit (at home)
and wait for my heart, that it might tell me the condition of
Memphis.

No task succeeds any longer in my hands:
my heart has departed from its place.
Come to me, Ptah,
and take me to Memphis.
Let me see you as desired.

I am awake, but my heart sleeps.
My heart is not in my body.
All my limbs are seized by evil:
my eye is weary from seeing,
my ear hears not.
My voice is husky,
all my words are garbled.
Be gracious to me! Grant that I revive.[11]

Lo, I do not wish to leave Thebes.
I have been taken away against my will.

I shall dance when I sail north,
when Thebes is with me
and the domain of Amun is all around me.

. . .

Bring me into your city, Amun,
for I love it.
I love your city more than bread and beer, Amun,
more than clothing and ointments.
The soil of your place is dearer to me
than the unguents of another land.[12]

O Thoth, bring me to Hermopolis,
your city, sweet of life,
while you nourish me with bread and beer,
while you protect my mouth while speaking.[13]

"What will become of us?" sigh daily in their hearts
those who are far from Thebes,
who dream all day long of its (i.e., Thebes') name. . . .
Sweeter is the bread of him who is there
than an abundance of goose fat.
It is sweeter . . . than honey,
one drinks of it until drunkenness.
See the condition of him who dwells in Thebes!
The sky doubles the breeze for him.[14]

How good it is to dwell in the southern city (i.e., Thebes).[15]

The delta Residence of the Ramessides is described thus:

Everyone has left his own city
and settled near it.
Its western part is the house of Amun,
Its southern part the house of Seth.
Astarte is in its east
and Wadjit in its northern quarter.
The castle in its midst is like the light-land of the sky.[16]

The nimbus of the holy city of god attracts settlers and visitors, as
stated in one of the poems about Memphis quoted earlier:

Every land comes to it.
Upper Egypt sails downstream to it,
Upper Egypt with sail and oar.

In the Middle Kingdom, Abydos was already praised as a holy city, as

> this isle to which one must make pilgrimage,
> the walls that the All-Lord has determined,
> blessed city since the time of Osiris,
> which Horus founded for his father,
> to which the stars in the sky must pay their due,
> mistress of the sky-dwellers,
> to whom the great ones of Busiris come,
> which resembles Heliopolis in blessedness,
> with which the All-Lord is satisfied.[17]

In the New Kingdom, someone wishes

> to reach Thebes the victorious,
> the eye of Re, mistress of temples,
> she is the light-land of the one with hidden names,
> his city, which he determined.[18]

"Solar eye," "light-land," and "primeval hill" were typical predicates of the holy city and were especially common for Thebes in the New Kingdom, as when Queen Hatsheput states

> I know
> that Karnak is light-land on earth,
> the illustrious primeval hill of the beginning,
> the light-eye of the All-Lord,
> his darling, which elevates his beauty
> and gathers his following for him.[19]

Tuthmosis III bears similar witness:

> For I know that Thebes is eternity,
> And Amun everlastingness,
> and Re the lord of Karnak.
> Southern Heliopolis (i.e., Thebes) is his radiant eye
> in this land. . . .
> It is eternity to be there.[20]

In a later text, Thebes is called

> the eye of Re, mistress of the lands,
> image of the sky,
> the one who left her, he alighted on her in the beginning.[21]

The rank of an Egyptian city was proportionate to its holiness, and its sacred rank was determined by its antiquity. The holy city lay on the primeval mound that emerged from the waters at the beginning of creation:

> Thebes is the model for every city:
> water and land were [mixed] in it at the beginning.
> Sand came to measure the fields,
> to make its soil come into being on the primeval mound,
> that the land might come into being.[22]

A Ptolemaic text says of Thebes

> When the earth was in the depths of the primeval waters,
> he (Amun) waded on it (Thebes).
> It dispelled his weakness entirely
> when he rested on it.
> It was the "place of life" that became the primeval mound,
> which rose up in the beginning.[23]

The city was the first and oldest work of creation, and it essentially preceded the actual creation, which was possible only through and from it. In an old text, the creator god describes the primeval condition before creation: "When Heliopolis was not yet founded that I might be in it." For the Egyptians, a city was a temple located on the primeval mound, the home and domain of an autochthonous deity.

What did this concept of city as divine dwelling mean in the lives of the people who dwelled in cities? We must accept literally the statement that it was precisely in its aspect of divine dwelling that a city bound people to one another and made them feel at home. The temple was the center of civil municipal administration in Egypt. City-dwellers belonged to the temple as lay priests; they were the "hour-priests" who served in the temples in monthly rotation. These citizen hour-priests were under the authority of the full-time priests, and these in turn were under the charge of a mayor or royal administrative official. The tie that bound individuals to their city was a religious one, and this is perhaps why it was so patent in Egypt. It was not just deities who had special ties to a locale. The Egyptians of pharaonic culture were not only not nomadic, they elevated sedentariness to a principle and practically a *summum bonum*. In their view, their highest goal in life was to be buried in the city where they had been born. For the Egyptians, their city was the decisive socializing framework. Even those who had made something of themselves at the royal court would boast of their "good name" in their city, for it was their city that retained their memory, thus keeping them alive even after death.

We only half understand this valorization of sedentariness, the Egyptians' intense feeling for "home," if we do not view it in conjunction with its opposite, which is known by the Greek term *ana-choresis*: people would abandon their homes and workplaces and go wandering off.[24] This was certainly no "wanderlust": the people uprooted in this manner did not take off of their own free will. The blame lay rather with the oppressive rent, taxes, and corvée labor requirements with which the rural population was burdened. Famine and civil war, as occurred in what we call the "Intermediate Periods" of Egyptian history, also led to such "internal migration."

Fear of punishment prompted many officials who were compromised or had fallen into disfavor to flee. Such a case underlies the Story of Sinuhe, the most famous ancient Egyptian literary work, as well as the Moscow Literary Letter, which is one thousand years later in date. Such flight was treated as desertion and severely punished. From the Middle Kingdom, we have lists of prisoners, peasants who had fled and been sentenced to forced labor. We also know of cases in the New Kingdom in which peasants who had been oppressed and beaten by their overseers took flight. In such cases, their abandoned fields remained unworked. This was a catastrophic loss to the Egyptian economy: not only did those left behind rely on these fields for sustenance, but as a rule also some functionary or resident member of the official elite. Officials of the Middle Kingdom were therefore expressly enjoined:

> Do not oppress the peasant with taxes!
> [. . .] If you bleed him, he will wander off.[25]

On the contrary, peasants should be treated well, for

> these are the people who produce what is;
> one lives by the work of their hands.
> If it is lacking, misery prevails.[26]

The late Demotic wisdom text on Papyrus Insinger from the Ptolemaic Period, an era that was especially affected by the problem of anachoresis, devotes an entire chapter to a warning about "abandonment of the place where one lives." Its chief argument is the loss of social integration into one's community. Only in one's own city is one known, regarded, and respected. Those who give up this advantage expose themselves to the ridicule, contempt, and insult that befall unknown individuals, socially unintegrated strangers. These admonishments are introduced by the statement, "The god in a city is the one on whom the death and life of its inhabitants depend."[27]

The city god is here expressly implored to take control of the burning problem of desertion. This is a very late text, to be sure, but the concept and institution of the city deity were present in Egypt from the beginning. The earliest carving found in Egypt, which is apparently western Asian in its style, is inscribed with the word *niwty*, "belonging to the city." Scholars have surely been correct in seeing this as a representation of a city god, a *nṯr niwty*, a "god belonging to the city." The concept of the city deity was one of the most ancient elements of Egyptian religion, which came to the fore again late in Egyptian history; an integral component of the deep layers of popular religion, it outlasted all historical changes and predominated again at the end.

2.2. *The Temple*

Space attained a sacred character through the local dimension of the divine realm, through the fact that the deities were resident in locales. This sacred character was connected with the Egyptian concept of a city as the locus of a divine lordship, but it attained architectonic form only in the temple. Now that we have illustrated the Egyptian concept of city by recourse to texts, we must turn to the concept of temple with the help of ground plans. Though we know very little about the appearance of Egyptian cities, we may assume that they contained no characteristic structures aside from the temples (except for capital cities with their royal palaces). The temples, and especially the chief temple of the city deity, represented the urban character of a settlement. We should recall the castle-like nature of the temples, whose high enclosure walls and pylon towers loomed visibly over the flat land from quite a distance away. In the topography of a settlement, the enormous, dominating character of the temple stood out clearly vis-à-vis all other manifestations of human building activity. Just as someone beholding the structure of medieval European settlements, with their innumerable castles, can deduce the feudal structure of medieval society, we can infer a theocratic feudalism from the appearance of the Egyptian landscape—especially from the New Kingdom on—with its countless fortress-like temples. As lords of the cities and proprietors of huge landed estates, the deities dwelled in castles on their "primeval mounds," determining the appearance of the land so exclusively that it was possible to conceive of Egypt as a single huge temple, the "temple of the entire world."

2.2.1. ECONOMIC CONCERN AND DIVINE DWELLING

Temple constructions of the New Kingdom, such as the Ramesseum, the mortuary temple of Ramesses II (Figure 1), best convey the picture of a divine fortress. In the midst of the entire complex, the temple itself, the divine dwelling, was a sandstone construction that extended westward from the huge pylon on its eastern façade. The buildings that filled the remaining space within the enclosure wall were made of sun-dried mud bricks. These were magazines that belonged to the

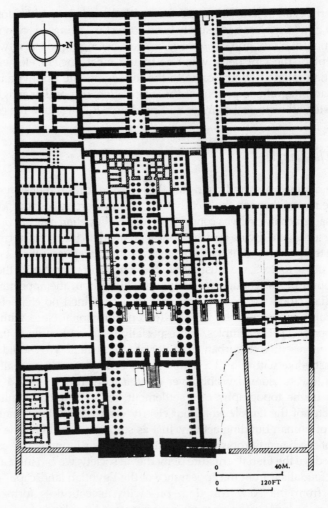

FIGURE 1. Plan of the Ramesseum. From W. S. Smith, *The Art and Architecture of Ancient Egypt* (Harmondsworth, England, 1958), p. 218, fig. 71.

temple as an economic concern. The Egyptian language made a distinction between these two aspects of an Egyptian temple. The word *pr*, "house, household," like Greek *oikos*, designated the totality of a deity's possessions, not only the magazines but also the landed property and the workshops that were the source of the provisions that filled them. Unfortunately, we do not know how much land belonged to any individual Egyptian temple, though we do know how much land Ramesses III donated to them. To the figures given in the Great Papyrus Harris, we would have to add the unknown amount of holdings they already had to arrive at a picture of the entire extent of a divine household in this period. For the *pr* of Amun, which far exceeded all the others in size, we have the figure of more than 590,000 acres. But a household consisted not only of landed domains, which in the case of the *pr* of Amun were scattered throughout the land, but also of human beings who made their living from them. Besides the upper and lower clergy, there were others who "belonged to" the temple: peasants, shepherds, miners, and artisans. Ramesses III's endowment to Amun amounted to 86,486 "heads." To illustrate this aspect of the god as landed proprietor and head of a household from a text, we cite here chapter 60 of the hymns to Amun from a papyrus in Leiden:

> His is the southern and the northern land,
> he alone has conquered it with his might;
> his border is strong, in so far as he is on earth,
> [it reaches] to the breadth of the earth and the height of the heavens.

> The gods request their maintenance from him:
> it is he who grants them food from his offerings.
> The lord of fields, riverbanks, and acres:
> to him belongs every document of his cadaster,
> the beginning of the measuring cord to its end.
> He measures the entire land with his two uraei.
> For him are foundation ceremonies carried out,
> his is the royal cubit that measures the stones.
> He who stretched his measuring cord to the breadth of the earth,
> and founded the Two Lands where they are located,
> the temples and sanctuaries.

> Every city is under his shadow,
> so that his heart indulges in what it pleases.
> One sings to him in every dwelling,
> every workshop stands fast for him in love.
> One brews for him on festival days,
> in the night, asleep, one waits for midnight.

> His name goes round on the rooftops,
> his is the song in the night, when it is dark.
> The gods receive offering loaves from his *ka*,
> the richest god, who protects what is theirs.[28]

In the Egyptian language, the *pr*, the divine household, is contrasted with the *ḥwt-nṯr*, the "god's house." The latter designates the actual temple, which was built of stone, unlike the storehouses and workshops, and lay dwellings as well. Like the servants in a household staff, the priests were *ḥmw-nṯr*, "servants of the god." They lived on the divine offerings that were placed, but not actually offered, before the cult statue and then before other statues of kings and private persons that shared in the so-called reversion offering, and which were finally consumed by the priests. From indications of the remuneration of specialized workers in that period, it has been calculated that 600 families lived on the eighty sacks of grain that Ramesses III donated to the Theban Amun as a daily offering ration. Naturally, this figure does not refer to a single temple, but to all the temples of Amun scattered throughout the land. The personnel of a normal temple consisted of about ten to twenty persons who dwelled in houses inside the temple enclosure. There were also the lay priests, the "hour-priests" comprising a group about ten times larger, who served in the temple only periodically and lived outside it.

2.2.2. THE TEMPLE AS "CENTER" AND "WAY"

Some temples were made of brick, but as a rule, a temple was a monumental stone construction, at least from the New Kingdom on, and for the most part earlier as well. In Egypt, stone was confined to sacred architecture, which included both temples and tombs. The contrast between the sacred and the profane was thus strongly emphasized in architecture. As a representative monumental construction, a temple was laden with meaning. We shall try to derive information pertinent to the context here from ground plans and from texts. As in the case of Egyptian cities, the question of the essence of an Egyptian temple has no answer that is valid for all periods. In this case as well, it is advisable to begin with the later periods, specifically the Ptolemaic temples, and then ask to what extent their salient characteristics were also valid for earlier divine dwellings. The Ptolemaic temples afford the advantage of a clearly defined type: nearly the same plan and the same architectural concept underlies all the large temples of this architecturally active era. From the inscriptions in the temples, it emerges that their common ground plan was thought to be derived from that of a primeval temple designed by the creator god himself at the beginning of the world.

Let us look, then, at the temple of Horus at Edfu (Figure 2). Two elements clearly stand out: the monumental pylon and, at the opposite end, in the innermost part of the temple (which in this case stretches along a north-south axis), the sanctuary, a free-standing naos. According to the principle that we shall call "center," this naos is surrounded by five "layers": (1) a corridor, (2) a ring of thirteen rooms opening off three sides of this corridor, (3) another corridor area with connecting doors and stairs leading to the roof, (4) an outer corridor, and (5) the exterior walls of the temple. To the south, according to the contrasting principle of "way," the sanctuary is preceded by a series of (once again) five rooms and five connecting doorways: (1) an ante-

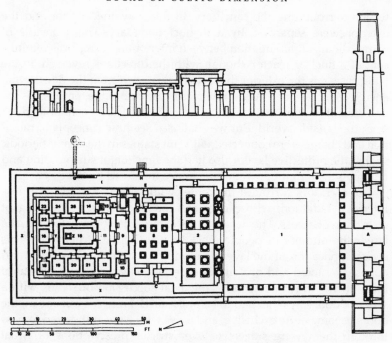

FIGURE 2. Elevation and plan of the temple of Horus at Edfu. From
S. Sauneron and H. Stierlin, *Die letzten Tempel Ägyptens: Edfu und Philae*
(Zurich, 1975), pp. 36–37.

room extending to the ends of the corridor surrounding the sanctuary,
called the "hall of the Ennead" (because the deities who dwelled in the
ring of chapels opening off this corridor were gathered there before the
chief god), (2) the offering room, (3) the inner hypostyle hall, (4) the Great
Hypostyle Hall, called the "Hall of Appearance," and (5) the colon-
naded court. Looking in from the outside, this sequence of rooms presents the appearance of a series of nested passageways, each
surrounding the ones inside. It seems as though a sort of central perspective has been constructed. From the exterior to the interior, the
rooms become ever smaller, while the floor becomes higher and the
ceiling lower. Corresponding to the diminution of space is an increasing darkness. The courtyard, which is flooded with light, is followed
by the crepuscular Hall of Appearance. The inner rooms lie in deep
darkness, with only isolated slits in the roof and the walls casting mysterious, spotlight-like beams of light.

The architectural technique of insulating and isolating the holy of
holies is connected with the notion of screening off. The profane, the
evil, and the impure were unable to penetrate the five layers of pro-

tection surrounding the sanctuary. In this way, the interior and the exterior were separated by a distinct boundary. This principle of extraordinary differentiation between interior and exterior is reminiscent of a nuclear reactor, though with the directions reversed: in the latter case, it is the exterior that is to be protected from the devastating energy collected deep inside, whereas in the case of the temple, it is the cult statues within that must be screened off from "contamination" from the outside world. But we shall also see how concepts of radiation and charge were connected with cult statues in these later periods, so that the protective layers also had the function of surrounding and retaining the radiant power of the image inhabited by the deity.

The corridors surround the center with several zones of ever less intensive radiation, whose decrease corresponds to a lessening of restriction of access. The nearer to the exterior a zone was located, the larger the number of people who were authorized to enter it. This social implication of the layering of interior and exterior, secrecy and openness, sacred and profane, is especially clear in the architectural form of the "way," or "route," the axial succession of rooms with a series of doorways that had to be penetrated. From the outside in, the doors become more exclusive, and those who were authorized to pass through them were subject to ever stricter prescriptions of ritual purity. This was not, however, a human route. Evidently, no priest ever penetrated this succession of doorways from the outside to the inside (except when carrying the divine image). Ordinarily, the outer doors remained shut, while the priests on duty, after purifying themselves in the sacred lake, entered through the side door. But when the temple doors were opened on festival days, it was the god who made his way through them as he left the temple in procession. The succession of rooms, halls, and courts gave architectonic form to *his* route, not that of humans. The forms of the centralizing enclosure and the symmetrical, axial succession of rooms emphasizing the processional route, correspond to the contrasting principles of arrest and movement as they related to the god.

The god resided in his temple in two forms: as a cult statue that remained in place and as a portable processional barque. The cult statue reified the god who rested in the innermost, the most sacred, the most screened-off heart of the temple; the barque hypostatized the god who emerged, who left the holy of holies on festival days, who proceeded outwards through the terraced zones of the ever-larger rooms and "appeared" in the profane outer world. For the duration of the festival, this "turn outward" blurred the starkly accented boundary between exterior and interior, or as it is expressed in Egyptian hymns, between "sky and earth." Evidently, the blurring of this otherwise sharply accentuated boundary was a part of the Egyptian concept of a religious festival. The appearance of the god, filling sky and earth with his splendor and inspiring all the world to rejoicing, sanctified the world outside. This idea of a turning to the outside on festival days and an opening of the otherwise hermetically sealed sacred gave the processional route its architectonic form, with spaces that grew ever larger from the interior to the exterior, through rooms, hypostyle halls, and the open courtyard.

The god's processional route also extended beyond the temple: a sacred avenue led straight to the river, the land's sole, yet perfectly sufficient, transportation route. Other, equally straight sacred avenues made a connection with other temples and holy places that the god visited during his processions. The festival outings thus encroached on urban planning. These processional avenues were of astonishing monumentality and were uncompromisingly laid out. In the New Kingdom, for example, three causeways, each about 38 yards wide and situated quite near one another, led from valley temples in the cultivated land to the three mortuary temples of Deir el-Bahari. These were not only perfectly straight, but they had exactly the same incline, which means that rises in the ground had to be leveled and depressions filled in. These avenues were paved with snow-white limestone and flanked by sloping limestone walls. Statues of the king lined the causeway of Mentuhotpe, and sphinxes that of Hatshepsut. In the Old Kingdom, the pyramids had been built with the same rigorous and uncompromising will to extreme monumentality as the religious structures of the New Kingdom. They, too, were signs of the divine on earth and sprang from the desire to establish a relationship between the heavens and the earth—or, as it is stated in the Hermetic tractate, to make the earth into the image (*imago*) of heaven.

If we compare the temple of Horus at Edfu to a typical divine temple of the New Kingdom, such as the temple of Khons at Karnak (Figure 3), the similarities and differences emerge clearly. The principle of centering by means of enclosure is less pronounced; the holy of holies is surrounded by secondary rooms and chapels, but not by isolating corridors and layers of walls. In fact, the concept of screening and isolation of the holy, as expressed in the centralizing concept of spatial ordering, is a typically late concept. The religion of the later periods was dominated by fear of profaning, of not heeding the prescriptions, of polluting the sacred. The rituals of this era—Protection of the House, Protection of the Body, Protection of the Bed, Protection of the *Neshmet*-barque, or Felling Apophis, Warding Off Evil, Felling Seth and His Following, and so forth—had a pronounced protective and exorcistic character.

In the temple of Khons, the motif of the processional route appears in precisely the same form as in temples built a millennium later, for it is a typical architectural concept of the New Kingdom. There are temples from this period in which the principle of the route is even

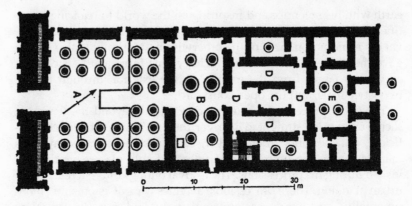

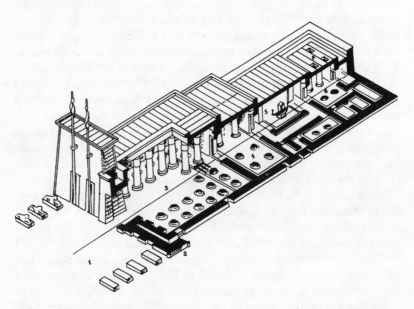

FIGURE 3. Plan and axonometric elevation of the temple of Khons at Karnak. Plan from K. Lange and M. Hirmer, *Ägypten: Architektur, Plastik, Malereri in drei Jahrtausenden*, 5th ed. (Munich, 1975), p. 143, fig. 61. Axonometric drawing from K. Michalowski, *Ägypten* (Freiburg, 1969), p. 571.

more dominant, such as the temple of Luxor. Temple plans that stress the notion of route set their festival function in the foreground. The importance of the festival associated with the temple of Luxor can be deduced immediately from a glance at its floor plan, and indeed, the festival of Luxor was probably the most important state festival during the New Kingdom.

But there was something further. Temples that stressed their route sheltered ambulatory, oracular deities. In Egypt, deities "spoke" through movement to make their wills known. Thus, the divine image moved toward the pretender chosen to be the successor to the throne or to be high priest or the official chosen to be scribe of the granary. Questions put to oracles had to be formulated in such a way that they could be answered by a simple yes or no. A forward movement of the divine image signified assent, a backward movement disapproval. Alternative responses were written down separately and presented to the deity, and the one toward which the statue turned was the correct one. This practice began in the New Kingdom at the same time that the new type of temple stressing the concept of route made its appearance, and it quickly spread throughout the land. But of all the oracles, that of the Theban Amun remained by far the most prominent. When we have dated records of oracular decisions, without exception, they occurred during religious festivals, thus showing that in Egypt, oracles were fundamentally connected with festivals. But this means that the form in which city deities exercised their de facto rulership—namely, oracles and divine jurisdiction—were intimately tied to the festivals and the associated appearances of the divine image in the open, and thus that their rulership reached beyond the temple enclosure and included the entire citizenry.

2.2.3. THE TEMPLE AS COSMOS

Much has been written about the cosmological significance of temples during the later periods of Egyptian history, making it the best known of all their aspects and functions. We can therefore limit ourselves to a brief summary of the most important facts. Essentially, the floor of these later temples represented the earth, and the ceiling the sky. Columns took the form of plants rising from the earth, and the dados of the walls were decorated with marsh plants or with processions of "fecundity figures," personifications of telluric fruitfulness that always face the inner part of the temple, bearing offerings. As the sky, the ceilings were decorated with stars or with astronomical representations. Between the floor and the ceiling, between earth and sky, stretched the decorations on the walls with their endless cult scenes filling this stony cosmos *in effigie* with action and life.

In the semantics of an Egyptian temple, there is a contradiction that is probably based in the structure of the sacred. Viewed from the outside, the temple is a highly protected area, an enclave of the sacred in a profane world, a tightly sealed vessel of radiant divine power that has mysteriously taken up earthly residence on this very spot. But viewed from within, this vessel of holiness separated from the world is itself the entire world. The temple represents a cosmos beyond which there is nothing more. The cult image filled the temple with an emanation of divine presence, while at the same time, the god filled the entire cosmos with the radiance of his manifestation. Certain Egyptian hymns lend perfect expression to this paradoxical structure:

> His face is unveiled in his temple,
> his cry penetrates to the end of the earth.
> His festival takes place in this sanctuary,
> his aroma plies the ocean.
> Lord of appearance in Thebes,
> his sovereignty fills the foreign lands.
> Sky and earth are filled with his beauty,
> his rays are flooded with gold.[29]

In another hymn, we read

> Your *ba* is mighty in Thebes,
> your sovereignty seizes the south.
> Your name is holy in Heliopolis,
> the north is filled with fear of your power.[30]

The cosmic symbolism of Egyptian temples rests on this antinomy between interior and exterior, between local ties and the omnipresence of the divine manifestation. The naos in which the cult statue rests is the remotest part of the sky, where the gods and goddesses dwell. The doors of the shrine are the celestial gates through which the sun god passes in the morning. The remainder of the temple is the world that the sun god floods with light when he appears in the east. Naos and temple thus have an internal-external relationship to one another. When the doors of the shrine are opened, the priest recites

> The door-leaves of the sky are opened on earth,
> so that the foreign lands and Egypt might gleam by means of his forms of manifestation.[31]

At the same time, however, the temple as a whole is a "'heaven' on earth":

> Come in peace, that you might unite with your house, your great light-land (*akhet*) on earth.[32]

"The form of the temple is like the sky with the sun,"[33] as it is put in a text of the Ramesside Period. From the New Kingdom on, innumerable texts emphasize that the temple is "like the *akhet* of the sky" or an "image of the celestial *akhet*."

The temple was a "sky" on earth, but at the same time sky *and* earth. It was a vessel of sacredness in the profane world, and it *was* the world that the omnipresent god filled to its limits. The symbolism of the temple and the concept of the divine were interrelated. The temple was an image of the cosmos, and the god who dwelled in it was a universal god. In chapter 9, we show that this concept of the divine made its appearance in the Ramesside Period, which explains why the cosmic character of temples, not only as an image of the sky but also of the world as a whole, asserted itself ever more clearly down through the later periods of Egyptian history. In the late temples, the world was present for the god in his house. Above all, that world was the land, or as the Egyptians put it, "the entire land" or the "Two Lands," that is, the land of Egypt, which had always been equated with the earth as the ordered realm of the world.

Processions of personifications of the forty-two nomes of Egypt, in long, geographically ordered (from south to north) rows, are depicted offering the products of their nomes to the chief deity of the temple. Geographical hymns establish a relationship between this chief deity and the succession of principal deities of each of the forty-two nomes, who are again enumerated in the same geographically ordered sequence. There are also representations of the chief deities of temples in the forms and names in which they were worshiped in each of the forty-two nomes. Just as the land of Egypt was called a temple in the later Hermetic text, here the temple was portrayed as the land of Egypt. This signified a strong emphasis on and dramatization of the local dimension of the divine. Unlike the temples of the New Kingdom, which cut a piece of the heavens out of the earth and offered it to deities as their dwellings, the later temples settle the deities specifically in the land. It is for this reason that the land was included in the temples in the form of geographical processions and litanies. The entire land waited on the deities in their temples, in return for which it was blessed with the beneficent effects of the divine presence.

Just as temple architecture actualized the cosmic aspect of the earth with its plant-shaped columns and its friezes of plants, so the processions of gods actualized the land in its social aspect. This also expressed the Egyptian view of the world, which interpreted the cosmos as a society. This was also true of the sky, whose cosmic aspect was represented on the ceilings of the temples. The social aspect of the heavens was represented by the secondary deities, the *theoi synnaoi*, who were worshiped in the chapels surrounding the holy of holies. To me, this point seems especially characteristic of Egyptian temples. No deity was the sole occupant of his or her temple. The great morning liturgy, which greeted the god appearing in the sky and the cult statue's awakening in the temple, enumerated in the form of a litany all that constituted this "sphere of belonging." The refrain was repeated seventy-eight times:

> Awake in peace, may you awake peacefully,
> Horus of Behdet awakes in peace.
> The gods awake early to adore your *ba*,
> O exalted winged beetle who ascends to the sky!

> It is he who "opens the sphere" in the sky goddess,
> and fills the earth with gold dust,
> who comes to life in the eastern mountains and descends head first
>   into the depths in the western mountains,
> who sleeps daily in Behdet.[34]

Each recitation of the refrain was followed by one of the following:

1. twenty-six theological aspects of Horus
2. the names of the ten subsidiary deities (*theoi synnaoi*): Hathor, Harsomtus, Khons, Min, Sokar, Osiris, Isis, Mehit-Tefnut, Nephthys, and Nekhbet, who are summarized as "the deities who are front of you and behind you, the Ennead surrounding your majesty," the falcon mummies of the sacred animals of the past, the deceased divine forebears
3. the various parts of the god's body
4. the emblems, crown, and insignia of his regalia
5. the city, and the temple with its halls, chapels, pillars, doorways, statues, reliefs, and barque shrine.

In the local dimension—that is, in the temple—we encounter the divine in an expressly polytheistic form. The temple shelters the god as a multiplicity, as a member of the divine realm that is itself a part of his all-encompassing essence, just as the temple could be considered as a part of the divine person. In the temples of the New Kingdom, the multiplicity of chapels surrounding the holy of holies already points to the underlying polytheistic concept of the divine.

In addition to the cosmic and social aspects of Egyptian temples, there was also the mythic. The temple recalled a mythical place, the primeval mound. It stood on the first soil that emerged from the primeval waters, on which the creator god stood to begin his work of creation. Through a long chain of ongoing renewals, the present temple was the direct descendant of the original sanctuary that the creator god himself had erected on the primeval mound. An origin myth connecting the structure with creation is associated with each of the larger late temples. These myths expressed the concept of divine autochthony, for the gods had inhabited the land since creation. Each temple was not only the center, but also the origin of the world. Yet the same temples also contained inscriptions containing concrete historical information. Thus, in an inscription in the crypts of the temple of Hathor at Dendara, we read of the precursors of the present temple that a temple from the time of Tuthmosis III had stood on this very spot, and that for his part, he had renewed a temple from the reign of Cheops.

Such successions of temples are also known archaeologically. On the island of Elephantine in the extreme south of Egypt, exemplary excavation technique and favorable circumstances have made it possible to reconstruct the architectural history of a temple that includes all the periods of pharaonic history—a stroke of luck that despite the uniqueness of the temple enables us to draw conclusions about the basic outline of general developments in ancient Egypt. At the outset, this local sanctuary was associated with a natural phenomenon, a niche formed by three huge granite blocks that were nearly 12 feet high. Here, a small brick hut measuring about 5 feet × 7 feet was constructed at the very beginning of pharaonic history, ca. 2900 B.C.E. (Figure 4). Later, a forecourt was added. More than one thousand years later, the limestone temple of Dynasty 12 continued to respect the natural setting of the niche in the rocks. It was not until five hundred more years had passed that the sandstone temple of Queen Hatshepsut made a radical break with the previous dimensions of the building and was built over the blocks of granite, which had in the interim been covered by more than 3 feet of deposit. Yet in the many unusual features of its ground plan, this temple still reflected a reference to the original sanctuary, for a descending ramp maintained its relationship to the niche in the rocks. It was the Ptolemaic temple that, another millennium and a half later, followed the conventional layout of its time on a level some yards higher, thus obliterating the unique aspect of the original layout.

This temple is an impressive example of what archaeological reality can lie behind the mythical or historical tradition of the temple inscriptions in an individual instance. The spade did not uncover the "primeval mound," but rather a series of successive temples that reached back over three millennia to the threshold of history. Seen the other way around, the temple was an organism that was ever growing, or more precisely put, in a process of augmentative renewal. In the beginning, there were primitive huts, which were recalled down into the latest periods in representations and in religious emblems or signs in the hieroglyphic writing system. But the temple architecture itself was filled with such archaic reminiscences. The most obvious examples are the torus molding and the cornice, the most common and best-known hallmarks of Egyptian architecture. These are renderings in stone of primitive methods of building with bundles of reeds. A temple was the reification of a cultural memory, a half-mythical, half-historical

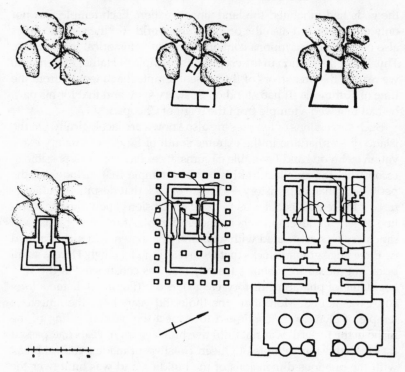

FIGURE 4. Plans of the various stages of the temple of Satis at Elephantine. From W. Kaiser, "Stadt und Tempel von Elephantine, siebente Grabungsbericht," *MDAIK* 33 (1977):65, fig. 1.

awareness from the unbelievably remote origins of pharaonic Egypt. Standing on its primeval mound, it pointed back to the building methods employed at the beginning of history. It was an image of the cosmos not only in the spatial sense, but in the temporal sense as well.

2.3. *Image and Cult*

2.3.1. *Descensio*: EGYPTIAN THEORIES OF THE CULT STATUE

The words "image" and "cult" point to the very heart of Egyptian religion. The center around which everything revolved, the basis on which everything rested, was neither holy scripture, nor shamanistic visions, nor ecstatic or mystic experiences of something wholly other, but rather the cult, the daily routine of an endlessly differentiated service rendered to the deities in the forms in which they were locally resident, their cult statues. If the Egyptians were famed in antiquity for serving their deities not only *pia mente*, "with a pious attitude," but also *sedula religione*, "with incessant cultic worship" (*Asclepius* 23), if they seemed to Herodotus to be *theosebes*, the most "pious" of all peoples (*Histories* II 37), these statements rest on the observation that nowhere else in the world was so much done for the divine, or so continuously. The text of the Hermetic tractate *Asclepius*, which we used as the starting point of our treatment of the "local" dimension of divine presence, also refers to cult activity when it calls Egypt the "image of heaven" and the "temple of the whole world," for it immediately qualifies these comparisons:

> . . . aut, quod est verius, translatio aut descensio omnium, quae gubernantur atque excercentur in caelo.
> . . . or, better, the conveying or descent of all that is regulated and carried out in heaven.[35]

The concept of image (*imago*) is immediately clarified: what is intended is action, not something static. Celestial activities are carried out on earth, and Egypt is a temple because it is the land where this is done according to heavenly directives. This activity is the cult, and specifically the statue cult. This passage from the Hermetic tractate is connected with a discourse regarding statues: they are the "gods who are in the temples," and their maker (*fictor*) is human, just as the highest god is the creator (*effector*) of the celestial deities.

Although this late text, which is not, strictly speaking, an Egyptian one, can serve only as an entrée into genuine Egyptian views concerning image and cult, it is nevertheless worthwhile to consider it briefly. Have we read it correctly? *Homo fictor est deorum qui in templis sunt* (man is the maker of the gods who are in the temples)—are the divine images a homemade "fiction" of humankind? This statement is deliberately provocative. It occurs in a dialogue, and the other interlocutor, Asclepius, acknowledges, *confundo, o Trismegiste*: "I am confused." Incredulous, he asks, *statuas dicis*, "Do you mean the statues?" Yes, but *statuas animatas sensu et spiritu plenas*, "statues alive with sensation and filled with spirit," which are prescient (*futurorum praescias*) and can give oracles, grant dreams, and cause and cure maladies. The statues, we are told, have two natures, one divine and one material, one above and the other below humankind. As creators of these statues, humans are reminded of their own divine origin, and by piously tending and worshiping them, they make the divine at home on earth.

What we learn about image and cult from Egyptian sources is surprisingly similar to the concepts of *descensio* and *translatio*. In the Morning Song from Edfu cited earlier, it is said of Horus:

> He comes from the sky each day
> to behold his image on its Great Seat.
> He *descends* (*hꜣi*) on his image (*sḥm*)

and mingles with his cult images (ʿḥmw).[36]

A similar text from Dendara says of Hathor:

> She flies down (ʿpi) from the sky
> to enter the *akhet* of her *ka* on earth,
> she flies down onto her body, she joins with her form.[37]

This divine *descensio* affected not only the cult statue, but all the representations in the temple, even those on the walls:

> She unites with her forms
> that are carved in her sanctuary.
>
> She alights on her forms
> that are carved on the wall.[38]

A text from Dendara referring to the representations in the Osiris chapel is especially explicit:

> Osiris . . . comes as a spirit (ȝḫ),
> to unite with his form in his sanctuary.
> He comes from the sky flying like a sparrowhawk
> with glittering feathers, and the *ba*s of the gods with him.
> He descends as a falcon on his chamber in Dendara . . .
> In peace, he enters his august chamber
> with the *ba*s of the gods who are around him.
> He sees his mysterious form depicted in its place,
> his figure engraved on the wall;
> he enters into his mysterious form,
> alights on his image . . .
> and the *ba*s of the gods take their places beside him.[39]

Time and again in the temple inscriptions of the Graeco-Roman Period, we encounter not only a terminology of descent that places deity and image in a vertical relationship and corresponds to the antinomy of heaven and earth in the Hermetic tractate, but also a terminology that expresses a double nature. The texts speak of the *ba* of the god, which alights on his *sekhem*. We translate *ba* as "soul"; Egyptians believed that this was the form in which people lived on after death, not on earth, in the tomb, and in the memory of the community, but in the next world, in the sky. *Sekhem* literally means "power," and probably also "sign of power" and thus "image." We read, for example, at Esna:

> His *ba* descends from the sky onto his earthly image,
> His majesty alights on his *sekhem*.[40]

And at Dendara:

> After his *ba* came from the sky to see his monuments,
> his heart united with his cult images.[41]

> After his *ba* came to the house of Re,
> it united with his image on the wall.[42]

The texts describe the relationship between the *ba* and the image as "uniting," "fraternizing," and "embracing." Hermann Junker coined the concept of "installation" or "indwelling" (*Einwohnung*), which has since become common in Egyptology. The concept is in fact quite well taken, for it expresses the specifically Egyptian concept of the "local" dimension of divine presence and supplements our all-too-static concepts of "native" or "autochthonous" in reference to the performative, eventful nature of this presence. The gods do not "dwell" on earth, which would merely be a condition; rather, they "install" themselves there, and specifically, they "install" themselves in their images: this is an event that occurs regularly and repeatedly, but with the collaboration of humankind, on whom the cult is dependent. Junker coined the concept of "indwelling" in reference to text passages that describe a deity's *ba* as descending from the sky and uniting not only with the cult statue, but also with the representations in the reliefs on the walls. These reliefs depict scenes of the cult: the deity descends from the sky as a *ba* to participate in the cult in the form of these images.

Clearly, in these late temple inscriptions we are dealing with a fully formed theory that distinguished between the deities and their representations and established the relationship between them with a nuanced terminology. Just as in the Hermetic corpus, it is a matter of *descensio*, "descent." The deities were in the sky as *ba*s, and their images were on earth; in the cult, they "installed" themselves in the temple daily. We must now examine to what extent this theory was an accomplishment of the Graeco-Roman Period, or, as Morenz and others have felt, was also true for earlier periods. The concept of installation/indwelling has its origin in beliefs about the dead. In texts of Dynasty 18 (ca. 1400 B.C.E.), we read statements such as "May my *ba* alight on my images (*ꜥḥmw*) in the monuments I have made."[43]

In this and later periods, there was a common mortuary concept that the *ba* of the deceased would descend from the sky and alight on the mummy. Thus, for instance, we read in a late, widely used mortuary text, "Your *ba* ascends to the sky in the company of the *ba*s of the gods and descends again on your mummy in the cemetery."[44]

Because of the analogy between the sun's course and the fate of the dead, on which the mythic organization of the sun's course is based (this will be discussed in detail in connection with the "mythic" dimension), similar concepts are also found in the older solar religion. At night, the sun god descends from the sky and into the netherworld as a *ba* to unite with his corpse. In the theological explanation of this process, Osiris was understood to be the netherworldly corpse of the sun god, so that it could be said of both the sun god and Osiris that his *ba* was in the sky and his mummy in the netherworld. Building on these concepts, though admittedly in another direction entirely, in the thirteenth and twelfth centuries a theology was developed of Amun as a cosmic deity who, as *ba*, image, and mummy, filled the three-tiered cosmos of sky, earth, and netherworld. This concept became generalized, and in later periods, all deities had a *ba*, an image, and a corpse, thus filling the cosmos with their three forms. In the later periods of Egyptian history, these various beginnings evolved into a theory that conceived of the relationship of deity and image in terms of above and below, sky and earth, *ba* and mummy, and correspondingly, of the process of "indwelling" as a *descensio* (*h3i* "to descend," *ḥni*, "to alight").

This opposition of above and below, sky and earth, divine substance and cult statue come into play in a distinctive manner in a ritual called Uniting with the Sun (*ḥnm itn*), which was carried out several times a year on the occasion of major religious festivals. The priests would carry the portable statues up to the temple roof to be bathed by the sunlight and thereby charged, as it were, with divine substance for a fresh period of time. Hymns that were sung on these occasions also explain this ceremony as a descent of the *ba*, which unites with the deity's earthly image and takes up residence in the temple. A verb was even derived from the noun *ba* to designate the statues' condition of being enlivened by divinity and being filled with its spirit. What is striking about this concept is that not only statues of the sun god, but all divine statues, were enlivened by contact with the sunlight. It is as though all divine *ba*-substance was concentrated in the sun, from which it was beamed into the cult statues of the deities.

One would search in vain in earlier periods for precursors of this ritual or the concepts expressed in it. Only one passage seems to express a similar view of the relationship between the sun and the divine statues. It is in the Instruction of Ani, which is probably from the early Ramesside Period (first half of the thirteenth century B.C.E.):

> The god of this land is the sun in the sky.
> (Only) his symbols are on earth.[45]

This statement has been taken as an expression of purest Amarna theology. The "symbols," however, are the divine statues, which were categorically excluded from Amarna religion. In fact, we see here the beginning of a concept that already closely resembles that of the later periods: the sun as the celestial concentration of all divine substance, and the many earthly divine statues in which, in the specific refractions of the polytheistic religion, this substance took on a form accessible to humankind. The actual locus of this viewpoint is the New Solar Theology of the New Kingdom, which we discuss in chapter 9.2. But even here, we find no trace of a ritual that could be in any way connected with the late Uniting with the Sun.

Typically enough, though, we find what are at least echoes of it in the funerary cult, in connection with a very ancient ritual that, it would seem, was based from the very beginning on a conceptual distinction between divine enlivening and the material substance of the cult image. The Egyptians called this ritual, which was even carried out in connection with the Uniting with the Sun at Esna and Kom Ombo, the Opening of the Mouth. It was a comprehensive sequence of rites, some of them quite archaic, whose goal was to endow the statue with a soul and to quicken it. Its roots were surely in the funerary cult, for the principal actor was the son, who, *inter alia*, had to sleep by the statue to see his deceased father in a dream. As early as the Old Kingdom, however, it was carried out on divine images as routinely and repeatedly as the Uniting with the Sun ritual in the Ptolemaic Period. In the New Kingdom, the ritual was expanded to include scenes from the solar cult that were evidently to be enacted in the forecourt of the tomb (and temple?), in the light of the sun. One scene is an offering litany with censings for all the gods and goddesses, ending with the sun god and all the deities of his barque and his circle. The other is a censing that was performed only for Re-Harakhty, the sun god. It is certainly these rites that are meant when we read in funerary wishes of this period,

> May your mummy be set up before the sun god
> in the forecourt of your tomb.[46]

With its nuanced rites and concepts, the mortuary cult was a "preparatory school" for theology, and through ritual activities related to tomb statues, Egyptians learned to distinguish between deities and their cult statues. In the Ptolemaic Period, the Opening of the Mouth was even carried out on the temple itself as a living, and repeatedly to be enlivened, receptacle of the divine essence!

With regard to the classical Egyptian concept of the essence of divine images, the text that first comes to mind is the so-called Memphite Theology. The text is preserved only in a copy from Dynasty 25, yet there was once a consensus that it reproduced a much older original going back at least to the Old Kingdom. Today, however, scholars are inclined, with good reason, to regard it as a formulation of the New Kingdom or even of the period in which it was copied down. This text, which is a theological tractate about the Memphite deity Ptah as creator god, states,

He "bore" the gods, he created the cities, he founded the nomes,
he placed the gods in their cult places,
he established their offerings and equipped their sanctuaries,
he made their "bodies" according to their wishes.

So the gods entered their "bodies,"
of all kinds of wood, all kinds of minerals, all kinds of clay,
and of everything that grows on him (the earth = creator god),
in which they took form.[47]

The text begins by confirming, with remarkable clarity, the triad of city, temple, and cult image that our treatment has identified as the basis of the local dimension of divine presence. In what follows, the process of "indwelling" is described as an "entering" (not a *descensio*, "descent"), and a clear distinction is drawn between the two "natures" of divine images: the gods on the one hand, and on the other, their "bodies" of more or less perishable earthly materials. The text unequivocally expresses what we must emphasize as the basic Egyptian concept regarding this point: *The statue is not the image of the deity's body, but the body itself.* It does not represent his form, but rather gives him form. The deity takes form in the statue, just as in a sacred animal or a natural phenomenon. The statues were not made, but "born." This was not said only in the case of the creator god Ptah; in royal inscriptions, "to bear" is practically a technical term for the fashioning of a cult statue, but even simple craftsmen or artisans say of themselves that they "bore" the statues of deities or the deities themselves. The profession of sculptor was designated "one who makes live," that is, "quickener," and the quickening ritual of the Opening of the Mouth constitutes the last stage in the preparation of the statue. The Egyptians never blurred the distinction between image and deity, but they took it in a different direction and to a different level from that to which we are accustomed. We shall return to this point later.

Yet another text supplies us with information regarding the Egyptian concept of a deity's "indwelling" in a cult statue. As in the case of the statement from the Instruction of Ani cited earlier, it belongs to the genre of wisdom literature, which even in Egypt is to be distinguished from religious texts in the stricter sense. The central theme of the Instruction for Merikare, which has come down to us in manuscripts of Dynasty 18 but is surely based on a Middle Kingdom text, is the problem of requital. In this connection, it states

Generation after generation passes by among humankind,
but the god who knows characters has hidden himself.
There is none who can repel the blow of the "lord of the hand"
(requital);

he strikes (without) eyes seeing it.

Revere the god on his way,
(the god), who is made of precious stones and made (lit., "born") of
bronze
like water that is replaced by other water.
But there is no stream that allows itself to be hidden;
it destroys the canal in which it was hidden.[48]

Here, a distinction is made between the hidden god as lord of requital
and the god made of stone and bronze, the cult statue. This distinction
is clarified by another one, that between standing water in an artificial
canal or pond and a living stream that cannot be dammed. Does this
distinction not intimate the double nature of the cult statue?
Humankind is directed to the "god on his way," that is, to the local
dimension of his presence, to the cult. Here and in this form shall they
revere him. But at the same time, they must know that the god who is
present, dwelling in his cult statue, reigns everywhere in his hiddenness and can at any time burst forth from this "channeled" form in
which he dwells like a river that overflows its dam. Here, there is no
talk of sky and earth, *ba* and image, but rather of hiddenness and presence, of human "enactment" and divine spontaneity. The simplification
and in a certain sense the trivializing of this mysterious antinomy in the
sense of an above and a below was the work of priests of later eras.

2.3.2. *Translatio*: FUNDAMENTALS OF THE EGYPTIAN CULT

The essence of the Egyptian cult has been called a "response," a
human "reaction" to the ever-present, supereminent effect of the
divine. This interpretation might do justice to the Egyptians' own
understanding. For them, the deities were no fictions, but genuine
powers. Nor did they view cult activity as a symbolic enactment, but
rather as a genuine encounter that, as is clear from many of the relevant texts, they experienced with fear and trembling, but which also
filled them with wonder, joy, and pleasure. For the Egyptians, the cult
activities that seem so routine to us were emotionally charged in a way
that we can describe only as a reaction to the prior occurrence of a
spontaneous manifestation of the divine. But a closer look shows that
we must make a distinction. Festival rituals were expressly "reactive";
the deity took the initiative, and the rites were accompanied by strong
emotions of wonder and joy. The daily cult ritual, however, was pre-
dominantly "operative": the priest awakened, greeted, worshiped,
purified, anointed, and dressed the cult statue and provided it three
times daily with the huge variety of foods of the daily offerings. Even
in the Egyptians' own understanding, the character of a symbolic

enactment clearly predominated in this portion of cult activity. This activity was directed to a cult statue inhabited by a deity. The priest's acts did not respond to the process of "indwelling" that was occurring, but rather accompanied and confirmed it. Indeed, the divine acts can be understood as a response to this activity. The ritual brought the divine effects down to earth, or—if we wish to do without the "above-below" metaphor of the later theology—brought them into a sphere that was accessible to human activity. If this cult activity were suspended, the deities would withdraw, leaving behind only the material substrate of their presence as an empty, inanimate form. The daily cult ritual corresponded to the local dimension of divine presence less in the sense of a response than that of an invitation and confirmation.

Egyptian cult, even the daily cult ritual, was a complex affair. The latter comprised rites of clothing and offering, and the clothing rites alone consisted of a good forty-five individual acts. Every action was broken down into its smallest constituent elements, and each of these was isolated as an individual rite. Thus, for instance, the first nine acts of the morning clothing ritual in the New Kingdom consisted of

1. lighting the flame
2. taking up the arm-shaped censer
3. placing the pan on the censer
4. placing incense in the flame
5. going to the sanctuary
6. breaking the cord
7. breaking the seal
8. sliding the doorbolt
9. "revealing the god" (opening the door-leaves of the shrine).[49]

The offering ritual was scarcely less comprehensive. It consisted of preparatory rites whose goal was to purify the offerings, the actual offering rites, praises of the deity, and concluding rites. To go into these in detail here is impossible, so I shall confine myself to an exposition of the basic structures of the ritual activity. In view of the amount and complexity of the material, it should be evident that counterexamples can be cited for just about any generalizing statement. Nevertheless, I feel it is legitimate to seek a generalizing perspective. It seems to me that three points are worth stressing in this connection.

First, the daily cult ritual was personal service to the lord of the temple, evidently modeled on the ceremony in which the king was clothed in the morning. As the lord of his house, the god was greeted, revered, and tended to. The ritual was thus rooted in the basic concept of the deity as resident in a locale; it is not directed toward a distant divinity who must be summoned, but rather to one who is present and resident. Its concern is with the well-being and satisfaction of the deity and thus with the requirements of the possibility of his earthly residence and local presence. The Egyptian word *ḥtp* (*hotep*), which means both "offering" and "satisfaction," is a central concept in the ritual.

The second point is that the ritual—and this is probably its most distinctive characteristic—*was not conceived of as a communication between the human and the divine, but rather as an interaction between deities*. In the spells with which the priest regularly accompanied his actions, and which were evidently as important to their success as the actions themselves, he assumes the role of such deities as Horus, Thoth, Anubis, and Harsaphes. In particular, the individual presentations (*hotep*) around which the ritual principally revolves are designated "eye of Horus," and everything from unguent to the foreleg of an ox was an object of cultic presentation. This remarkable process, which had its origin in the mortuary cult, deserves further comment.

We can begin by considering some examples of verbal interpretation of cultic acts. When fat is placed in the fire of the burnt offering to make the flames leap higher, it is said,

> Abundance comes, joined with abundance,
> Horus arises to cure (*sꜥḏ*) his eye
> in its name "fat" (*ꜥḏ*).[50]

When meat is then placed on the fire, it is said,

> The breast is the eye of Horus,
> the leg is the testicles of Seth.
> As Horus is satisfied with his eye,
> as Seth is satisfied with his testicles,
> so is the god satisfied with his meat.[51]

The same comparisons with the eye of Horus and the testicles of Seth are next applied to the offerings of beer, white bread, cakes, and wine. The concluding purification with the *nemset*-vessel includes the statement, "take to yourself the eye of Horus," and the censing is accompanied by the words

> The incense comes, the divine aroma comes,
> its aroma comes to you,
> the aroma of the eye of Horus comes to you.[52]

Even the "reversion of offerings"—that is, the presentation of the offerings that had been made to the god to the other divine statues and their ultimate consumption by the priests, and thus the removal of what had been brought—is related to the eye of Horus:

Your enemy retreats before you.
Horus turns to his eye
in its name "reversion of the offerings."
[...]
Take the offering of the king.
May the eye of Horus flourish with you![53]

At the end, when the torch is extinguished, it is said,

This is the eye of Horus,
through which you have become great,
you flourish through it,
you gain might through it.[54]

When the offerings are proclaimed, that is, when each of the items brought and offered to the god is announced in a litany-like manner, nearly every one of these announcements begins with the formula, "Take to yourself the eye of Horus!"

The verbal accompaniment of the individual presentations rests on the principle of explanatory transposition of what is happening into the divine realm. It is thus that an item being offered becomes the "eye of Horus." The latter is extremely multivalent; here, it probably stands above all for the notion of plenitude of life force. The oldest texts that mention it stem from the royal mortuary cult of the Old Kingdom and are preserved to us in great number in the Pyramid Texts. I believe that this is also the actual origin of this symbolism. The eye of Horus is the mythological interpretation of the gift of the lost life force that the son and successor restores to his deceased father and predecessor across the threshold that separates this world from the next. The eye of Horus symbolizes the life force that has been lost, the lack that death has inflicted on the recipient of the cult. Robbed by Seth, it had to be restored by Horus. Thus, for example, in a spell of the Pyramid Texts that was recited along with an offering of figs, we read

Osiris Wenis, take to yourself the eye of Horus,
which he has rescued from the hand of Seth.[55]

Here, the words for "fig" (*išd*) and "rescue" (*šd*) constitute a pun. The eye was torn from Horus by Seth and was restored to him by Thoth, but it was also restored to Osiris by Horus (and Thoth). This restitution was the embodiment of every alleviation of lack or need, from the extreme need of the deceased lying in the tomb to the cult statue's need to be waited on.

When the priest proffers an object—a loaf of bread, a jug of beer, a piece of meat—and explains it as the "eye of Horus," he thus enters into a divine constellation that originated in the relationship between the living son (Horus) and the deceased father (Osiris). This is the constellation that spans the gulf separating this world from the next. Here, too, as in the case of the theology of cult statues, the mortuary cult shows itself to be the "preparatory school" of theology. The mortuary cult supplied the model for bridging two spheres of existence: between the living and the deceased in their tombs, between humankind and the deities in their temples. And when the god is given the eye of Horus, it invigorates his life force as well, healing him in his need.

The third point, which flows from what has preceded but needs to be stressed separately, is that in Egyptian ritual, speech explicitly and performatively accomplishes this transposition of the cultic events into the divine realm. Via an older world of concrete rites and cult objects, the royal mortuary cult of the Old Kingdom systematically established a mythic world of meaning. We return to this in chapter 4. Speech was a preeminent means of making the otherworldly realm of meaning manifest in the this-worldly realm of symbolic objects and actions. Just as the deceased, as an element in this life, was displaced into the divine realm, so a deity, as an otherworldly power, could "install" himself or herself in a cult statue so as to act as an element in this world. Speech established a relationship between this and the other world—between sky and earth, to use the categories of the later theology—by interpreting cultic acts as divine or celestial events. Thus was accomplished what the Hermetic text designates *translatio*, the transference of celestial events to the terrestrial realm.

Finally, it must again be stressed that cult was based on the polytheistic structure of Egyptian religion. It was construed as activity carried out in the framework of divine constellations, between deities, and thus also as entailing a multiplicity of deities. Moreover, it was directed toward deities not in the comprehensive plenitude of their distant and hidden essence, but in the specific, well-defined special form of their individual local presence and cultic "indwelling." Expressly and often, the priest emphasizes, "I have compared your essence to no other god."[56] Cult statues also had to reproduce the distinctive traits of the deities. As they themselves wished, the creator god had fashioned the statues so as to resemble them. Multiplicity and variety prevail everywhere in this dimension.

The same was true of the temple and the city. A temple was, as a rule, inhabited by many deities and sheltered its principle deity along with the "sphere of belonging" to which he or she belonged as an animated being, at least according to the view of the later periods. A city was also inhabited by various deities. Numerous deities resided in the plurality of cities, and the total of the cities combined with the multiplicity of the deities residing in them into the unity of the land on the one hand, and on the other, into the unity of the pantheon. In

Egypt, there was no single Memphis or Thebes in the sense that there is a single Jerusalem, a single Rome, or a single Mecca, but rather a multitude of religious centers, each of them a holy city in its own right. And just as the polytheistic structure of the religion is clearly revealed in the geography of settlements and the architecture of temples, it also determined the meaning and form of cult activity.

CHAPTER 3

The Cosmos

3.1. Cult and Cosmos: Performance and Event, Symbol and Reality

Turning from the cultic or local dimension of divine presence to the cosmos, the latter at first appears in many ways to be the exact opposite of the cult. The cult was an essentially human performance in which gods and goddesses benevolently participated, "indwelling" (to use the late terminology) in the cult images human hands had fashioned for them by descending on them from the sky as *ba*. By contrast, the actual divine performance was the cosmos, the embodiment and result of what the deities did of their own accord. In this opposition, cult seems to be a human attempt to intervene in cosmic events, to influence them in a manner beneficial to society through offerings and prayer. As we have seen, such a perspective, in which cult and cosmos were polarized, was especially characteristic of the theology of the Ptolemaic temple inscriptions, which interpret the dichotomy as sky and earth. They portray the temple as the symbol and image of the cosmos, with the result that the rituals enacted in them could symbolically intervene in cosmic events, that is, in the world of the divine as it occurs in the form of the cosmos. The cosmos was essentially the sky, a distant, otherworldly realm, in a certain sense transcendent, and accessible to humankind only through the mediation of symbols. The actual dimension of divine presence was the cult.

With this theology of the cult, which was perhaps carried rather too rigorously to its logical conclusion, it would be difficult to convey the idea of the cosmos as a dimension of divine presence. Yet it was precisely this concept that was expressed in an ancient polemical statement directed against cult images and their worship: "The one and only temple of God is the cosmos."[1] Despite this theological position regarding the natural world, which has been carried with equal rigor to its logical conclusion, and which dismisses temples and cult images to seek the divine in nature alone as the temple built by God for himself, we should not classify Egyptian religion as a "natural religion." We must avoid such oppositions, moreover, if we are to understand

Egyptian religion not in its late, but in its classical expression. The logic and rigor of a system of thought that views "cult religion" and "natural religion" as opposites seems foreign and inappropriate to the earlier periods. Classical Egyptian religion was a little of each, and just as the preceding chapter was devoted to the cult, the present one deals with the sense in which Egyptian religion was a religion of nature.

3.2. Cosmography as Theology

A natural religion exists in the cosmic dimension of divine presence. It experiences nature as a hierophany, as a manifestation of divine powers. This concept is current in the contemporary world, or has again become current as the exact antithesis of our own religious tradition, which is stamped by Judeo-Christian beliefs. This has occurred via undercurrents preserved until modern times in alchemy, Hermetism, and neopagan movements of late classical antiquity; via the somewhat nostalgic transfiguration of pagan Greece in the German classical period, particularly in Schiller's poem "The Gods of Greece," with its striking and potent diagnosis of a "nature that has lost its gods"; and finally and most important, via attempts to understand this "loss" by means of scholarly analysis as a process of secularization or disenchantment, notably in the work of Max Weber. In its capacity as a natural religion, Egyptian religion was in no way unique; it was but one of innumerable expressions of the religious in an un-demystified world. As such, though, it had its own individual, culture-specific aspects, and these are dealt with in the discussion that follows.

The Egyptians' relationship to nature was characterized by an unusual wealth of detail and by a precision of observation and description, yet also by a peculiar narrowness of interest. The scenes depicting animals in the tombs of Old Kingdom officials are well known; they would do honor to a zoological textbook, so seldom is there any doubt as to the zoological classification of any of the animals represented. In contrast to a textbook, though, the animal world is not portrayed for its own sake, but in a partial manner that is determined by a specific horizon of relevance: what is represented is that which is important for human nourishment. There can be no question of a zoological textbook in these tomb reliefs, however true to nature they might be. This is just one symptom of an attitude toward the world that appears at all levels, and that struck the open-minded Greeks as rather exceptional. Because of the Egyptians' limited interest in nature, the Greeks felt that the Egyptians were *philochrematos*, "utilitarian," in contrast to themselves, who were *philomathés*, "scientific." Instead of obtaining precise information about the origin of the Nile, the Egyptians were content with an abstruse theory according to which the Nile flowed from the netherworld at Elephantine and at a place in the area of present-day Old Cairo called "Babylon" in Greek. Because the interest of the Egyptians was confined to the Nile of Egypt itself, it included the detail that Upper and Lower Egypt were each provided with a special Nile that had a source of its own. The Egyptians seem never to have inquired into the reasons for the most striking and puzzling natural occurrence in their land, the annual rise and fall of the Nile. The Greeks were surprised that the Egyptians either were satisfied with answers that could not withstand experience, as in the case of the source of the Nile, or had not first posed specific questions that the Greeks asked, as in the case of the Nile inundation. How astonished they would have been, had they known what questions the Egyptians posed instead, or had they known of the detailed maps the Egyptians made of the netherworld and other regions far removed from any human experience! This was obviously no question of bringing the world into the realm of experience, but rather of interpreting what lay beyond the realm of experience: it is clear that a concept such as *philochrematos*, an interest directed purely to practical utility, does not do justice to Egyptian culture.

3.2.1. COSMOGRAPHY OF VISIBLE REALITY

Egyptian interest in nature and the resulting style of cognition and theorizing was religious in its orientation; put more precisely, it was a solar theology. The actual locus of Egyptian "natural history" and cosmography was the cult of the sun, which was the source of the iconological principles and the concrete models for the reliefs that we admire in the tombs, as we know from fragments from the sun temples of Dynasty 5. The kings of this dynasty (ca. 2500 B.C.E.) constructed pyramids that were much smaller than those of their predecessors Khufu and Khephren, building instead sanctuaries for the sun god, whose cult was connected to their own mortuary cult. They also made "Son of Re" a regular component of their titularies. A legend attached to them, according to which they were sired by the sun god himself, who chose the wife of one of his priests to bear the first three kings of the dynasty as triplets. Dynasty 5 was the apogee of solar religion in ancient Egypt. In the sun temple of Neuserre, the fourth king of the dynasty, there was a relief-decorated corridor that has come to be called by the German term *Weltkammer* ("chamber of the world") because of the program of its decoration. The fragments that have been found display a huge number of animals carved in the finest relief style: wild animals, such as antelopes, gazelles, ibexes, cheetahs, panthers, and wild cattle; domesticated animals, such as cattle, donkeys, goats, and sheep; and all possible kinds of birds and watercourses filled with species of fish. People are also depicted, occupied with catching or raising these animals, and inscriptions serve as captions to the scenes. The repertoire of scenes seems to go far beyond those of the private tombs, though evidently not beyond their thematic framework, which can be connected, broadly speaking, with the notion of food supply. In their precision and detail, these reliefs are the high point of achievement in this respect in ancient Egypt. But they also disclose the special intensity of interest—limited in scope as always—of the Egyptians of this early era as they confronted nature.

The relief fragments from the Weltkammer of Neuserre are connected to the cycle represented by the three seasons of the Egyptian year: Inundation, Winter, and Summer. The thematic framework of the reliefs is the concept of representing all the characteristic events that occur in each of the seasons: the growth of plants, the reproduction of animals, the movements of migratory birds and fish in the Nile, and the seasonal occupations of humankind. These long rows of horizontal registers arranged one above the other are all preceded by the personification of the season they illustrate. Among these events, for example, is the migration of the *mugil*-fish (mullet), which swim upstream from the Mediterranean to Aswan in the spring and back downstream to the delta in the fall. In his masterful treatment of the fragments, Elmar Edel was able to restore what is preserved of the inscription accompanying the autumn migration: "Departure of the *ḥskmt*-mugil and the *ḥbȝ*-mugil from the nomes of Upper Egypt, swimming northward to eat the *sȝ*-plants in the waters of the delta."[2] The entire composition has the unmistakably didactic character of a comprehensive codification of the knowledge that the Egyptians had acquired over the course of centuries (millennia?) regarding the seasonal events in their natural environment.

What is this textbook of natural history doing in a sanctuary? In addition to the primary reference to the provisioning of humankind and the secondary reference to the three seasons of the Egyptian year, there is another, fundamental semantic framework of reference: the sun god. It is he to whom the personifications of the seasons offer all the provisions they have to contribute in this cycle of representations. It is the sun god who is lord of seasons and provisions, and it is his creative will that brings forth all the growth and reproduction. This clearly emerges from one of the inscriptions reconstructed by Edel, the caption of a scene depicting pelicans:

> When the night sun spends the night in the temple domains,
> mating is not permitted.
> When the sky opens,
> the way is clear for the will to create,
> and he reigns again over all phalli and vulvae.[3]

This passage clearly states what all these scenes are about: the manifestations of the divine creative will that gives rise to the seasons and
all that comes into being during them. The Egyptian word for this creative will, *ḥw*, means "will," and also "word" and "abundance."

Sanctuaries were erected to the sun god in later periods, but they
no longer included representations of this type. Instead, corresponding theological considerations regarding the world of nature are to
be found in literature. The relationship between the creative will of
the sun god and the provisioning of humankind underlies a section of
the Instruction for Merikare, which is probably a text of the Middle
Kingdom (ca. 1800 B.C.E., but perhaps already ca. 2100 B.C.E.):

Well provided for is humankind, the cattle of the god,
It was for them that he created heaven and earth;
he repelled the greed of the waters
and created air so that their noses would live.
They are his images, which have come forth from his body.

It is for them that he rises in the sky,
for them he makes plants and animals,
birds and fish, that they might eat,
he slaughtered his enemies and took action against his own children,
for they plotted rebellion.

It was for their sake that he made light,
and to see them, he sails [in the sky].
He erected a chapel behind them,
when they weep, he hears.

He made rulers in the egg for them
and overseers to strengthen the back of the weak.
And he made magic for them as weapons
to ward off the blow of events,
guarding them night and day.

He slew the refractory of heart among them,
as a man smites his son for the sake of his brother,
The god knows every name.[4]

We treat this important text in chapter 8.3. Here, we confine ourselves
to the one point that connects it with the representations in the Old
Kingdom Weltkammer: the solicitous, human orientation of the divine
creative will, which expresses itself not only in the course of the sun,
but also in the inexhaustible creation of nourishment on earth.

Another text, which is perhaps somewhat later (it is first attested
ca. 1600 B.C.E.), a hymn to the Theban Amun revered as sun god and

equated with Re, can be compared to the Old Kingdom Weltkammer reliefs in the loving detail of its portrayal of life as it is daily created and maintained by the sun god:

> You are the sole one, who has created all that is,
> the single sole one who created what exists;
> from whose eyes humankind came forth,
> from whose pronouncement the gods came into existence.
>
> Creator of the fodder on which cattle live, and the tree of life for
>   people.
> He who creates what the fish in the river live on
> and the birds who populate the sky.
> He who gives breath to the one in the egg
> and sustains the young of the serpents,
> who creates what gnats live on,
> and worms and fleas as well,
> who provides for the mice in their holes,
> and sustains the beetles in every piece of wood.
>
> Greetings, you who accomplish all this,
> the single sole one with many arms,
> who spends the night awake while all the world sleeps,
> to seek what is beneficial to his flock![5]

The description of nature in this lyric hymn to the sun is characterized by the same serene and pastoral spirit as the reliefs of the Old Kingdom, which maintain the effectiveness of this great god down to the minutest detail. From a literary point of view, the famous Great Hymn of the heretic Akhenaten represents the acme of this tradition. Admittedly, one hesitates to adduce a supposedly heretical text as evidence for a tradition that had stretched longer than one thousand years, from the middle of the third millennium B.C.E. down to the Amarna Period (ca. 1350 B.C.E.). It can be shown, however, that the revolutionary coup entailed in the religion of Amarna was directed only at the cultic and mythic dimensions of the divine realm. It treated the cosmic dimension as an absolute, and its theology placed the world of nature at center stage.

Akhenaten's Great Hymn to the Aten—which we need not quote at length here, because it is available in many reliable and accessible translations—supplies perhaps the best indication of the object of the Egyptians' interest in nature. It was not concerned with discovering hidden causes and interrelationships, but rather with explaining the phenomena by means of the all-encompassing potency of the sun god, which it tracks down in the most obscure of details. The inquiry does not proceed from individual phenomena to their context, but rather from the context—solar theology—to the phenomena. The world is not explained, but rather "read," that is, an interpretation is offered of how divine creative power manifests itself in the world: in the mysterious existence of the embryo in the womb, for instance, or of the chick in the egg, which can be heard peeping while it is still in its shell and can run about as soon as it leaves it—but also in larger things, such as the variety of races and languages, and in the utilitarian provision of rain, a "Nile in the sky," to sustain those peoples who do not have a share in the terrestrial Nile. If something is "explained" here, it is not nature, but rather the deity who makes himself manifest in it.

The significance of this text from Amarna lies not only in the poetic warmth and vividness of its depiction of nature, but also in the fact that it takes a further step and formulates the theological importance of the phenomena it depicts, as we see in the following verses:

> You created a million forms out of yourself, the sole one,
> cities and towns,
> fields, roadway, and water.[6]

Here, the world that the god not only touches and illuminates with his rays, but brings forth, is conceived not just as nature, as a "biosphere," as otherwise in this tradition, but as space that his light makes capable of habitation, development, and use by humankind. The biosphere is included in these million forms, as the lines just cited makes clear. A related formulation in another hymn from Amarna states explicitly

> You have made the sky on high so as to ascend to it,
> to see everything you create, O sole one,
> while millions of lives are in you, to sustain them,
> for the sight of your rays is the breath of life for noses.[7]

Light has the power to form and give life; it creates forms and breathes life into them. In the Great Hymn, moreover, the seasons are also explicitly identified as creations of the sun god:

> Your rays nourish all the fields;
> when you rise, they live and grow for your sake.
> You create the seasons to allow all your creatures to develop,
> winter to cool them,
> summer, that they might feel you.[8]

Nothing testifies more impressively to the actual direction and depth of this interpretation of reality than the fact that it not only includes the visible world as a creation of light, but also time as something created by the movement of the sun god. Here, too, the antecedents stretch far back; in a magical text from the Middle Kingdom (ca. 1800 B.C.E.), the sun god says of himself, "I am the one who separates the years and creates the seasons."[9] We are thus probably not mistaken if we view the Old Kingdom as the origin of this theology of nature and understand the latter as the verbal articulation of the point of view whose visual expression we encounter in the reliefs of the Weltkammer.

The Great Hymn uses a term we have rendered "forms" for that which the sun god creates with his rays and his movement. The actual Egyptian term, *kheperu*, is derived from the verb *kheper*, "to come into being," so that it can mean "coming into being," "becoming," that is, self-development or self-unfolding in time. When the text interprets all of the million-faceted reality as a self-unfolding of the sun god in the time created by his movement, it is a theological position that stands or falls with the monotheism of this revolutionary episode. We deal with this problem, which is theological in the narrower sense of the term, in detail later. But the basic concept that the sun god brings forth a created world for the sake of humankind through his light and his movement was evidently the underlying principle of the interpretation of the world in solar theology from its very beginning. This created world, in and on which humankind lives, constantly emerges from the sun god in the sense of his *kheperu*. Hence, it is clear why the Egyptian form of concern with nature, with the production, codification, and transmission of a knowledge of nature, had its locus in the cult of the sun. In the last analysis, it was a matter of the *kheperu* of the sun god.

There is a group of formulae in which we can discern unequivocally the central importance that the *kheperu* of the sun god possessed in Dynasty 18: the throne names of the Egyptian kings. These names, which the kings assumed at their coronation, traditionally contained a statement about the sun god Re and thus represented a sort of motto according to which the king could act and which was supposed to secure the blessing of the sun god on his reign. Unlike all previous dynasties, the throne names of the kings of Dynasty 18 were almost exclusively formed with the component *kheper*, or *kheperu*[10]:

3. Aakheperkare	"Great Is the Development of the *Ka* of Re"	Tuthmosis I
4. Aakheperenre	"Great Is the Development of Re"	Tuthmosis II
5. Menkheperre	"Constant Is the Development of Re"	Tuthmosis III
6. Aakheprure	"Great Are the Developments of Re"	Amenophis II
7. Menkheprure	"Constant Are the Developments of Re"	Tuthmosis IV
9. Neferkheprure	"Beautiful Are the Developments of Re"	Amenophis IV

10. Ankhkheprure	"Alive with Developments Is Re"	Smenkhkare
11. Nebkheprure	"Lord of Developments Is Re"	Tutankhamun
12. Kheperkheprure	"Developing in Developments Is Re"	Ay
13. Djeserkheprure	"Holy of Developments Is Re"	Haremhab

This uniformity is itself quite striking, and even more so the decided preference for the term *kheper*. In light of our considerations up to this point, we should see in it a strong and unequivocal declaration of belief in visible reality, in the world of nature as the sun god's creation, in which he develops into a million-faceted plenitude through the power of his life-creating rays and his time-creating movement. This world is extolled as "great," "constant," and "beautiful"—nothing could better suit the theology of this period. Dynasty 18 was the golden age of natural religion, of the cosmic dimension of divine presence, which was, in a radical fashion, made into an absolute in the Amarna Period. To conclude this excursus on the term *kheperu*, we may again recall the hymn to Osiris, in whose opening lines I perceived something of an Egyptian formulation of the three dimensions of presence, and which also stems from Dynasty 18. There, we read

> Greetings, Osiris, lord of everlastingness,
> king of the gods, with many names,
> with holy *kheperu* and mysterious images in the temples.

Here, along with the verbal (names) and the local-cultic (images) dimensions, is the cosmic dimension, the "mysterious" and not directly perceptible "unfolding" of the god in time, which can only be inferred by a penetrating interpretation of the reality of nature.

3.2.2. COSMOGRAPHY OF INVISIBLE REALITY

The theme of the reliefs in the Weltkammer of the sun temple of Neuserre is the world illuminated by sunlight and the ordered expressions of life in the course of the tripartite seasonal rhythms of nature, which is moved by divine creative will. A thousand years later, in the royal tombs of the New Kingdom, descriptions of the cosmos appear that do not relate to the visible upper world *summoned* by the sunlight but to the netherworldly sphere *traversed* by the sun god. One of these cosmographies of the netherworld, the Book of Nut, is an astronomical representation with descriptive excurses on individual phenomena. It contains the Egyptian theory of migratory birds, which recalls in many ways the texts that accompany the reliefs in the Weltkammer and sheds a highly characteristic light on the Egyptian style of contemplating nature. Referring to the northern sky, the text states

> Compact darkness, the cool water region (ḳbḥw) of the gods,
> the place from which the birds come.
> They are on her (the sky goddess Nut's) northwest side to her north-
> east side,
> they open onto the netherworld, which is on her northern side.[11]

The representation displays two ovals in this outer zone of the sky, which the rays of the sun cannot reach. In one of these are three young birds. The caption describes the ovals as "nests that are in the cool water region."[12] Then, regarding the birds

> The faces of these birds are like those of people,
> but their form is that of birds.
> They speak to one another with human speech.
> But as soon as they come to eat plants and nourish themselves in Egypt,
> they alight under the brightness of the sky and take on their bird form.[13]

Thus, we have here a theory of migratory birds. The Egyptians knew that these were not native to Egypt, but rather came from the north at specific times of the year. But they conceived of this "north" as a region of the sky, not of the earth. Beyond the Egyptian horizon, there stretched no other lands or seas; rather, the sky approached the earth and opened onto the netherworld. If the birds came from there, as could be observed annually, then they did not inhabit this other-worldly northern region as birds, but as otherworldly creatures who transformed into birds only on penetrating into the Egyptian realm, where the sun god shines. Their otherworldly form coincides with that of the *ba*, the "soul," which had the form of a bird. This must not mean that the migratory birds were viewed as reincarnations of the souls of the dead. The other regions of the cosmos were also inhabited by *ba*s, which are evidently not to be understood as those of the deceased, but rather inhabitants of otherworldly realms that communicated with this world, like that of the distant north. In the east dwelled the "*ba*s of the east," whom another cosmographic text describes as follows:

> The baboons who announce Re,
> when this great god is born
> in the sixth hour in the netherworld.

> They appear for him only after they have taken on their form,
> while they are on both sides of this god
> and appear for him until he goes down in the sky,

dancing for him and leaping for him,
singing for him, making music for him, making a joyful din for him,

When this great god appears before the eyes of the people,
they hear the joyful words of *wetjenet*.
It is they who announce Re in the sky and on the earth.[14]

The apes who were at home far to the southeast of Egypt, and who could be observed setting up a cry at dawn, thus also counted as otherworldly creatures who assumed their familiar form only at daybreak and inhabited a region that opened on the sky and the netherworld. The same was also true of the "western *bas*"—they had the form of jackals, and they received the sun in the west and towed it through the netherworld.

These concepts have the same structure we encountered in the Egyptian theory regarding the sources of the Nile. From the Egyptian point of view, the Nile did not come from terrestrial regions somewhere to the south of Egypt, but rather from the netherworld, and it communicated in some mysterious manner with Nun, the "primeval water" surrounding the cosmos that had emerged from it. Nun was to be found in this world as well, under many guises. He could be found in the water table; rain was connected with him; and it was even said that people were immersed in Nun in their sleep:

We live anew (at dawn),
after we entered Nun,
and he rejuvenated us as one who is young for the first time,
the old man being shed
and a new one donned.[15]

To the Egyptians, nature was curiously open in directions that set it apart from our concept of nature, in the direction of culture—following from the principle of the "social interpretation of nature," which we shall not go into here—and in the direction of the supernatural. To them, nature was "super-natural" in a way that fundamentally prevented a concept of nature. The sun was a god: his movement, his rising and setting, were interpreted as action that sprang from a will. The Nile was also a god whose acts were deliberate when his floodwaters crested and fell. The Egyptians did not experience the divine in nature in inexplicable, exceptional cases like rainbows, earthquakes, solar and lunar eclipses and the like, but in the regularity of diurnal and annual cyclical processes. Nature was not something distinct from the gods, something they created, over which they exerted influence, of which they had charge. Although statements to this effect abound, inextricably connected with them, and sometimes in the very same texts, we find the concept that deities were themselves these natural elements and phenomena. The Egyptians did not view their gods and goddesses as beyond nature, but rather in nature and thus as nature. The deities were "natural"—that is, cosmic—to the same extent that nature or the cosmos was divine.

Egyptians took an interest in nature because and in so far as they lived by it and were dependent on it. Crops and livestock constituted the subsistence of Egyptian society. We can easily imagine the central importance they attached to phenomena such as light, warmth, the Nile inundation, the cycle of vegetation, and the fecundity of soil and cattle. Their efforts had to be aimed at turning scarcity into abundance on the basis of the possibilities allowed by nature. Even today, little has changed in that regard; only the means of optimizing subsistence from nature have undergone radical change. In ancient times, the means were first and foremost not technological, but religious. The abundance for which the Egyptians strove was celebrated in the cult so as to achieve it in reality. Cutting back the offerings in the most minor provincial temple would result in famine throughout the land. The Egyptians interpreted their dependence on the life-giving, beneficent powers of their natural environment along religious lines as a dependence on deities who had continually to be "satisfied." Nature was the manifest end of a chain of interactions that related the deities to one another and whose network constituted the divine realm. It was here that cult intervened, to support these life-giving beneficent powers with hymns and gifts.

The cult, and more specifically, the cult of the sun, was thus the home of Egyptian cosmography, of descriptions of the cosmos that were related to this world in the fragments from the Weltkammer of the Old Kingdom sun temple and to the next world—and almost exclusively to the netherworld—in the royal tombs of the New Kingdom. The latter compositions are known to scholars as the Books of the Netherworld, and they have been most often interpreted as royal mortuary texts or "guides to the netherworld" because they were recorded in royal tombs. In reality, however, they are codifications of cosmological knowledge that belonged to the solar cult and constituted the basis of its successful practice. The sun cult is to be understood as a laudatory, supportive counterpart to the course of the sun, accompanying it with hourly offerings and recitations.

A major part of the Egyptians' astronomical knowledge served specifically to measure time, especially the lunar month, whose beginning rested on observation, not calculation, as well as the hours, whose length varied—for day and night, from sunrise to sunset and sunset to sunrise, were always each divided into twelve segments of equal length. Above all, however, this knowledge was related to the course of the sun, which was conceived of as a journey through the sky and the netherworld and described down to the last detail. The oldest and most widely used Book of the Netherworld enumerates the 900 deities and beings who come nightly into contact with the sun god, precisely specifies the length of each of the distances he covers in one hour (e.g., 745 miles), and cites verbatim the words he exchanges with those in the netherworld. All this elaborate store of knowledge, so oddly compounded of observations, speculations, and mythological interpretations, had a cultic function. The priest of the sun had to know its course to be able to accompany it in the cult and thereby keep it in motion, and it was this knowledge that authorized him to make these collaborative interventions in the cosmic process. We are clearly informed of this by a text that sets down the role of the king as solar priest in the same descriptive manner that characterizes the cosmographical literature. Knowledge stands at its center:

> The king knows the mysterious words
> that the eastern *ba*s speak
> when they make loud praise for Re
> at his rising, his appearance in Light-land;
> when the doors are opened for him,
> the gates of the eastern Light-land,
> so that he might travel on the roads of the sky.
>
> He knows their forms and their embodiments,
> and their home in God's-Land.
> He knows the place where they stand,
> when Re begins his journey.
> He knows the words that the two crews speak
> when they tow the barque of the Heavenly One.
>
> He knows the birthings of Re
> and his self-generation in the waters.
> He knows that mysterious gateway from which the great god emerges.
>
> He knows the one in the morning barque
> and the great image in the evening barque.
> He knows your landing place in Light-land
> and your course in the sky goddess.[16]

Whence does the king—or the priest who represents him in the cult—derive this knowledge? From a literature that describes its own function thus (I cite here the title of the Amduat):

> Knowing the *ba*s of the netherworld,
> knowing the mysterious *ba*s,
> knowing the gates and the roads the great god travels,

knowing what is done,
knowing what is in the hours and their gods,
knowing the course of the hours and their gods,
knowing their "transfigurations" for Re,
knowing what he cries out to them,
knowing the flourishing ones and the annihilated ones.[17]

What use does the king make of this knowledge? The Amduat is explicit regarding this as well. Repeatedly, at each stage of the knowledge displayed in this manual of the netherworldly route of the sun, its use is stressed:

He who knows it goes forth in the daytime . . .[18]
He who knows it descends into the realm of the dead . . .[19]
He who knows them is a well-provided *akh*-soul[20]
He who knows this text approaches those in the netherworld . . .[21]
He who knows them can pass by them[22]

And so forth. These remarks can be summarized in the form of the following basic concepts:

1. Knowledge of the circumstances of the beings in the next world conveys the possibility of sharing in their living conditions. Thus, he who "knows their thrones in the west" becomes one who "assumes his thrones in the netherworld"[23]; he who knows those who are provided with clothing "is one who has clothing in the earth"[24]; he who knows the ones provided with offerings "belongs to the food offerings in the netherworld, he is satisfied with the offerings of the gods in the following of Osiris"[25]—most of the remarks are of this type. He who knows those in the netherworld belongs to them and shares in their living conditions as if he were one of them.
2. Knowledge of the dangers that threaten in the next life serves to protect against them. "He who does not know it cannot repel the demon Wildface."[26]
3. Knowledge of the netherworld permits unhindered freedom of movement in this space. "He who knows them by their names passes through the netherworld to its end."[27]

The concluding remark summarizes the aim of the entire book:

He who knows these mysterious representations
is a well-provided *akh*.
He ever exits and enters the netherworld
and ever speaks to the living.[28]

This is not, however, priestly knowledge, but rather knowledge that, as the Egyptians conceived it, the dead had to have at their disposal if they were to overcome the dangers of the transition to the next life and be admitted as members in full standing in the community of the netherworldly. Remarks to this effect are common in the mortuary literature:

> He who knows this spell
> will be like the sun god in the east,
> like Osiris within the netherworld,
> He will enter the circle of fire,
> and no flame will ever stand in his way.[29]

> He who knows this spell
> will enter to them,
> being a holy god in the following of Thoth.
> He will enter any sky he wishes to enter.

> But he who does not know this spell on any way that is to be passed,
> will be struck by a deadly blow
> that is determined (for him) as one who does not exist,
> who receives no *maat*, forever.[30]

Knowledge "socialized" the deceased in a realm that was conceived of as a community. It identified him to those in the afterlife as one of them and lent him power over demons who could be dangerous to him. Knowledge of the netherworld conferred a netherworldly identity on him as a "holy god in the following of Thoth," the god who was the guide of souls and the learned one, the quintessential knowing one. Knowledge of the sun's course also conferred a netherworldly identity: "He who knows it is a *ba* of the *ba*s with Re."[31]

It is thus no surprise that until now, the "science" in the Books of the Netherworld of the Amduat type has been understood as exclusively royal mortuary literature. Although the form of the learned descriptions is wholly different from that of the mortuary texts, which are literature meant to be recited, the function of knowledge, the knowledge of the cognitive content of these texts, is apparently exactly the same as in the mortuary literature. And considering the context of the placement of these Books of the Netherworld in the royal tombs of the New Kingdom, it cannot be denied that as mortuary literature and as a sort of parting gift to these kings, they fulfilled aims similar to copies of the Book of the Dead that were placed in the tombs of the ordinary dead to provide them with the knowledge they needed. And yet, the text regarding the knowledge of the sun priest leaves no doubt that precisely the same knowledge that is recorded in the Amduat played a role in the cult of the sun. The same store of knowledge served both to authorize the sun priest and to equip the deceased king for the afterlife. How is this double function to be explained?

With regard to the importance of knowledge, cult and mortuary beliefs had a common basis. This common denominator lay in what can be designated with the help of the concepts "identification" and "participation." Just as knowledge of the netherworld qualified the deceased to associate with its occupants as one of them, so the cosmographic knowledge of the priest qualified him to approach the sun god as a member of the latter's social sphere in the divine realm. Knowing the words and actions of the "eastern *bas*," he becomes one of them, as it were, and faces the sun god as a baboon:

> I have sung hymns to the sun god,
> I have mingled with the solar apes,
> I am one of them.[32]

As we have already seen in our treatment of the cultic dimension of divine presence—and we shall return to it again in connection with the mythic dimension—cult is to be understood as communication and interaction purely on the level of the divine realm. The priest enters into the social constellations of the world of the gods to associate with the divine.[33] In the case of the solar cult, it is said that he takes his place in the barque of the sun god, in his immediate celestial and netherworldly vicinity. His knowledge authorizes him to do this. Knowledge socializes the priest in the divine realm and includes him in cosmic processes so that he can favorably influence them as

> Harakhty's assistant, who smites the enemies of the sun with the
>   intensity of his words,
> who causes that the barque proceed in peace.[34]

3.3. Natura Loquitur

What has been shown here in the case of the solar cult can probably, *mutatis mutandis*, be generalized to the attitude of the Egyptians toward nature and the cosmos as a whole. They viewed nature and cosmos—it is not advisable to make a distinction between the two—as an active network of beneficent, malevolent, and ambivalent forces in which deities were at work, both with and against one another. The function of cult was to support the beneficent and avert the harmful, thus intervening in this network of actions. Underlying the cult was a concept of the world that we might call "dramatic," and this in two respects: because the world consists of acts, the work of a deity in action occurs in everything that happens, and humankind, in the person of the king, participates actively in this dramatic reality; but dramatic also in the sense that because reality is continually at play, the result of a success must always be repeated and can in no way be understood in and of itself. Given the prospect of a "virtual apocalypse" that proceeds from the ever-present possibility of a standstill, a catastrophe, every sunrise is an event to be greeted with rejoicing:

> The earth becomes bright, Re shines over his land
> he has triumphed over his enemies![35]

This dramatic view of reality not only takes the possibility of catastrophe into account, it also deliberately uses it so as to avert catastrophe or—in magic—to put pressure on the gods. Thus, in a spell to heal serpent and scorpion bites, a physician (as priests of the goddesses Sahkmet, all physicians were also magicians) threatens, for example, to cause the sun barque to "run aground on the sandbank of Apophis" and describes the results of such a standstill:

> The sun barque stands still and fares no further,
> The sun is still where it was yesterday,
> food is shipless, the temples blocked,
> sickness there will turn disruption back
> to where it was yesterday.
> The demon of darkness roams about, time is not divided,
> the figures of shadows can no longer be observed.
> Springs are blocked, plants wither,
> life is taken from the living,
> until Horus recovers for his mother Isis
> and my patient also recovers.[36]

By means of such recitations, the patient and his illness became involved in the cosmic drama, just as cultic recitations involved cultic acts in the network of cosmic actions. If the patient suffered, nature suffered, not automatically, but because of a sympathetic interrelation that the magician can establish or construct because he has knowledge of the larger context and is initiated into the network of actions, into the drama of reality. The patient is identified with Horus and thus inserted into a constellation and a mythic situation in which Horus, the embodiment of the helpless child, is bitten by a serpent or a scorpion and cured by his mother Isis through her magical power. The magician was able to establish this connection and induce the gods to intervene by means of the catastrophe he invoked.

Such texts, recited in connection with magical or cultic dramatizations, represent nature, drawn into empathy, as a "waste land," as T. S.

Eliot called his poem, which was based on a different mythology but a corresponding concept of the world:

> The earth is made waste,
> the sun does not rise,
> the moon does not appear, it no longer exists,
> The ocean sinks, the land spins round,
> the river is no longer navigable.
> The entire world moans and cries,
> gods and goddesses, humans, transfigured ones, and dead,
> small and large cattle cry out loud . . .[37]

This ritual text is concerned with the death of Osiris, which brings the life of the cosmos to a standstill. But just as the sorrow of the gods makes the world desolate and life dry up, their joy inspires radiance and abundance. "Heaven laughs! The earth rejoices," sings the opening chorus of an Easter cantata by J. S. Bach on the theme of the resurrection of Christ, thus still displaying some consciousness of a dramatic interrelationship that connects God and humankind, cosmos and creature. Quite similarly, at a very early date, Egyptian texts began to celebrate the resurrection of the king, who has emerged from his tomb and ascended to the sky, as a theophany. Here, though, sky and earth participate in this event with mixed emotions, for the appearance of a new god upsets the balance of the world:

> The sky speaks,
> the earth trembles,
> the earth god quakes,
> the two divine domains cry out loud.[38]
> The sky is cloudy,
> the stars are covered (?),
> the bow-lands quake.
> The bones of the spirits of the earth tremble.[39]
>
> The face of the sky is washed,
> the Nine Bows are radiant.[40]

In the same form, but turned entirely toward the joyful and thus contrasting with the "waste land" portraits of the cultic lamentations and the magical spell cited above, hymns depict the condition and the mood into which the world has been placed by a deity appearing in a religious festival:

> The sky is gold, Nun is lapis lazuli,
> the earth is strewn with turquoise at his rising.

The gods look on, their temples are open,
people fall into astonishment at the sight of him.

All the trees sway back and forth before him,
they turn toward his eye, their leaves unfold,
the fish leap in the water,
they come from their channels out of desire for him.
All the game animals dance before him,
the birds beat with their wings.
They recognize him in his goodly hour,
they come to life at the sight of him daily.[41]

Thus is described the sunrise; a similar text from a thousand years later describes a festival procession:

The sky is in festival,
the earth is malachite,
the temples are strewn with faience . . .[42]

Texts also describe the death of the king and his ascent to the sky (as in the Pyramid Texts cited earlier), or even his ascension to the throne, as in this text of Ramesses II:

The sky trembled, the earth quaked
when he took possession of the kingship of Re.[43]

All these were events that were inserted, or could be included, in the dramatic context of the process of reality, events that were reflected in nature and had an effect on the cosmos. It was this context that preoccupied the thoughts, observations, and speculations of the Egyptians. It was the object of the store of knowledge that the temples accumulated, elaborated, and codified, a knowledge of the world that was as much theology as cosmology. What the Egyptians feared and strove to avert was not the end of the world, but the collapse of this context. They had thus to be learned, knowledgeable, and incessantly involved in action. Quite appropriately, Philippe Derchain has remarked that this conviction was drawn from an indeterminate feeling that the dramatic global relationship they conceived of, this unity of all that existed, would collapse if they stopped thinking of it. As Derchain formulates it, in this world that was always of the imagination, ritual had the function of preserving its integrity.[44]

But this is not a matter of a specific cultic and ritual world of conceptions, as we might perhaps assume from the function of the texts cited up to this point and the social context of this entire cosmographical discourse. It is rather a matter of a more general mentality and picture of the world, as emerges from an entirely different realm of discourse: "waste land" laments that refer not to cult and myth, but rather to history. Around 2000 B.C.E., after the collapse of the Old Kingdom, the experience of anarchy, confusion, and food shortages gave rise to a literature that took the form of rhetorical laments over the condition of the land as a chaos, a topsy-turvy world, with its social order reversed, everyone at war with everyone else, deeds of brutality, impoverishment, and misery. Nature played a large role in these laments, particularly in the Prophecies of Neferti:

> The sun is covered and does not shine,
> that people might be able to see;
> one cannot live when clouds cover (it). . . .
> Egypt's river is dry,
> one crosses the water on foot.
> . . .
> Water becomes riverbank,
> and riverbank becomes water.
> The south wind will contend with the north wind,
> and the sky will be in a single wind storm . . .[45]

> Re will separate himself from humankind.
> Though the hour of his rising will still exist,
> one will no longer know when it is noon,
> for no shadow will any longer be distinguished,
> no face that sees [him] will any longer be dazzled.[46]

Deprived of its gods, who have withdrawn from it, nature will continue, but humankind will be obliged to survive in a world that has lost its cohesion, and thus its luster and its order. In the Egyptians' experience of reality, the collapse of kingship triggered the same crisis as that evoked by the magician when his patient was bitten by a serpent and that represented by cult in the cycle of the annual festivals. Astonishingly enough, we again encounter this very mentality and concept of the world, and in part even the same formulations and images—though in other languages—more than two thousand years later. The Potter's Oracle, which has come down to us in Greek, laments

> The Nile will be low, the earth unfruitful;
> the sun will be darkened,
> because it will not wish to see the disaster occurring in Egypt.
> The winds will bring misery on the earth.[47]

The most impressive portrait of nature deprived of the gods and uninhabitable by humankind is found in the Hermetic tractate

Asclepius, which was the starting point of our discussion of the cultic dimension. This text is also an apocalyptic prophecy. We may recall the context, which had to do with the reality of images, of cult images as deities dwelling on earth, and cult as a reproduction of celestial events. Then, the apocalyptic vision ends in a future in which this harmony of heaven and earth, of divine creative power and human piety, will fall apart. The gods will withdraw to heaven and terminate their cultic presence. The cosmos (*mundus*) will no longer be an object of wonder and prayer. When the gods effect their "painful separation" (*dolenda secessio*) from humankind,

> The earth will shake, and the seas will be unnavigable,
> the sky will no longer be crossed by stars,
> the stars will forsake their courses,
> every divine voice will be silent, forced into silence.
> The fruits of the earth will be spoiled and the soil no longer fruitful,
> and even the air will hang heavy and close.[48]

This is not a description of the aftermath of a nuclear war, but rather of a "disenchantment of the world" that seemed to loom on the horizon in the third and fourth centuries C.E., during the controversies between Gnostic, Jewish, and Christian movements. The typically Egyptian association of cult and natural religion is nowhere made as explicit as in this text. Human piety was directed equally toward cult statues and nature, that "inimitable work of God, that glorious construction . . . instrument of divine will," and the deities' "installation" on earth occurred in both cult statues and nature, where "everything in the visible world that is worthy of worship, praise, and love is united in One." From the end of the Old Kingdom to the end of antiquity, the theme of all these laments was the unholy condition of a world that humankind had rendered uninhabitable by offending against the harmony of a socially conceived reality, by contravening the principle of solidarity. The principle of plenitude that made the world a flourishing paradise was *Maat*, the "Right." Its opposite devastated the world, because the gods renounced their dwelling, not only in the temples of the local dimension, but also in the life-giving powers of nature in the cosmic dimension.

3.4. Cosmos and Time

Our consideration of the Egyptian concept of "cosmos as drama" has already made it clear that the Egyptians did not conceive of reality as primarily spatial and material, but as temporal and performative, as a living process that was represented most impressively in the course of the sun. Cosmological thought and concepts centered on the sun's course were thus expressed principally in temporal terms. The Egyptians had no concept of "space" in the sense of a primary category of cosmic totality, but rather one of "time." In a typically Egyptian manner, this was a double concept, expressed by two words. The Egyptians had a penchant for expressing totalities as a union of pairs. Egypt itself was called the "Two Lands," "South and North," and the "Two Banks." The concept of the entire land as a political totality was expressed as the "Uniting of the Two Lands." Analogously, the fullness of time as a cosmic totality was expressed by a pair of words, *neheh* (*nḥḥ*) and *djet* (*ḏt*).

The meaning of this disjunctive concept of time and its two components cannot be translated by any pair of words in Western languages. The Egyptian terms in no way correspond to our "time" and "eternity"; this distinction derived from Greek ontology (eternity as the punctually concentrated presence of being, which unfolds in time as the process of becoming) was not only foreign to Egyptian thought, but even contrary to it. *Neheh* and *djet* both have properties of our "time," as well as of our "eternity," and as a practical matter, either can sometimes be translated as "time" and sometimes as "eternity." The terms refer to the totality (as such, sacred and in a sense transcendent and thus "eternal") of cosmic time. To clarify this concept of time and its religious implications or semantic range, we must heed an important distinction. We are so accustomed to the notion of infinity that we think of "totality" as finite and bounded. The Egyptians, however, viewed "totality" as the opposite of finite and bounded. To them, the boundaries of totality were not contrasted with the unbounded, but with the "whole," with "plenitude."

In chapter 17 of the Book of the Dead, a compendium of Egyptian mortuary beliefs in the form of a series of questions and answers (an initiate's examination?), the expression "all being" is explained as "neheh and djet." What this means is that neheh and djet designate the comprehensive and absolute horizon of totality. They refer to the temporal totality of the cosmos, but it was in this way that the concept of "cosmos" or "being," that is, of reality, was comprehensible to Egyptian thought and capable of articulation. This totalization of being on the temporal level is so foreign to us that some scholars have proposed that djet and neheh mean "space" and "time." This is not correct, however; both are unequivocally temporal concepts, and in Egyptian thought, they represented the whole of reality.

It should thus not be surprising that we have no equivalent for this pair in our own languages or in our own concept of time. Our dichotomy of time and eternity is based on Greek ontology and Christian dogmatics, and our concept of time rests on the system of tenses in Western languages, which express the notions of past, present, and future. Instead of these three temporal divisions, the Afroasiatic family of languages has two divisions, which are called "aspects," and therein lies the path to the meaning of *neheh* and *djet*. Naturally enough, these terms can be brought into associative connections with various modern words, but they cannot really be translated. That would require a linguistic treatise, which we shall spare ourselves here. The closest we can come is a pair of concepts such as "change" and "completion/perfection," somewhat in the sense of Rilke's sonnet to Orpheus:

> Even though the world keeps changing
> quickly as cloud-shapes,
> all things perfected fall
> home to the age-old.

In Egyptian, "change" was *kheper*, and "completedness" was *tem*. Both concepts were embodied in the gods Khepri (the "becoming one") and Atum (the "completed one"), who were combined into a dual god at an early date and who stood, in the theology of the course of the sun, for the morning sun (Khepri) and the evening sun (Atum). The two were identified with the temporal concepts *neheh* (change) and *djet* (completedness). Entry into the plenitude of cosmic time was thus wished for the deceased with the words

> You unite with *neheh*-time
> when it rises as the morning sun,
> and with *djet*-time
> when it sets as the evening sun.[49]

We can also illustrate the Egyptian disjunction of time with the help of the concepts "come" and "remain." It is often said of *neheh*-time that it "comes": it is time as an incessantly pulsating stream of days, months, seasons, and years. *Djet*-time, however, "remains," "lasts," and "endures." It is the time in which we distinguish the completed, that which has been effected in the stream of *neheh*-time, which has matured into completion and has changed into a different form of time that will undergo no further change or motion.

The concept *neheh* can still best be connected with our everyday notion of time. For us, time is less something that comes than something that goes by, but in any case in motion. It is difficult to conceive of *djet*-time, and this is probably why it has often been explained as "space." Thus, any attempt to clarify this category for the modern reader requires effort that could easily imply that the ancient Egyptians concerned themselves with forming subtle scholastic concepts. There can, however, be no question of this. The natural evidence for *djet*-time, which is so entirely lacking to our way of thinking, was there in abundance for the ancient Egyptians. To them, it was anchored in the world of experience and concepts in at least three ways: in their language, in the mortuary cult, and in the figure of the god Osiris. Thus, for example, nothing seems more "natural" to us than the concept of the past. An important component of the "evidence" for the past lies in the fact that it has a reality as a category in the tense systems of our languages. Originally, at least—there were profound changes in the second millennium B.C.E.—the Egyptian verbal system knew no past, but rather a category I prefer to call "resultativity." "Resultativity" refers to the self-contained nature or *completion* of an action or occurrence—in this, it corresponds to our "perfect"—but also to the *continuation* of the resulting condition in the present. This linguistic category corresponds exactly to and is the grammatical basis for what *djet* signifies on the conceptual level: the enduring *continuation* of that which, acting and changing, has been *completed* in time.

This correlation of grammar and concept construction would be left dangling in the air, of course, if we were unable to point to a grammatical counterpart to the concept of *neheh*, or better put, if the conceptual distinction as such could not be discovered in the verbal system of the language. The complete table of correlations looks like this:

Concept	*Djet* "continuation of the completed"	*Neheh* "change" and "occurrence"
Temporal categories	*Resultativity* "continuation of the result of completed actions or occurrences"	*Virtuality* "occurrence in and of itself"
Underlying aspectual opposition	perfectivity	imperfectivity

In the framework of a study of Egyptian religion, this explanation will have to suffice. It can illustrate the interrelationships to which this proposal refers, though it is not enough to substantiate the thesis itself. The latter lies rather in the area of "language, thought, and concept formation in the ancient Near East," to cite the title of a monograph by the Assyriologist Wolfram von Soden. But what my proposal maintains is that the dichotomy of the concepts of time so characteristic of Egyptian thought was correlated with the aspectual system of the Egyptian language, and thus that a sort of natural evidence for it existed in the minds of the speakers of this language.

Resultativity is not just a grammatical category, but also an attitude, toward the world in general and toward time in particular. Such an attitude, though aimed in a different direction, has been described by Mircea Eliade in his book *Cosmos and History*, and in many other works as well, as an aversion to history and contingency, a striving to transcend "profane" time through repeated integration into the "sacred" time of ever-recurring origins. According to Eliade, this is the concept of time in mythic thought, and as such, it is part of the heritage of all humankind. From the narrower but perhaps more precise perspective of the Egyptologist, we can say that this is not "the," but rather "an" Egyptian concept of time, namely, *neheh* and the entire realm of values and concepts connected with the course of the sun. *Neheh* is the time of "eternal return," and as a cultural attitude, it is expressed in rituals that ornamentalize time, making time congruent and thus sublimating it through the regular repetition of constant patterns of activity.

Ancient Egypt scarcely differs in this respect from any other early or traditional culture that is characterized by "mythic thought." It might be that in Egypt, these matters were more complex than in other cultures, or it might be that Eliade unduly oversimplified the temporal concepts of other cultures (I cannot judge), but in Egypt, this mythic-ritualistic conception of time and this attitude toward it stood in stark contrast to that which was based on the category of resultativity. As a cultural attitude, resultativity expressed itself in a striving for attainment, and above all, for the preservation of a result, of a final form ready to be eternalized. This striving expressed itself in forms of cultural expression that are virtual symbols of ancient Egyptian culture: hieroglyphs, pyramids, mummies. The writing system, the massive monumentality of the funerary architecture, and mummification of the dead are among the manifestations of this interest in permanence and endurance. Connected with the enormous efforts and expenditures that were put forth was a conceptual realm centering on the notions of imperishability and immutable continuance. The central meaning attached to biography as the "state of having become" (*kheper*) of the fixed and monumentalized end form of a life points to the typical structure of resultativity. The concept of "eternity" and the monumentalization of the dead stood in a relationship of polar opposition. Theory was the basis of practice, but for its part, theory also had a basis and a meaningful embodiment in practice.

This entire complex of concepts and values took form and assumed religious meaning in the god Osiris, just as the complementary complex of ideas and attitudes revolving around the idea of eternal renewal centered on the god of the sun and his course. Just as Nietzsche attempted to reveal a dichotomy in basic Greek cultural attitudes by invoking the gods Apollo and Dionysus, we may speak— and presumably more correctly—of the "Osirian" and the "solar" in ancient Egypt. These two gods were juxtaposed to one another as a pair who comprised a dominating, antinomic constellation. Osiris was the god of the *djet* aspect of time. He could even be called *djet*, just as he was sometimes referred to as *sf*, "yesterday." "Yesterday": that which has taken on form, that which has been realized, that which endures, in contrast to "tomorrow" and *neheh*, the names of the sun god as that which comes and is possible. But Osiris had yet another aspect, so that as god of resultativity, of immortal continuation, he bore the epithet "Wennefer," which means literally, "he who remains matured." In the conceptual realm peculiar to Egypt, the temporal category we have designated "resultativity" could have found no clearer or more pregnant expression than in this epithet of Osiris (which lived on in the Christian name Onnophrius). For what could a formulation like "he who remains matured" mean, other than the imperishable and immutable continuation of that which has been completed in time? Applied to a concept in the name of a god, a category of time assumes a sacred, numinous, divine significance. In the idea (and the experience) of the god Wennefer, the temporal category of resultativity is associated with the desire for immortality. Osiris was the god of the dead. An idea of immortality aimed at continuity and endurance took form in his person. He reigned over a temporality—an eternity—in which all that had been completed in the light of the sun and in the temporality of another god remained immutable and imperishable.

This other god was the sun god. He embodied the virtuality of *neheh*, just as Osiris embodied the resultativity of *djet*. In the endless cycle of his rising and setting, his coming into being and passing away, his death and his birth, he was always in a process of coming, of experiencing flux in the periodic rhythms of pulsating time of day and night, months, seasons, and years. In his person, the temporal category of virtuality assumed a religious intensity of importance and sacredness: as the inexhaustible supply, the immeasurable plenitude of time in contrast to human boundedness, immortality as unceasingness, as "ever again," or "day after day," as the Egyptians put it.

It is crucial that these two gods did not represent alternatives. One could not make a choice between "solar time" and "Osirian time" as perhaps, according to Nietzsche's (and perhaps even the ancient Greek) conception, one could lead either an Apollonian or a Dionysian existence. Or, if the notion of "decision" seems inappropriate, no one could be destined to be born into one or the other form of time. Rather, Re and Osiris—apparently unlike Apollo and Dionysus—formed a constellation. They were what they were only in relation to one another. Only the two together yielded reality, and it was only their combined effect that gave rise to the complex of *neheh* and *djet* that humankind experienced as "time": a periodically consummated union of the two aspects, change and completion, from which reality proceeded as a sort of continuity of the life of the cosmos. The Egyptians thus conceived of time as a combination of "solar time" and "Osirian time" that had its origin in the active, combined effectiveness of the two gods.

The Egyptians imagined the constellation in which Re and Osiris work together as embodiments of the two antinomic or complementary aspects of time, as a *ba* and a corpse, by analogy with the two aspects of the person in which the deceased led an eternal life, "going in" and "going out" as a *ba* in the *neheh*-time of the sun and "enduring" as a corpse in the *djet*-time of Osiris. *Ba* and corpse would unite at night, the *ba* alighting on the mummy in bird form, thus ensuring the continuity of the person. In the constellation of Re and Osiris, this model was applied to cosmic totality as a sort of formula. Night after night, as a *ba*, Re would "go in" and "go out," that is, descend into and emerge from the netherworld; and around midnight, he would unite with Osiris, the corpse that lay continuously in the deepest depths of the netherworld, thus ensuring the continuity of the cosmos. In this constellation, the Egyptian concept of time as eternal life and the continuity of the reality of the cosmos took on the vividness, the succinctness, and the depictability of reality as it was lived. It could be described in hymns, represented, and even ritually performed. Such a ritual, preserved on a late papyrus in the British Museum, culminates in the consummation of the union of Re and Osiris:

It is a great mystery,
it is Re and Osiris.
He who reveals it will die a sudden death.[50]

The ritual was performed in the "House of Life," and as recognized by Philippe Derchain, who published the text, it served to maintain life.

The Egyptian language had no word for the all-embracing, abstract horizon of totality described by our concepts "cosmos," "world," and "reality," just as it had no word for "time" or "space." Instead, we encounter not a concept, but a constellation: not (just) of concepts, but (also) of gods. This constellation lends expression to the religious meaning of the cosmos and the cosmic reality of the gods, whose multiplicity—here reduced to a duality—is inevitable. There was no god whose *ba* was the sun and whose corpse was Osiris, at least not originally and from all time. The cosmos existed through the combined effectiveness of these gods. Inasmuch as they lived, they collaborated. In the ultimate abstraction, this life was conceived of as a union of *ba* and corpse, that is, of an eternal life attained even by the deceased. Time was the consummation of this eternal life. For the ancient Egyptians, life was the ultimate reality, not being, as in Greek philosophy, and not release from the cycle of rebirth and the veil of *maya*, as in Indian thought. Instead of eternity of being, there was continuity of life, in which humankind played a part and had its share; a salvation that was not attained through "*heilsgeschichte*," but actualized as ritual.

3.5. The Divinity of the Cosmos and the "Cosmicity" of the Divine: The Cosmos as Dimension of Divine Presence

In the preceding sections, I attempted to show that, and in what way, the cosmos, or nature, was a sacred (that is, capable of hierophany) object of religious experience and worship for the ancient Egyptians. It was especially important to make it clear that we must not conceive of this sacredness as symbolic. The cosmos was not a sign of the sacred, a space or (to be more concrete) a "television screen" on which the sacred made its appearance; rather, it *was* the sacred itself. The cosmos was the sacred as the horizon of totality, of the whole that encompassed the fragmentary—and as such, profane—existence and everyday experience of humankind. This whole—and this is critical in understanding a polytheistic religion—was conceived of not as a unity, but as a multiplicity, and not as (personal) form, but as act or correlated acts, as the joint effort of a multiplicity of deities, as "drama" in which all the deities played greater or lesser, that is, principal or subordinate, roles. We must now consider what this "dramatic" concept of nature, which viewed reality as the collaborative effort of divine actions, meant for the ancient Egyptian concept of the divine.

The thesis of the cosmic dimension means that in just the same way as essentially every (although perhaps not in each and every case) deity in the full sense of the Egyptian concept of the divine had a cult place and thus a cultic/local dimension of the unfolding of his or her essence, so every deity was essentially caught up in the drama of the cosmos, the network of actions that constituted Egyptian reality, making his or her contribution to both the visible and the invisible spheres of the world. We cannot test the heuristic value of this thesis on each one of the more important figures of the Egyptian pantheon here, so we shall confine ourselves to a selection of problematic instances.

First, there were deities with cosmic forms of manifestation whose most distinctive contribution to the "success" of reality lay on a level other than the cosmic. Thoth, for instance, was the god of the moon, but his cosmic traits were relatively unimportant. First and foremost, Thoth was the god of writing and reckoning, the patron of scribes and (basically the same thing) officials. The pronounced intellectuality of this god in no way contradicted his cosmic form of manifestation, however, but stemmed directly from it. In the complexity and precision of its phases, the moon was the reckoner par excellence of time, and as such, a distinctively intellectual heavenly body. Its intimate relationship to the calendar also connected it with everything pertaining to calendrical matters—calculation, planning, counting, measuring, weighing, distributing, and so forth—making the moon god the ideal patron of the profession responsible for all these matters. In the framework of our inquiry into the cosmic dimension of the divine as a heuristic model, the essence of Thoth, god of writing and calculation, bureaucratic punctiliousness, exactitude, supervision, and knowledge reveals itself as "moon-ness," as the religious interpretation of the moon and as such part of the comprehensive religious interpretation of the cosmos, that which we are calling Egyptian polytheism in this chapter. Ptah is a similar instance. Ptah was an earth god, but in his case as well, his cosmic traits were less important than his role as patron of a profession: that of artists and craftsmen. Ptah embodied the primeval permanence and creativity of the earth, the unity of what the Greeks distinguished as matter and form. As embodiment of "matter," Ptah was at the same time and above all the inventor of forms. In the figure of Ptah, we see an expression of a religious interpretation of the earth that made no distinction between form and matter and that inserted *homo faber* into nature by explaining nature itself as *deus faber*.

What we have learned from these examples and can extend to the Egyptian concept of the divine more generally is that the cosmic dimension of the divine was not confined to the sheer materiality of cosmic elements such as earth, air, water, and so forth, or to celestial bodies such as the sun and the moon, but rather that it referred to specific complexes of actions, traits, attitudes, and qualities that were interpreted as cosmic phenomena "in action" and in which humankind also participated. Nut was not so much the sky as what the sky did, giving birth to the heavenly bodies and hiding them within herself, not so much the goddess of the sky as mother goddess and goddess of the dead. Hathor, the other goddess of the sky, embodied its heavenly splendor and was the goddess of love, beauty, and the intoxication that could transcend the mundane. Re, the sun god, was the god of kingship.

The contributions of some deities to the cosmic drama, however, is difficult to determine. The god Anubis, for example, had a very specific function, one that is more unequivocally expressed than is the case with most of the other deities of the Egyptian pantheon. He is (like Osiris) a god of the dead and of the necropolis, though unlike Osiris, he was not the ruler of the dead, but rather the patron of embalmers, mummifiers, and mortuary priests. In contrast to the lunar intellectuality of Thoth, the solar-based royal rule of Re, the chthonic creativity of Ptah, or the celestial charm of Hathor, this specific complex of activities, qualities, and competencies is not easy to relate to the cosmic dimension. Anubis's specific activities contributed to the success of reality—and in a most important way, considering the central role of the funeral in ancient Egypt—but these activities did not manifest themselves in nature.

Nevertheless, Anubis also had a specific form that separated him from the human realm and related him to a cosmic sphere. The jackal was the animal of the western desert in the Egyptian picture of the world, just as the baboon belonged to the eastern desert. The "*ba*s of the east," the baboons, greeted the sun god at his rising, and in like manner, jackals towed the solar barque through the netherworld as the "*ba*s of the west." The jackal stood for the realm of the dead, which the sun god entered in the evening. As a cosmic sphere, the realm of the dead had many forms, for the Egyptians divided it into a number of aspects and regions. One of these was Anubis. Considered as a force of nature, he was the god of the transitional zone between the world above and the netherworld; this zone was called the "holy land" in Egyptian, and Anubis was its designated lord. In his cosmic dimension, Anubis *was* this transitional zone, not just its lord, and conversely, embodied in his person was the specific activity of this area of the cosmos, as it was represented in the religious and dramatic interpretation of the world, that of overcoming this transition from the world above to that below, from life to death.

Because we meet with this same structure in the case of deities of rather different sorts, we must maintain that it was a basic structure of the Egyptian concept of the divine. Just as deities ensured the unity of the land in their capacity of local lords, so, as natural forces, they ensured the unity of the cosmos. Just as the entirety of the land was conceivable only as the unified multiplicity of the deities who dwelled in it, so the entirety of the cosmos was conceivable only as the combined effectiveness of differentiated powers. Just as the sacred character of Egypt rested on the fact that deities resided in its locales, so the divinity of the cosmos rested on their activity; that is to say, cosmic phenomena were represented as their actions.

CHAPTER 4

The Verbal
or Mythic Dimension

4.1. The "Name Formula"

Under the rubric of the verbal or mythic dimension of divine presence,
we shall inquire into the manner in which the sacred was expressed in
language, just as we have inquired into its cultic-local dimension in
terms of the forms of its earthly presence and into its cosmic dimension in terms of the forms of its cosmic manifestation. Here, verbal is
the more general category, and mythic the more concrete and specific.
We can begin by assuming that myth was a typical manner of representing the sacred verbally (though, of course, it was not the only manner, and myth had functions other than to conceptualize the sacred),
and that by "myth" we are to understand "divine history," that is, narratives dealing with the divine. There are problems with regard to this
concept in Egypt, as we shall see, so that it is preferable to set aside the
adjective "verbal," which is more general but entails fewer assump-
tions. The Egyptian text from which our tripartite classification of the
dimensions of the divine realm proceeded subsumes the verbal articulation of divine essence under the concept of name, which is a highly
apposite designation for the verbal dimension. In its *names*, the sacred
was present in a sense similar to its presence in *cult statues* and its
developments (that is, its cosmic-natural manifestations). Naming
names was perhaps an earlier and more direct means of establishing
presence than telling tales. In any event, the former played a substantial role in Egyptian cult and theology, in the simple form of litanies
that list names and in the elaborate form of hymns.

The Egyptian theory of the name was based on the principle that
an essential relationship existed between the name and the named.
The name was a statement regarding essence, and even a heraldic
device, as we have seen in the example of the throne names assumed
by kings at their coronation. The relationship between name and
essence ran in both directions: everything that can be gathered from a
name says something about the essence of the named, and everything

that can be said about the essence of a person can be ascribed to that person as a name. The Egyptian concept of the name thus included what we understand by "predicate."

There are many indications that in Egypt, the cultic naming of the name of a deity was the original form of hymnic praise. In any event, the earliest hymns consist of litanies in which various divine names are inserted into an otherwise unvarying refrain:

> May you awake in peace,
> Purified One, in peace!
> May you awake in peace,
> Horus-of-the-East, in peace!
> May you awake in peace,
> Eastern *ba*, in peace!
> May you awake in peace,
> Harakhty, in peace![1]

Hymns containing name formulas are an especially characteristic type; nothing shows more clearly the special features of the Egyptian concept of the name and the use to which it was put. The principle of the name formula consists of establishing a relationship between a god or goddess (G), an action (A), and an object (O) in the visible (usually the cultic) sphere. O is made the name of the deity, usually with the help of a wordplay involving A and O. The following examples from the Pyramid Texts serve to illustrate:

	A	O
They (the gods) will fraternize with you in your name of *snwt*-shrine.	Fraternize (*sn*)	*snwt*-shrine
They will not turn you back in your name of *itrt*-shrine.[2]	turn back (*tr*)	*itrt*-shrine
Horus is *ba*, he lays claim to his father in you in your name of Ba-repit (-palanquin)	to be *ba* (*bꜣ*), lay claim (*ip*)	*bꜣ-rpit* (palanquin)
Your mother Nut has spread herself over you in her name of Shetpet.[3]	spread (*pšš*)	*Št-pt* (place name)
Horus has enlivened you in your name of He-of-Anedj.	enliven (*sꜥnḫ*)	He-of-*ꜥndt*
Horus has filled you with his eye in his name of Divine Offering.[4]	fill (*mḥ*)	(place name)
		offering (*wꜣḥt*)

You are given to your mother Nut in her name of Tomb; she has embraced you in her name of Sarcophagus; you are brought to her in her name of Mastaba.[5]	give (*rdi*) embrace (*ink*) bring (*siˁ*) 	tomb (*ḳrst*) sarcophagus (*ḳrs*) mastaba (*iˁ*)
Horus has elevated you in his name of Henu-barque; he carries you in your name of Sokar.[6]	elevate (*f ꜣi*) carry (*ṯni*)	Ḥnw-barque Sokar (*Zkri*)

The rules of this procedure are clear: the names are cult objects (palanquin, barque, tomb, sarcophagus) and places (shrines, cities). Less often, they are actual divine names (Sokar, the god of the Memphite necropolis) or even cosmic regions, as in the following text:

To be spoken:
§626 O Osiris King Teti,
stand up, lift yourself!
Your mother Nut has borne you,
Geb has wiped your mouth for you.
The Great Ennead protects you,
they have placed your enemy under you.
§627 "Carry one who is greater than you," they say to him in your
name of Great Sawmill (*itf ꜣ wr*, a sanctuary).
"Elevate (*ṯni*) one who is greater than you," they say to him
in your name of Thinite Nome (*Ṯni*).
§628 Your two sisters, Isis and Nephthys, come to you to make
you well,
you are complete (*km*) and great (*wr*)
in your name of Bitter Lake (*Km wr*).
You are green and great
in your name of Sea (*W ꜣḏ wr*).
§629 See you are great and round (*šn*)
in (your name of) Ocean (*Šn wr*)
See, you are circular (*dbn*)
in your name of "Ring-That-Encircles-the-Northern-
Lands."
See, you are round and great
in your name of Great-Circle-of-the-Setting (a body of water).
§630 Isis and Nephthys have protected (*z ꜣ*) you in Siut (*Z ꜣwt*),
for you are its lord in your name of Lord of Siut, because you
are its god in your name God.
§631 They pray to you, be not far from them
in your name of Divine Beard (*Dw ꜣw*).

They join with you, that you not be angry (*dnd*)
in your name of *Dndrw*-barque.

§632 Your sister Isis comes to you,
rejoicing for love of you.
She sits on your phallus,
so that your semen enters her,
sharp (*spd*) as Sothis (*Spdt*).
Horus-Sopdu has come forth from you
as Horus who is in Sothis.

§633 He is well (*akh*) for you through him
in his name of Akh-(spirit)-in-the-*Dndrw*-Barque.
He protects you in his name
of Horus-Who-Protects-His-Father.[7]

Without further details, the individual cultic episodes of the ritual
that underlies this text cannot be reconstructed. Moreover, here we
are concerned only with the principle that such texts follow; for this,
some summary comments suffice. The text has to do with the burial
ritual of the king, and more specifically—as is clear from the history
of transmission of this spell—with ceremonies conducted at night in
connection with anointing and mummification. The corpse of the
king is addressed as Osiris, and the officiants are designated with the
names of various deities. Someone serving as a bearer plays the role
of the "enemy" (Seth), and the corpse's secretions are bodies of water,
lakes, seas, oceans. The high point of the nocturnal ritual is the resurrection of the corpse for the engendering and conception of the successor to the throne, Horus, who is present in the form of the actual
crown prince and successor. In these texts, we are dealing with a curious process of explanation in which the originally cultic sphere, with
its priests, cult objects (barques, shrines), and acts (embalming, mummification, etc.), is semantically transformed by a distant, divine
realm of meanings. There are truly archaic rites (for example, in connection with the Opening of the Mouth ritual) that do not yet display
this transformation by means of a sphere of meaning stemming from
the divine realm. Thus this clearly emerges as a secondary process
that must have occurred during the centuries that comprised
Dynasties 3 through 5 (ca. 2750–2500 B.C.E.). With the division of the
sacral realm into a "here" and a "there," that consciousness of a symbolic structure of the sacred emerged that we have already encountered in our treatment of the cultic and cosmic dimensions, and which
we described with the concept of "installation/indwelling."

In spells containing name formulas, the name serves to create a
relationship between the two spheres, the cultic sphere "here" and the
sphere of the divine realm "there." We must note in this connection
that the great majority of these names are anything but established

names of Osiris. Rather, they are coined on a purely ad hoc basis and are to be understood as assigning a role. Neither Osiris nor the deceased king was ever otherwise called the Bitter Lake or the *itrt*-chapel. They bore these names only in the circumscribed framework of the respective ritual acts. That these are generally called "names" points to the verbal nature of the phenomenon. Over and above the phenomenon of the cultic and cosmic spheres in which the sacred makes its appearance, the "name" is a specifically verbal phenomenon. It points to the particular power of language to create relationships and to the verbal aspect of the dimension in which these relationships are constituted. This relationship between the present and the distant was spun from the most basic material of language— phonemes. In the overwhelming majority of instances, the name and the word that designates the ritual act related to one another by assonance; both have one or more phonemes in common.

The extent to which this type of wordplay was characteristic of cultic speech in Egypt was entirely different from that of the name formulas. The latter was a widespread but specific phenomenon, whereas outside of name formulas, wordplay occurs everywhere that cultic acts are accompanied by recitations—or, more precisely put, where speech is interwoven with cultic acts, as long as a transformation of the rite by a distant sphere of meaning emanating from the divine realm was spoken of. The wealth of wordplays demonstrates how those who composed spells for the cult worked self-consciously with language—with substance (sound) and with form (phonemic structure) of expression—to bring the cultic and the divine spheres into a relationship with one another. They testify to a belief in the possibilities of language, a consciousness of language that is foreign to us, for we have come to understand the conventional nature of the signs of language. We speak of "plays" on words because we experience such a use of language, which undermines the conventionality of signs in a cunning and usually amusing manner, as playful. In Egypt, however, wordplay was regarded as a highly serious and controlled use of language, for language was understood to be a dimension of divine presence.

4.2. The Akh-*Power of Speech: Transfiguration as Sacramental Interpretation*

Hymns with name formulas belong to a genre of liturgical recitations that the Egyptians called "transfigurations" (*sꜣḫw*). The Egyptian term *s-ꜣḫw* is a causative form derived from the root *ꜣḫ*, which has a complex of meanings: "to radiate," "to be light," "to be spirit." Also derived from the root is a noun, "*ꜣḫw*" (*akhu*), "radiant power," "spiritual power," which refers in particular to the power of words. This word also contains the kernel of a whole theory of language, and we need only take a closer look at the relevant texts to expound it. Here, of course, this can only be done briefly and to the extent that it permits conclusions regarding our inquiry into language as a third dimension of divine presence.

Akhu refers to the specific power of the *sacred word*, in the sense of Gustav Mensching's well-known definition of "myth" as the "visualization of the supernatural in spatiotemporal events, mediated through the word, which is therefore sacred word." Only the radiant power of divine words had the ability to illuminate the sacred, the divine meaning of cultic, and even cosmic, events and acts, the otherworldliness in this world. As a verbal power that emanated from speech, *akhu* was a means that deities, especially deities of knowledge, such as Isis, Thoth, and Re, had at their disposal. With the radiant power of their sacred words, Isis and Thoth could exorcise the enemy and stop the sun in its course, and Isis could heal her suffering child Horus and revive the dead Osiris. In the cult, speech also made use of this power of language, in that it was expressed as the language of deities.

Investigating the history of "transfiguration spells" that refer to cultic acts and objects with the help of name formulas and wordplay, we come—as Siegfried Schott in particular has indisputably demonstrated—to spells that were themselves uttered in the context of these very cultic acts, that is, to "dramatic" texts. In particular, name formulas served as transformations of dramatic texts. Instead of the dramatic form

A speaks to B
"I have brought you C"
remark: D (a cult object)

B is addressed with a name formula:

A brings you C in your (or A's) name D.

For example:

dramatic:

Horus to Osiris:
"This is the mighty eye of Horus, take it in your hand!"
remark: breaking the red jars[8]

explanation:

Horus has given you his mighty eye,
he has placed it in your hand.[9]

The dramatic element in these cultic spells consists in the fact that they are uttered as divine speeches by priests who play the roles of the deities in question as they carry out the respective cultic acts. The words uttered while performing the cultic acts are thus the words of deities, sacred words whose radiant power makes it possible to illuminate the otherworldly meaning of what is happening in this-worldly events. Plays on words were the preferred means to this end. The process can be illustrated with the help of an example from the Dynasty 13 Ramesseum Dramatic Papyrus, which contains a coronation ritual of presumably much earlier date.

The papyrus is divided into a register of illustrations and a register of texts. In the illustration of the scene that concerns us, a representation of a man and the caption "lector priest" appear, along with the words, "I have brought you the *qeni*-corselet." The illustration thus refers to the this-worldly sphere of the ritual proceedings. In the accompanying text register, we read

It happened that the *qeni*-corselet was brought by the lector priest.
This means: Horus, when he embraces his father and turns to Geb.
HORUS TO GEB: "I have embraced (*qeni*) my father, who is weary, until
    he becomes well (*seneb*) again."
OSIRIS
QENI-CORSELET
SENEB-(FRINGE?)
BUTO (the city where the mythic drama occurs)[10]

The words make possible what the illustration cannot achieve: they refer to both the this-worldly and the otherworldly spheres, describing the same action in each of them and connecting the two descriptions with a copula, here rendered as "this means," that serves as an equals sign. There follow the dramatic words that are to be spoken while the act of "bringing the *qeni*-corselet" is performed, and which translate these words in the divine speech that accompanies the priest in the illustration. This speech is composed of plays on words referring to the cult objects "*qeni*-corselet" and "*seneb*-fringe(?)," which are articles of the king's raiment. The uttering of this divine speech projects the action being carried out in this world into the divine realm. It is thus expanded by means of a prehistory and a post-history. From a simple act "here," an occurrence happens "there." Here, a corselet with a fringe(?) is brought, and there, a father who is "weary," that is, dead, is embraced so that he will become well again, that is, restored to life. The action "here" and the occurrence "there" are related to one another by symbolic representation. The action means the occurrence. The relationship is effected through words, explicitly in the descriptive comment on the scene ("a cultic act is performed, this means: an occurrence in the divine realm"), and implicitly in the recitation as words of the god to be spoken while performing the cultic act. I designate this procedure, which is usually labeled "mythicization of ritual" in Egyptology, as "sacramental interpretation."

The process of "transfiguration" consisted in preparing an extract, as it were, from these rituals. Texts thus arose that represent lengthy, related divine speeches and refer exclusively to the divine realm. They make no mention of cultic acts and confine themselves to events in the divine realm, which they sum up and expand on. The listing and fleshing out of these events, which always center on the deceased king, were supposed to confirm and certify his own transposition into this divine sphere. All the blessings that these occurrences in the divine realm bring about are heaped on the addressee of these spells. Through them, he becomes a "radiant spirit of light," a "transfigured one"—this is the meaning of the Egyptian designation of this genre of spells, for as already mentioned, it is a causative form of the root $ȝḫ$, akh—a member of the divine sphere. The process of sacramental interpretation, in which an otherworldly, divine meaning becomes manifest in cultic act, takes on a life of its own in these transfigurations, for this meaning no longer refers to the individual act, but is, as it were, heaped on the addressee. Thus arises the form of a hymnic status-characteristic of the deceased, which praises him by describing him as the center and the beneficiary of a number of divine constellations:

Oho! Oho!
Lift yourself, Teti,
take your head, collect your bones,
gather your limbs,
wipe the earth from your flesh!

Take your bread, which does not grow moldy,
your beer, which does not become sour!

When you approach the doors that bar the commoners,
Khenti-menutef comes out to you
to grasp your hand.
He takes you up to the sky,
to your father Geb.

He (Geb) rejoices at your presence,
he stretches out his hands to you,
he kisses you, he takes you on his lap,
he places you at the head of the imperishable spirits.
Those whose places are mysterious worship you,
the great ones gather by you,
the watchers rise before you.[11]

We need only juxtapose this mortuary text from the middle of the third millennium B.C.E. to any solar hymn from the New Kingdom, approximately one thousand years later, to affirm the similarity of the two texts, for a common method of Egyptian cult hymns entails the principle of transfiguration:

Hail, Re!
Praise to you, Atum,
at your beautiful coming, appearing and mighty!

You have traversed the sky, you have reached the earth,
you have joined the sky at dusk.

The two chapels of the land come bowing to you,
they sing praises to you daily.
The western gods rejoice at your beauty,
those whose places are mysterious worship you,
the great ones gather by you,
They sing you (the song) "Take Care, Earth."
The inhabitants of Light-land row you,
those in the night-barque transport you,
they say "Welcome" to you in the presence of your majesty:
"Welcome, welcome, having arrived in peace,
hail to you, ruler of the sky, lord of the West!"

Your mother Naunet embraces you,
she sees her son in you as Lord of Fear, Great of Majesty.
You descend in life in the night sky.
Your father Tatenen elevates you,
he wraps his arms around you, that you may be transformed and
    divine in the earth,
he gives you as a venerable one to Osiris.[12]

Here, a cosmic process (sunset), not a cultic one, is sacramentally inter-preted, in the same ways and in part with the same turns of expression as in the mortuary text. The actions of the addressee are integrated into divine events: praise of the westerners, embrace by the mother (serv-ing to recognize the newcomer as son, like the fatherly embrace by Geb in the mortuary text), and elevation by the father. The solar hymn does not describe sunset; rather, it transfigures it, in the same manner as the mortuary text, using the radiant power of the sacred word to illumi-nate the otherworldly, divine meaning of an event in the world per-ceptible to humankind.

The Egyptian idea of the radiant power of the sacred word, which visualized divine events in this-worldly actions and made it possible to overlay the objective, earthly realm with meaning from an otherworldly conceptual realm, developed, on the basis of the sacramental interpretation of ritual, into the whole universe of discourse of cultic speech that composed the mortuary and temple liturgies. The radiant power of speech made the divine realm, in all its otherworldliness, capable of being approached, conceptualized, and represented, and speech was thus a dimension of divine presence. Because the Egyptians had the concept of the sacred word, the sacred was not ineffable to them, although the utterance of the sacred word, the use of the radiant power of speech, was bound up with the strictest of requirements. Only deities could make use of the "radiant power of words" (*ȝḥw typyw-rȝ*), along with the king, insofar as the latter acted as a god, and the priests to whom the king delegated his priestly function, when they appeared in divine roles and were authorized to use sacred words.

4.3. Sacred Words and Sacred Knowledge

Our account of language as a dimension of presence began with two Egyptian concepts: *akhu* "radiant power" and *ran* "name." Sacred, radiantly powerful words report an otherworldly, divine sphere of meaning that is imposed on the reality of this world in a manner that explains and thus makes sense of it. Instead of supplying definitions, Egyptians would state names, that is, the sacred and secret names of things and actions that the priests had to know to exercise the radiant power of the words. A highly characteristic, and certainly early, form of handing down these names is the commentary ("this means"), as exemplified by the Ramesseum Dramatic Papyrus, which records knowledge that unfolds on two levels: that of appearances and that of meanings, or names. This becomes clear in another example from this text:

> It happened that the pillar was erected by the royal messengers.
> This means: Horus commanded his children to raise up Seth under
> Osiris.[13]

The comment is intended for the priest; it is not sacred word, inasmuch as it was not recited in the cult. The only things recited were the dramatic speeches that one deity addressed to another and that functioned entirely on the divine level of meaning. But as a rule, these were formulated in such a manner that we can recognize elements of the cultic level in their very sound. Thus, in our example, Horus says to his children, "Let it endure (*ḏd*) under him!"[14] The word *ḏd*, "endure," refers to the pillar (*ḏd*).

This structure of knowledge of phenomena and their mysterious meanings ("names") deriving from the divine realm also occurs in mortuary texts intended to provide the deceased with knowledge necessary for the journey through the afterlife. In these texts, the deceased person for the most part represents himself in his divine role, his "name"; in the most elaborate form, he transposes his body limb by limb into the divine realm:

My head is a vulture,
    that I might ascend and rise to the sky;
the sides of my head are the stars of the god,
    that I might ascend and rise to the sky;
my pate is [. . .] and Nun,
    that I might ascend and rise to the sky;
my face is Wepwawet,
    that I might ascend and rise to the sky;
my eyes are the great ones at the head of the *bas* of Heliopolis,
    that I might ascend and rise to the sky;
my nose is Thoth,
    that I might ascend and rise to the sky . . .[15]

And so forth. Twenty further identifications follow, down to the "soles of the feet," which are equated with the two solar barques, and the "toes," which are identified with the *bas* of Heliopolis. To journey to the sky, the deceased had to present himself before a ferryman, who subjected him to a thorough interrogation:

O, Mahaf ["He Who Looks Backwards"], waken Aqen for me!
Who is it who speaks?
It is I, one loved by his father; the father of my father already loved
    me. It is I who awaken him [i.e., the father = Osiris] for you when
    he sleeps. It is I who attach his head for you, it is I who open his
    mouth for you [the deceased represents himself as Horus, who is
    able and willing to save his father Osiris from death]. Waken
    Aqen for me! See, I have come!
Why should I waken him?
It is he who is to bring me the ferry that Khnum assembled at the
    head of the winding canal.
Is that all you can say to me, that I should awaken him for you? The
    ferry is in pieces, no reeds are to be found for it!
Then fetch fresh reeds from the tail of Seth [this is the corresponding
    thing in the divine realm, the secret name of the reeds that are
    lacking; to pronounce it produces what is desired].
Where should the lacing be fetched for it?
Then fetch that twig that came out of Upper Egypt, which Horus
    and the Ombite (i.e., Seth) joined together on that goodly day of
    the Opening of the Year.
But where should *mdȝm* be fetched for it?
The lower lip of Babi!
From where should the leather strips for it be taken?
Then fetch the two hands of the Mistress, that she might make
    them! . . .[16]

And so forth. Piece by piece, the ferry is called by its names in the divine realm and magically assembled.

In making the crossing, the deceased had to avoid the net that demonic gods had spread between sky and earth to trap the bird-souls of the dead. This, too, could only be done by knowing the secret names, that is, the divine meaning, of all the particulars of the net:

> For I know the name of the place where it is hung after netting the fish:
> it is the riverbank in the sky on which every god sits.
> I know the name of the place where it is stored after netting the fish:
> it is the papyrus in the hand of Osiris.
> I know the name(s) of the float above and the sinker below:
> they are the kneecaps of Osiris and the fingertips of Geb.
> . . .
> I ascend to the sky among the gods,
> I bring and repeat the word of the god.[17]

Thus, a growing store of knowledge arose in connection with the principle of the sacramental explanation of cultic acts, a doctrinal system into which anyone wishing to associate with the gods—king, priest, deceased—had to be initiated. The divine meaning that lent the radiant power of divine speech to the words uttered by the priests as they performed their cultic duties became, in the mouth of the deceased, a code word, a password that enabled him to make his way past the dangers of the next world. Naturally, we are best informed of the store of knowledge available to deceased persons, for it was placed with them in writing in their tombs, and grave goods have survived well-preserved in Egypt. We correctly understand the actual religious meaning of this knowledge only if we recognize that these mortuary texts are a reflection of a much more comprehensive priestly literature that is lost to us, in part because it was mostly handed down orally due to the secret, sacred nature of the name and of divine speech, and in part because we have yet to find a single temple library, whether archive or scriptorium, with the written codification of this knowledge preserved in situ. Such depositories and scriptoria existed, however, in every religious center of any importance. We have already encountered this problem in connection with the cosmos as a dimension of divine presence and with cosmography as the literary genre in which knowledge of cosmic phenomena and the divine actions manifested in them was codified and handed down. Here, too, it is tombs that have preserved this knowledge to us in the form of grave goods: the royal tombs of the New Kingdom. In this case, however, there are clear indications that the actual locus of this literature and this knowledge was the solar cult.

The world of the deities of Egypt was not an object of belief, but rather of knowledge: knowledge of names, processes, actions, and events that were superimposed, in a manner that explained and made sense of, saved, and transfigured, on the realm of manifestations in the cult and in nature, a realm that was no longer directly sacred but only still sacred in a symbolic sense. This knowledge made the deceased invulnerable, and it purified the priest for contact with deities and authorized him to make use of the "radiant power on his mouth." Knowledge referred to speech and its use in the cult. The commentary in the Ramesseum Dramatic Papyrus discloses to the officiant the relationship between the words that he utters and the actions that he is to perform or, in any case, to accompany with his speech. Cosmography describes the cosmic process of the course of the sun using sacramental interpretation, lending it a sacred meaning, so that the priest could accompany it with hourly recitations. By means of these hymns, he was able to foster the course of the sun by working with it, because, legitimized by his knowledge of meanings stemming from the divine realm, he could illuminate the sacred sense of visible processes through the radiant power of his words.

Language as a dimension of divine presence was divided into two aspects: knowledge and speech. In the cultic dimension, the gods make their appearance as cult statues and lords of the manor, and in the cosmic dimension, they are natural phenomena; in the mythic dimension, they are names, or they are a text that stands behind the world of appearances, interpreting and making sense of it. We shall return to this concept, for it played a major role in the development of theological discourse. It is said of the gods that they emerged "from the mouth" of the creator god and that they are the names he gave to the parts of his body. In the theology of creation, the meaning-imparting "text," the speech act of the creator god, precedes the world of appearances in need of meaning, in precisely the sense of the Platonism characteristic of mythic thought, as noted by Mircea Eliade.

4.4. Speech and Personality

To the extent that the "text" that lends cohesion to the world of appearances in a way that gives meaning to it assumes the form of *history*, and to the extent that the share of an individual deity in it intensifies into *destiny*, the concept of *myth* suggests itself for that which we have been describing from various points of view with words like "divine realm," "sacred word," "sphere of meaning," and so forth. This degree of narrative integration of elements—processes, acts, events—is difficult to determine. Texts referring to this sphere, whether in the descriptive, commenting form of sacred knowledge or in the dramatic form of sacred words, are not narratives. Quite gradually at first, there developed in religious texts a narrative form in which individual events made their appearance as episodes in a comprehensive narrative context, a myth. The end and zenith of this development is marked by a text written in Greek: Plutarch's record of the myth of Osiris. It is possible, of course, that myth had a venue of its own in oral tradition and was adopted into texts recorded in writing only in the form of qualifications, citations, and allusions. Despite the remote antiquity to which the corpora of the Coffin Texts and the Pyramid Texts, as well as the Ramesseum Dramatic Papyrus stretch back—as far as the beginning of the third millennium B.C.E.—we must nevertheless consider the possibility that myths took form only gradually at first. Evidently, both interpretations are valid, without in any way excluding one another.

There is an abundance of clear, differentiated, and empirically substantial concepts regarding the functions and accomplishments of myth. Until now, however, we have had no clear idea of what might have preceded myth, according to its second meaning. Herein lies the great importance of Egyptian texts for the history of religion—if only we free ourselves from attempting to see fragments, *membra disjecta* of a finished mythology, in them and instead understand them as precursors of myth. What constituted the meaning, the function, and the achievement of such precursors, which were not yet histories but only events, not yet destinies, but only roles? And how might we describe these pre- or para-narrative forms?[18] Taking advantage of the most obvious, best-documented example, if we collect all the mentions of Osiris in Old Kingdom texts related to the mortuary cult, the core of their meaning turns out to be a constellation in which Osiris plays the role of the deceased father and Horus that of the loving son. Clearly, this is a transposition into the divine realm, that is, a sacramental interpretation, of the original and most fundamental constellation of the mortuary cult. What is special about this constellation—we can also say, its function or achievement—is that it embraces this world and the next. Thus, it became the model for cult more generally.

> Awake, awake, O my father Osiris!
> I am your son who loves you,
> I am your son Horus who loves you!
> See, I have come to you to bring you
> what he (Seth) took from you.[19]

With these words, the mortuary priest makes an offering of bread. The deceased plays the role of Osiris here, the priest that of Horus, and the offering that of the "eye of Horus," which Seth took from Osiris and which Horus must recover from Seth in order to restore it to the deceased as its rightful owner. The explanatory reference to the divine constellation lends the cultic act the meaning of a restitution:

the offering becomes the return of what was stolen, a symbol of the life force that the avenging son wins back for his father from his murderer. In the same manner, when figs are presented during the ritual meal, the priest says,

> Osiris Wenis, take for yourself the Eye of Horus,
> which he has rescued from the hand of Seth.[20]

The words with which the priest "brings the *qeni*-corselet" in the coronation ritual of the Ramesseum Dramatic Papyrus have the same restitutive purport:

> I hold in my embrace this father of mine,
> who has become weary, that he might become hale again.[21]

Scholars have always wished to see such statements as citations from a myth, allusions to a story substantially identical to that recorded by Plutarch three thousand years later. But if we begin from the actions these texts accompany and sacramentally interpret, we have less the impression of an abbreviation or a garbling than one of an expansion. The offering was conceived of as a restitution: this is the central point around which what follows is arranged in the sense of an expansion. Restitution presupposes a loss, and the basic roles are thus:

- the recipient of the offering, who has experienced a previous loss
- the agent who inflicted this loss on him
- the avenger who redresses this loss.

What has been lost is life force. The recipient is thus dead, and with the offering, he regains his life force. As personification of the cause of death, the agent is a scapegoat whose punishment serves to reverse death itself; or, in any case, the destruction he has caused is canceled, and the event can be assimilated within the framework of an existing order of meaning. In this constellation, the recipient and the avenger are related to one another as (deceased) father and son, and the agent confronts them as the brother of the father. I thus call it the "Hamlet constellation," not in the sense of a direct dependence of Shakespeare's play on the Egyptian myth (which was familiar to the European Renaissance via Plutarch), but rather in the sense of an anthropological generalization. Nearly all the rites of the mortuary cult can be explained in light of this constellation, but its importance extends further. We have already seen the deceased, who is ascending to the sky, legitimate himself before the reluctant ferryman as the son who has come to heal the fatal wound of his father. Above all, it was the king's role as son—beginning with the mortuary cult of his father or predecessor, which was still predominant during the Old Kingdom—that was extended into the divine realm as a whole. In Egypt, as we have already repeatedly stressed, cult was a royal monopoly that the king delegated to the priests. Performing his cultic acts, the king (or the priests standing in for him) played the role of the son who stood face-to-face with all the deities, who were conceived to be his fathers and mothers.

As is perhaps already clear from this example, constellations served to bestow meaning. Broad areas of cultic acts become meaningful in light of constellations like that representing the (deceased) father and his son. Put otherwise, the self-explanation of social activity was articulated into constellations in this early period. This was true not only of ritual activity but of activity in general, in so far as it was experienced as meaningful. Thus, for example, at Napata in Nubia, a king of Dynasty 25 (ca. 700 B.C.E.) described and commemorated a journey made by his mother to Egypt using formulations that explained the event in light of the constellation of Isis and Horus:

She was in Nubia,
the king's sister, sweet of life,
the king's mother Ibala—may she live!
I had gone far away from her
as a youth of twenty years,
when I came to Lower Egypt with his majesty.
She journeyed north
to see me again after a long time.
She found me crowned on the throne of Horus,
having received the crowns of Re:
the two uraei were joined on my brow,
and all the gods formed the protection of my body.
She rejoiced over the masses when she saw the beauty of his majesty,
like Isis when she beheld her son Horus,
    crowned on the throne of his father
    after he had become a young man
    in the falcon's nest at Chemmis.
Upper and Lower Egypt
and all the foreign countries bowed the head before this royal mother.
She was in a festive mood over the masses,
great and small,
they rejoiced before this king's mother and said,
"Isis received her son Horus,
just as the king's mother has now united with her son,
the king of Upper and Lower Egypt Taharqa—may he live forever—
beloved of the gods [and goddesses].
You will live forever
by command of your father Amun,

the energetic god who loves the one who loves him,
who knows the one who is devoted to him,
who caused that your mother be united with you in peace
and that she see the beauty that he created for you.
O mighty king, you are alive and well,
just as Horus lives for his mother Isis,
you endure on the throne of Horus
forever and ever."[22]

From about fifteen hundred years earlier, there is an alabaster statuette depicting Pepy I on his mother's lap, referring in another
medium to the same constellation. It was a basic fact that the central
constellations of the Egyptian divine realm were representable and in
fact represented in both word and picture. In an inscription of Sethos I
(ca. 1300 B.C.E.), the king describes the relief decoration of a chapel he
had erected for his deceased father Ramesses I:

His mother is with him without cease,
those who departed before him are gathered before him.
The beloved brother of the king stands before him,
I am his son, who keeps his name alive.
The mother of the god, her arms are around him
like Isis when she united with her father.
All his siblings are in their places,
he rejoices, for his people are around him.[23]

Representations can be translated into language, and the common
theme is the constellation.

We have described the structure of sacred, "radiantly powerful"
speech as a differentiation and correlation of a level of appearances
and a level of meaning. With the help of the concept of constellations,
it is now possible to fill this abstract structure with concrete content.
What sacred words bring to language and actualize are constellations,
in the light of which any given action becomes meaningful. The genre
of transfigurations, which developed from these brief divine speeches
uttered in ritual, is nothing other than the verbal realization of constellations in which the deceased is embedded thanks to the rites performed on him, and in whose framework the acts of which these rites
make him capable are performed. This can be seen, for instance, in
spell 373 of the Pyramid Texts, cited earlier (see the text cited at note
11), which has to do with Osiris as deceased son and Geb as his father
in the afterlife, and with the act of paternal recognition that Geb carries out on his (as it were) newborn son by placing him on his lap and
caressing him. This recognition is followed by public homage; this,
too, occurs in a highly typical constellation that reappears in a similar

manner in a widespread hymn to the setting sun (see the text cited earlier at note 12). The following transfiguration is typical of the descriptions of the deceased given in these texts, in that it is oriented to characteristic constellations:

> O king Pepy,
> go, that you may be transfigured (*akh*),
> that you may have power as a god,
> as successor of Osiris!
> . . .
> You have your *wrrt*-crown on you,
> you have your *mizwt*-crown on your shoulder;
> your face is before you,
> praise precedes you,
> the followers of the god are behind you,
> the nobles of the god are in front of you,
> they sing, "the god is coming, the god is coming,
> king Pepy is coming to the throne of Osiris,
> that *akh*-spirit in Nedit is coming,
> the power in This."
> Isis speaks to you,
> Nephthys calls to you,
> the transfigured ones come bowing to you,
> they kiss the earth before your feet
> in fear of you, o Pepy,
> in the cities of Sia.
>
> You ascend to your mother Nut,
> that she might take you by the hand,
> that she might show you the way to Light-land,
> to the place where Re is.
> The gates of the sky are opened before you,
> the gates of the cool celestial water open before you.
> You find Re, who has stood up to await you.
> He takes you by the hand
> and leads you to the two shrines of the sky.
> He places you on the throne of Osiris.[24]

These texts have a double reference. One is to a ritual event that they explain and transfigure—here, probably a procession of the sarcophagus or a statue of the deceased; in spell 373, an offering of food. The other is to constellations in the divine realm, which they describe. It is the latter that concern us. The texts represent the deceased as someone who plays roles in constellations in the divine realm, as the point of reference of divine actions: in brief, as a person, with being a person understood here as complete integration into a "sphere of belonging" (a term I introduced in my treatment of the local dimension, that is, of a deity as lord of a temple). Personality and integration into constellations are closely connected to one another. Transfigurations "construct" the person of the deceased in the divine realm by describing the constellations into which he enters and is integrated, whether actively or passively, just as other texts put together a ferry and a net out of their names in the divine realm.

In this context, it is important to note that it is the person of a deity that is constructed in these texts referring to the deceased, his corpse, his mummy, his coffin, or his statue. In the sacramental interpretations of these radiantly powerful spells, we see the many ways in which the cult performed in this world represents the passage of the deceased from the world of the living into the tomb, the necropolis, the realm of the dead, as an ascent to the sky, reconstituting his personality, which fell apart at death, as that of a god, whose social sphere the divine realm now constructs in specific constellations. We can sense a stage in the history of burial customs that must have preceded the principle of sacramental interpretation. In that stage, the deceased king was not integrated into the divine realm as a new god, but rather took his earthly court with him to the grave as his "sphere of belonging." The corresponding concept of the person is thus older than the texts that first speak to us of constellations in the divine realm in connection with sacramental interpretations of what occurs in rituals. Much can be said for the idea that this world of deities conceived as persons and related to one another in constellations—that is, the classical form of Egyptian polytheism—developed during the course of the emergence of the Egyptian state, that is, in the first half of the third millennium B.C.E. We have no evidence for the preceding, "prepersonal" phase in the history of Egyptian religion, and formulating hypotheses about it does not have a place within the framework of this discussion. Only one thing is important: with the coming into being of the *persons* of deities—that is, with the personalizing and thus the anthropomorphizing of the Egyptian concept of the divine—*polytheism* came into being. As a person, a deity had need of a "sphere of belonging." He became a person only by being integrated into constellations. As a person, a deity was not conceivable without reference to other deities. He was Osiris only in relation to Horus and Seth, that is, the dead father. Each new constellation—and only additional constellations!—enriched his essence: constellations with Isis and Nephthys, with Geb and Nut, and with the sun god. The same was true of all the other deities, insofar as they were viewed as persons.

It seems to me that this qualification is essential. Personality is only one aspect of divinity. The history of religion knows many forms of apersonal concepts and experiences of the numinous. The animal, plant, and fetish forms of many Egyptian deities point to a preanthropomorphic and thus probably also prepersonal phase of the form of the numinous. From the point of view of the history of religion, personality is something that is achieved; according to the well-known dictum of the Dutch scholar of the phenomenology of religion, G. van der Leeuw, it is a relatively late one: "God was a latecomer in the history of religion." At least in the case of Egyptian religion, attributing personality to deities is less appropriate than speaking of "dimensions of divine presence," and in particular, of the linguistic dimension. Personality is not the essence of the deities, but rather an aspect of them, and specifically, the aspect that is accessible through language. By means of verbal explanation of their numinous reality, deities acquire personal contours, and the linguistic means by which they become persons occur in three ways: as speech about the gods and goddesses, as speech directed to them, and as speech they direct among and to one another. All three of these occur in the framework of constellations. If—as we continually read—an original monotheism preceded the classical polytheism, it must have been a silent one. A deity who speaks and who is accessible through speech is a deity who is a person, and to be a person means to be integrated into a sphere of what belongs to one, that is, into the constellations of the divine realm.

The advantage of this interpretation is that it frees us from assuming a change in the form of the divine, as though the gods had originally been apersonal "powers" and then, through an evolutionary process, transformed into deities who were persons. Personality is rather an aspect that accrued to them to the degree that religion assumed a discursive character and resorted to speech in the universe of religious discourse that was unfolding. The personality of the deities was a function of the linguistic dimension of divine presence, and their essence extended beyond it. Personality was an aspect of their accessibility and the ability to communicate with them.

4.5. *Language, Meaning, and Action*

I would now like to extend to the concept of action what was said in the preceding section about the relationship between language and personality. Deities are persons not only to the extent that they make themselves understood through speech and are thus open to understanding, but also insofar as they act. And the concept of a deity who acts already presupposes integration into the constellation of a "sphere of belonging." This context can be shown from a group of texts that do not refer to the king playing a divine role, as in the case of the Pyramid Texts and the ritual texts cited earlier, but rather to a genuine god: the hymnic (liturgical) and cosmographic representations of the course of the sun. These texts refer to the cosmic phenomena of the cycle of day and night, understood as the orbiting of the sun around the earth, in precisely the same sense of a sacramental explanation as the dramatic texts and the transfigurations that refer to the acts and objects of the cult. This analogy not only allows, but even compels us to generalize the concept of person in the ritual and mortuary texts and their process of sacramental interpretation and to classify them with the basic structures of the Egyptian concept of the divine, that is to say, of the verbal dimension.

We have already spoken (see chapter 3.2.2) of the representation of cosmic phenomena that solar hymns and cosmographic texts understand as the course of the sun. We can reduce them to a simple formula: they represent these processes as actions. Just like speech, and on the basis of speech, action is also a social and semantic phenomenon. Action must be meaningful and meaning must be communicated socially, and this presupposes a social and a semantic dimensioning of reality. Action occurs with respect to a partner in a common horizon of meaning with shared goals, expectations, and values. In the classical Egyptian conception, the social dimension of divine action is the divine realm. The partners in this action are those deities who enter into the relationship of a constellation with the deity who is the central theme in each given case—in the present case, with the sun god. This is not relatively self-evident. Deities could, after all, also act in reference to the human realm. With regard to the course of the sun in particular, nothing seems more obvious—if we already interpret it as divine act, and this again as the action of a solar deity—than to relate it to the world of humankind. The latter is in fact precisely the theme of a number of Egyptian solar hymns, of which the most important, the Great Hymn of Akhenaten of Amarna, is well enough known; we cited it in chapter 3.2.1. Then, we were concerned with demonstrating a "reading" of nature that recognized the working of a divine creative will in phenomena. Now, we must specify: insofar as the portrayal of a sole god presupposes that he accomplishes the work of the sun's course in its distant celestial pathway *alone*, this "reading" stands in diametric opposition to what underlies the multitude of traditional sun hymns by way of "implicit" theology. The monotheistic theology of Amarna stands in the tradition of an "explicit theology" that had long since conceptually distanced itself from the traditional concept of the course of the sun and drew the consequences of this opposition in a radical and intolerant manner.

I should like to summarize only briefly what was true of the traditional, classic concept of the course of the sun. It was interpreted as action within the framework of changing constellations in the divine realm. Just as in the transfigurations of the dead, in the solar hymns, the sun god was by no means always the one who acted. Quite the contrary, he plays a passive role in many constellations: he is born in the morning, he is greeted, towed along, worshiped, and embraced, and in the evening, he is received, once again embraced, towed through the netherworld, and again worshiped. In the morning, the active roles in these constellations are played by the mother who bears him, the sky goddess Nut, by the nurses who nourish him, by his celestial adorants, in particular the solar baboons, who worship him, and other deities who are occasionally included; in the evening, the active roles are his mother, who again enfolds him in her arms, the jackals who tow him through the netherworld, and the inhabitants of the netherworld, who worship him. In all this, the sun god is not purely passive; on the contrary, all these actions, even his birth, refer to some triggering act of the god, which is usually expressed by intransitive verbs: you rise, you arise, you appear, you shine, you set, you land. Between these intransitive-passive (from the point of view of the sun god) phases of his transit, lie the dominating, active phases of traversing the sky and journeying through the netherworld. Crossing the sky during the day journey brought the sun god into an antagonistic constellation with the enemy, who personified inimical powers, the "gravitation of chaos" (in any case, the personality of the serpentine enemy of the sun was quite limited) against which the order of creation had ever and again to be asserted anew. Auxiliary deities who fought the enemy entered into this constellation aimed at triumph, along with the divine realm generally, in the most comprehensive constellations imaginable, all of whom rejoice at the sun's triumph over the dragon of chaos:

The sky rejoices, earth is in joy,
Gods and goddesses are in festival
and give praise to Re-Harakhty
when they see him appear in his barque,
after he has felled the enemy in his attack.[25]

The nightly journey of the sun as a *descensus ad inferos* brought the sun god into constellations with the inhabitants of the netherworld, the transfigured dead. His light, and in particular his speech, awoke them from the sleep of death and allowed them to participate in the life-giving order that emanated from his course. But in this, the god himself experienced the form of existence of the transfigured dead and set an example for them by overcoming death. For in the depths of the night and the netherworld—and this was the most mysterious constellation of all—he united with Osiris, the son with the deceased father, the *ba* with the corpse, and from this union, he received the strength for a fresh life cycle.

Before I indicate the principle followed by this manner of representing cosmic processes, let us again look at examples. Here are two

that complement one another in that one ignores the evening and the
night phase, and the other passes briefly over the morning phase. Both
refer to sunrise, that is, they are addressed to the sun god as he rises:

	Phase	Constellation
Greetings, Re, when you arise,		
Atum at your beautiful setting!		
You appear, you shine on the back		
of your mother,		mother
having appeared as king of the Ennead	morning	Ennead
Nut greets you,		mother
Maat embraces you always.		daughter
You cross the sky broad of heart,		
the Lake of Knives is quieted.		
The rebel is fallen, his arms are bound.		enemy
The knife has penetrated his vertebra.	midday	
Re endures in favorable wind,		
the *Msktt*-barque has annihilated		barque
the one who attacked it,		
the southerners and northerners tow you,	evening	
the westerners and easterners adore you.[26]		
Greetings, Re, at your rising,		
Amun, Power of the Gods!	morning	
You rise and illuminate the Two Lands!		
You cross the sky in peace,		
your heart is broad in the *M'nḏt*-		
barque.		barque
You pass the sandbank of the Sea		
of Knives,		
your enemies are felled.		enemies
You have appeared in the house of Shu,		
you have set in the western Light-land.	evening	
Old age has taken your majesty,		
while the arms of your mother		mother
embrace you protectively.[27]		

Here are two extracts from a cosmographic book, the descriptions of
sunset and sunrise in the Book of the Night:

Setting in life by the majesty of this god,
spreading light and illuminating in the darkness,
opening the gate of the sky in the west,
removing the torch from the ground.
Seizing the prow-rope of the divine ship by the crew.
Making ovations by the gods of the netherworld.
Arrival at the first gate, "Mistress of Terror." . . . [28]

Emerging from the netherworld,
sitting in the morning-barque,
traversing the primeval ocean in the hour of the day "That Beholds
    the Perfection of Her Lord."
Transforming into Khepri,
rising to the horizon,
entering the mouth,
emerging from the vulva.
Shining in the gateway of Light-land in the hour "That Makes the
    Perfection of Re Shine,"
to create the sustenance of humankind,
of cattle and of all the serpents he has created.[29]

The principle underlying these representations of cosmic phenomena
can be described as the interpretation of processes as actions. The
sense of this method emerges from the analogy with mortuary texts.
Just as the latter transfigure the deceased's passage into the next life,
so these texts transfigure the course of the sun. And as in the case of
the deceased, the sun god is depicted as inserted into the constellations of a "sphere of belonging," and the divine plenitude of his personality is unfolded in actions that occur through him and to him in
the framework of these constellations. Cosmography comments on,
and hymns accompany, cosmic phenomena as a cycle of events in the
divine realm. Cosmographies expand on the sacred meaning of these
events with richly detailed information, whereas hymns summarize
them in brief strophes that almost always correspond to the phases of
the sun's course.

This breakdown of the continual cosmic process into the three
phases of the daytime and the fourth phase of the night already
appears to provide a form- and sense-imparting entrée into the raw
material of the cosmic evidence. That is not, however, correct. The
division of the sun's course into phases was evidently an age-old and
deeply rooted concept in Egypt, and it thus formed part of the material exploited by the religious discourse of hymns and cosmographies.
For the Egyptians, the daytime was divided into three periods, just as
the year was divided into three seasons. During these three periods,
the sun god changed his name and his form. As he himself states in a
magical text, he was

Khepri in the morning,
Re at midday,
Atum in the evening.[30]

As Khepri, he was a scarab-beetle, as Re, he was a falcon-headed man,
and as Atum, he was a ram-headed man; in these three forms, he was
at the same time child, adult, and old man. These are, of course,
already elements of a theological interpretation. But the division into
phases clearly belonged to the natural evidence that theology discovered and processed. This much emerges from the fact that Amarna
religion, with its extreme counterposition to the traditional theology
of the course of the sun, retained this phase structure. The segmenta-
tion of the cycle of day and night into phases was thus in itself prethe-
ological and constituted a part of the visible reality on which
theological explication, or "sacramental interpretation," built.

The decisive point of this interpretation, this investing of the phases
with religious meaning, was their dramatization as *events in the divine
realm*, as interactive complexes of actions in the framework of divine
constellations. It was against precisely this structure of constellations
that the Amarna countermovement was directed, indicating unmistakably that the framework is decisive here. The constellations in
which the "drama" of the sun's course was carried out were purely of
the divine realm. Humans, fauna, flora, visible nature, all of which are
depicted in the reliefs of the seasons praising the sun god in the
Weltkammers of the sun temples (see chapter 3.2.1), and on which the
solar hymns of the theological countermovement linger so insistently,
fade out in this form of representation. Even the solar baboons and the
jackals belong to another world. Nevertheless, for the Egyptians, these
representations of activity with which hymns depict the phases of the
sun's course were filled with references to their own world. I use the
words "representations" and "depict" not only because these texts
read like pictorial descriptions, but because a world of artistic images
accrued in close connection with them: depictions on the walls of
tombs, vignettes in the Book of the Dead, paintings on coffins, and
many others as well. The cosmographies are in any event always made
up of both texts and pictures. What the texts depict with verbal images
can be immediately translated into the pictorial language of art. We are
dealing with a conceptual articulation of meaning that can find expression in both word and picture. I call this form of articulation an "icon."
Icons are pictorial conceptions, artistic illustrations of divine
processes, actions, and events that can find concrete expression in both
texts and pictures. What the implicit theology of traditional Egyptian
polytheism made of the course of the sun was "icons": archetypal
illustrations of its redemptive meaning, by means of which the theology interpreted the phases of the cosmic phenomena.

This process is that of transfiguration, although with a reversal of direction. In mortuary texts, the deceased's passing into the next world is compared to the sunset, and the deceased can be addressed:

You are enveloped in the embrace of your mother Nut,
you are alive forever.[31]

Solar hymns represent sunset in a corresponding manner:

Your mother Nut embraces you,
she sees her son in you, "Lord of Fear, Great of Majesty."[32]

The icon of sunset represents the cosmic process in such a way that it can be the archetype of the fate of the dead. It invests actions and events in the divine realm with a formulation that makes them comprehensible on the level of the mortuary cult. The same is true of the morning icon, which symbolizes the overcoming of death and the renewal of life, rebirth from the womb of the sky goddess. Connected with it are Isis and Nephthys, the divine mourning women, whose laments and transfigurations raise the dead into the morning constellation of the course of the sun:

Isis and Nephthys lift you
as you emerge from the thighs of your mother Nut.[33]

The icons give the course of the sun a form that makes it possible to relate it to the world of humankind, for they bring to light a meaning in the sun's course that is common to both levels, the cosmic level and that of the fate of the dead; that is, events on both levels can be explained by means of them. There is a third level as well: kingship, which is dominant in the icon of midday. The sun god traversing the sky is the archetype of royal rule as triumph over evil, the victory of right and order, the *parousia* of Maat. Just as the icons of evening and morning sketch out the archetype of a successful outcome for individuals' hopes for immortality, so the midday icon of overcoming the enemy lends archetypal form above all to society and its interest in health, life, and well-being.

This iconography of the sun's course is to be viewed as the unfolding of the essence of the sun god into the dimension of language, as the multitude of names and forms in which things can be said about him and to him. In the context of our treatment of the "implicit theology" of the Egyptians, they had the function of an example. Just like the sun god, all the important Egyptian deities unfolded the plenitude of the essence of their personhood into constellations and actions. Language represented the divine realm as an interactive network of constellations in which "one acts and lives in the other." The iconography of the sun's course had—or acquired in the course of its development—more than a paradigmatic status in the whole of Egyptian religion: it became a sort of formulation of the cosmos, the central idea in the Egyptian picture of the world. The icons in which the three levels of cosmos, kingship, and mortuary beliefs found archetypal formulations of ideational content, and by means of which these levels became explicable in solar, royal, and mortuary texts, formulate the coherence of reality per se. The icons of the sun's course endow reality with coherence by relating the three levels or dimensions of meaning in which reality transpires to one another, that is, to common archetypes. They represent the cosmos as action. Reality is performative, and anything performed on one of its levels with respect to archetypal icons—sunrise, coronation, burial—has a share in the reality of events in the divine realm.

How did icons acquire this explanatory power to represent a sort of cosmic model? I believe that it is connected with the Egyptian concept of time. Unlike the Greeks, the Egyptians did not make a distinction between "time" and "eternity," or—what amounts to the same thing—between "being" and "becoming." For them, the decisive dichotomy was rather a cosmic "plenitude of time" and a transitory "span of time" allotted to every earthly being, or—what amounts to the same thing—life and death. The course of the sun was at the same time the pulse-beat of the world, which filled the cosmos with life force by means of the cyclic defeat of the enemy and of death. The constellation that lent the clarity of an icon to this idea was that of Re and Osiris. In the depths of the night, they unite as father and son, as the day at dusk and dawn, and as the two aspects of the plenitude of cosmic time that the Egyptians distinguished as *neheh* and *djet*. Time—or more precisely put—the *continuity of reality* had its origin in the cyclical uniting of *neheh* and *djet*, "virtuality" and "resultativity." Once the step was taken of explaining the course of the sun as the cyclical complexion of the two aspects "change" and "permanence," an all-embracing formulation was obtained. For that which exists is—according to one Egyptian definition—*neheh* and *djet*. This explanation might be very old. It is striking that the two sun gods who, as the morning and evening forms of the sun, make up with Re the triune deity embodied in the course of the sun have eloquent names that refer to the two aspects of time in a way that was clear and everpresent to the Egyptians themselves: Khepri means the "Becoming One" and Atum the "Completed One." Tangible here are the beginnings of a concept that developed into a comprehensive theory of time at the point when Osiris, the deceased father, was added as the embodiment of *djet*.

It is characteristic of the Egyptian picture of the cosmos that even as abstract an idea as the union of *neheh* and *djet* as guarantee of the continuity of cosmic life was articulated as a constellation, as the activity of two gods, and was even capable of being represented in art. This activity, too, was archetypically related to ideas about kingship and the dead. The activity was imaged in two ways: as the embrace by means of which the deceased father transmitted *ka*, the vital dynastic force, to his son, and as the uniting of *ba* and corpse. The *ka*-embrace was the archetype of the legitimacy of the king, who as "Horus appeared in the arms of his father Osiris." The uniting of *ba* (Re) and corpse (Osiris) was the archetype of individual immortality. This analogy between the fate of the dead and the course of the sun is explicitly stressed when the sun god says, in a cosmographical book,

> I cause the *ba*s to alight on their corpses,
> after I myself have alighted on my corpse,[34]

Humankind is not mentioned in the iconic representations of the sun's course that we find in the hymns, for this event transpires in constellations in the divine realm, and humans as such can never be partners in constellations of deities. The icons do, however, hold open the possibility of identification and participation. In the cult, humans enter into the constellations and play the roles of deities:

> I have sung hymns to the sun,
> I have associated myself with the solar baboons,
> I am one of them.
> I have played the second of Isis
> and heightened the effect of her radiant power (*akhu*).[35]

Political-social success and the fate of the individual after death are explained with reference to the meaning given form by the icons of the sun's course. The verbal dimension of presence lends coherence to reality, with the result that everything gains a share in the sacred meaning that here becomes speech. The sacred names and icons make this meaning—the continuity of life and the coherence of reality—not only thinkable and communicable, but also realizable, through the radiant power of the word. By reciting these icons in their verbal realizations as hymns, the priest—as stated in a formulation that expresses the Egyptians' own understanding of this act of speech—causes "Maat (the personification of the meaning in question here) to ascend to the sun god."

CHAPTER 5

Myth

5.1. Myth, Icon, and Story

"Icon": this is the name we have given to the form in which an occurrence in visible reality—in the cult or in the cosmos—is identified as
an event in the divine realm according to the principle of sacramental
interpretation. This event is represented as an interaction of deities
acting in the framework of typical and established roles and constellations. Thus, for example, sunrise is explained as a birth, and the
birth is represented as the interaction of the constellations mother and
child, child and nurse, child and adorants. Or, an offering is explained
as the restitution of life force, and the life force is represented as action
in the framework of the constellation of the deceased father, his son,
and an enemy. Icons are timeless or related to a "timeless present," for
they are the divine archetypes of actions that are continually carried
out in the cult and the cosmos. In the process, the icons are realized
by means of the radiant power of language. Every morning, the sun
is born anew; at every coronation, Isis once again nurses her son
Horus; with every offering, the Eye of Horus is again restored. In
icons, time is brought to a halt, or better, "ornamentalized" in the
form of an endless array of overlapping patterns. Individual events—
sunrises, coronations, cultic acts—overlap in relation to such icons.

Stories, however, are always related to a place in time, and they
occur in the past. For this reason, they can only be told, just as icons
can only be described. They are related to the mode of narration, just
as icons are related to the mode of description. Besides its reference to
the past, a story denotes a specific coherence that is essentially teleo-
logical: a chain of episodes is connected into a story in such a way that
it is directed toward a goal. It is not the fact that the episodes stand in
a cause-and-effect relationship, but that they lead teleologically to a
good or a bad ending, that determines the coherence of a story. The
cycle of icons related to the course of the sun is lacking not only in narrative reference (that is, to the past), but also in narrative coherence.
The icons of morning, the daily journey, the landing, and the journey
through the netherworld describe and explain an occurrence in the

present. Their relationship to one another results from this occurrence, in which daytime follows morning, and so forth. I call this type of coherence, which results, in ritual texts, from the constant sequence of cultic acts, "practical coherence," for its real existence is not in the text, but in the world of objects and facts to which the text refers. Moreover, their relationship to one another follows the principle of analogy, especially to the human life cycle (birth, adulthood, old age, death).

Egyptian myths combine the principle of icons and the principle of stories, "iconicity" and "narrativity." It would be an error to make a distinction between icons and myths. In Egypt, icons were the material of which myths were made, and stories were the form in which the material was unfolded. Icons could at any time be developed into stories, and stories could at any time be condensed into icons. This is the case when a mythic episode, for instance, that of Isis and the child Horus, occurs outside the myth of Osiris and develops independent meanings in various contexts. In contrast to Mesopotamian and Greek myths, the iconic fixity of Egyptian myths prevented their development into truly effective stories. Though they freed themselves from the practical coherence of ritual and cosmic events, they developed only a weak narrative coherence. Their episodes are only loosely related to one another, and their characters seem scarcely less fixed in their roles than in the constellations of icons. Their protagonists lack coherence, whether with respect to their actions (character, will, intentionality) or to their experiences (reflection, development, assimilation of their own past). Actions often remain strangely without consequences, and characters frequently change their minds without any motive that is apparent to us.

The most common definition of "myth" calls it a story about deities. Like many others, this definition can be easily disproved by referring to stories that are unquestionably myths but are not about deities, such as the myth of Oedipus. Scholars have therefore refrained from defining myth in the sense of an anthropological universal. For Egypt, however, the definition is valid. Myths were indeed stories told about deities, and only about deities. Relating myths was a form of contact with the divine, and myth was thus a dimension of divine presence and of religious experience. But myth was not "narrative (and thus explicit) theology." The theme of myth was not the essence of the deities, but rather—and this point seems decisive to me and is probably valid not only for Egyptian mythology—the essence of reality. Myths establish and enclose the area in which human actions and experiences can be oriented. The stories they tell about deities are supposed to bring to light the meaningful structure of reality. Myths are always set in the past, and they always refer to the present. What they relate about the past is supposed to shed light on the present. Their intent is not to relate the past for its own sake, but as a prelude to the present, diagnosing the present in the form of a genetic projection. They dress the statement, "the world is A," in the form

There was a time when the world was not-A.
Then certain events occurred.
Their result was: the world is A.

We can call this function of myth "explanatory," but we must be aware that this has nothing to do with transfiguration, but rather with explanation, with attributing meaning to reality. The many myths of "how death came into the world" are not intended to transfigure death, but rather to relate it to other features of present reality, such as scarcity, work, absence of the divine, and sexuality, and to fit it into a comprehensive diagnosis of the *conditio humana*. This "genetic explanation" of reality should not be confused with etiology. The difference between explanatory and etiological myths lies in the status of the initial question. The question of how death came into the world has a different status from that of how the robin acquired its red breast.

5.2. The Myth of the Heavenly Cow

The most detailed example of an explanatory myth from Egypt is the Book of the Heavenly Cow, which was recorded in several New Kingdom royal tombs and is probably to be ascribed to the genre of cosmography in its wider sense. It consists of a representation that depicts the solar barque on the body of the sky goddess in the form of a cow whose belly is supported by Shu, the god of the air, and whose legs are supported by eight *heh*-gods, who incarnate the atmosphere (Figure 5), along with a text that, with its 330 verses, was the length of a book (that is, a roll of papyrus) by Egyptian standards. In addition to the actual tale, it also includes detailed instructions for preparing the representation and reciting the text, such as are found in less detailed form in magical texts. Magic also plays a surprisingly large role in the mythic account. In a typically Egyptian manner, the myth is dramatized by direct quotations that take up more space than the account itself.

The situation at the outset, the ideal picture that is the opposite of the present condition, whose essence the myth wishes to demonstrate in the form of a genetic projection, is sketched at the beginning in a few sentences and displays an order that is already disturbed:

It happened that Re (arose), the self-created god,
after he occupied the kingship
when humans and gods were (still) together.
Then the people devised a plot against Re.

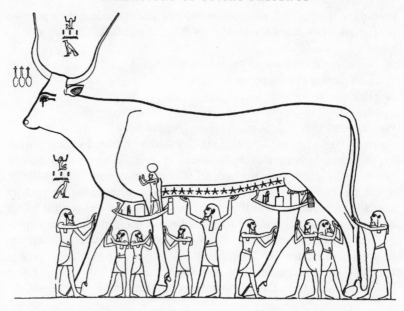

FIGURE 5. The heavenly cow. From A. Piankoff, *The Shrines of Tut-Ankh-Amon*, Bollingen Series 40 (New York, 1955), p. 142, fig. 46.

> His majesty was old:
>   His bones were silver,
>   his limbs were gold,
>   his hair was genuine lapis-lazuli.
> His majesty perceived the plot
>   the people had devised against him.[1]

The sun god convenes a meeting of the divine council. The following forty verses detail the deities' exchanges; Hathor, the fiery "eye" and the daughter of the sun god, is to kill the rebels. The action resumes with a single sentence:

> This goddess returned
> after she killed the people in the desert.[2]

A brief dialogue ensues between the sun god and his daughter, who has returned. With no transition whatsoever, the second part of the story commences. It has to do with the preparation of a drink made of beer colored blood-red; Re has seven thousand jugs of it poured out over the land to protect humankind, which has evidently not yet been completely annihilated, from the goddess. The ruse succeeds: in the morning, when the goddess sees the "blood," she drinks it and becomes intoxicated, forgetting humankind. This section contains a number of etiological asides regarding the origin of a cult, the preparation of an intoxicating drink on the festival of Hathor, and the "time of suffering." The first and the second parts of the story are separated not only by a night, but also by a change of heart on the part of the sun god, who evidently rues his decision to annihilate the human race. The text, however, makes no mention of this matter! The third part deals with the creation of the sky. It begins with an admission by the sun god: "My heart is too weary to be with them (i.e., humankind)."[3] This leads to the separation of sky and earth, deities and humankind. The sky is lifted up by Shu and his eight divine assistants in the form of a celestial cow along whose back the sun god travels. The humans, who remain behind on earth and are left to their own devices, go to war with one another, "and so slaughter came about among humankind."[4]

After detailed instructions on how to prepare the accompanying illustration and where each caption is to be placed, there is a fourth, concluding section containing a dialogue whose theme is the creation of the netherworld, which must be prepared for the nightly journey of the sun. Finally, the moon god Thoth is appointed as "vizier" and as the nocturnal stand-in for the sun. There are some final remarks concerning the recitation of the text; they serve to make the myth a mortuary text that can keep the reciter of these "divine words" alive even in the realm of the dead and transplant him among the gods, thus canceling the separation related in the story. Mythic processes are reversible, and when it is stated that the world is A and once was not-A, the original counter-picture can again be realized in the story. The text is a myth about original sin: it relates how things came to the separation of deities and humankind and thus to the sorrowful condition, characterized as "slaughter," of the humanity left behind on earth. Recitation of the text by the cognoscenti, however, removes the sin and the separation and "resocializes" humankind, though only after death, in the divine realm:

> He who recites this spell will be alive in the realm of the dead,
> and respect for him will be greater than (for) those on earth.
> If they speak your names,
> (the celestial supports) Neheh and Djet,
> they will say, "He is [truly] a god!",
> they will say, "He has reached us here on this road!"[5]

As noted, the Book of the Heavenly Cow consists of a text and a representation. The representation refers to the present condition of the world in the form of an icon: as a constellation and a construct of actions. We see the sun barque traveling, the gods of the air who serve as supports, and the all-encompassing celestial cow. The text refers to the past, a time when Re was king over deities and humans together. The relationship between the two, the iconic and the narrative element, is that of a prelude: the picture represents the present condition, and the text narrates what preceded it, thereby pointing the way to its alleviation. In making the world, as it has become, transparent by drawing the contrasting picture of its origin, the myth makes use of the radiant power of the word to facilitate the restoration of its original unity, at least for the deceased, who, equipped with it, can associate with deities.

5.3. The Engendering of the Child

We must carefully distinguish between the sense of a myth, that is, the meaning of the story, and the purpose of its physical recording (or oral performance). The meaning of the myth of the heavenly cow has to do with the topic of original sin; the human condition is anthropologically and cosmologically situated in a differentiated cosmos in which deities and humans occupy separate places, and this separation is connected with a sin, a rebellion of humankind, and also with the aging process of the sun god. This myth has historical roots; it has often, and without doubt correctly, been connected with the experience of the collapse of the Old Kingdom. But its recording in royal tombs of Dynasty 19 stems from a much later period and pursues wholly different goals. Here, the myth is used as a cosmological magical text for the king's ascent to the sky. The myth we shall consider in what follows is significantly different on both levels, that of history and that of its recording, from the myth of the heavenly cow. The story deals with the king, who overall plays no role in the myth of the heavenly cow. Furthermore, it does not refer to primeval time as the vaguely understood prelude to an equally vaguely understood present, but rather to the immediate prelude to the immediate present. The recording of the myth is not a part of tomb decoration, but rather of temple decoration, and its goal is not related to the deceased king, but rather to the living one. The four preserved records of it are in temples of the New Kingdom: the mortuary temple of Hatshepsut at Deir el-Bahari, the Luxor temple of Amenophis III, the Ramesseum of Ramesses II (now reused in the temple of Medinet Habu), and the temple of Khonspekhrod, the divine child of the Theban triad, in front of the temple of Mut (Dynasty 22?).

The story, which is not actually related in these attestations, but rather presented in a coherent series of tableaux, has to do with the divine descent of the royal child. Amun, king of the gods, decides to engender a new king in whose hands rule over the world will be placed, one who will build temples to deities and increase their offerings, and in whose time abundance and fertility will reign. A mortal woman strikes his fancy; Thoth, the divine messenger, ascertains that she is none other than the queen herself. He conducts Amun, who has assumed the form of her royal husband, to the queen. The queen is awakened by the aroma of the god and realizes who is beside her. After the god "has done all he desired with her," she praises him with these words:

> How great is your power!
> The sight of your countenance is noble.
> You have surrounded me with your radiance,
> your scent is in all my limbs.[6]

Amun forms the name of the future child from the words the couple exchange. He commands Khnum, the god who creates individuals and models humans on his potter's wheel, to fashion the child in his (i.e., Amun's) image. Khnum, along with Heqet, the goddess of childbirth, fashions the child. Thoth is sent to the queen to announce her pregnancy to her. Khnum and Heqet personally lead the expectant mother to the bed where she will give birth. A number of helpful deities and protective genies stand beside her as she gives birth. The deity of the "birthing brick" and personal destiny pronounces a blessing on the newborn child. The child is to be raised by the deities: Amun immediately sets it on his lap and recognizes his offspring, divine nurses suckle the child, and deities bestow blessings on it. As the child grows, it is circumcised, purified, and presented to the assembled deities of the land as the new king.

The preserved copies proceed with the story in a highly idiosyncratic manner, breaking it down like a drama or a sacred play into fifteen or seventeen scenes. The scenes represent the story in pictures, explaining it with narrative captions at the beginning and otherwise with the words that the deities exchange with one another, which are written beside them. The beginning corresponds exactly to what Hans Blumenberg has called "the categorical determination of the 'long-windedness' of mythological forms," that is, "the negation of the attribute 'omnipotence.'" Amun, the omniscient god, falls in love with a mortal woman and is obliged to inquire as to her identity. Amun, the omnipotent god, is obliged to assume the form of the king to gain access to the queen. All this is no theological statement, but rather narrative strategy in the service of dramatic tension. Then, with the fifth scene, the form of representation takes something of a turn: the deities merely play their typical roles in the framework of established constellations, just as in the sequence of scenes depicting the course of the sun or those serving as sacramental interpretation of ritual. For this reason, scholars have taken these scenes, too, as the representation of a ritual. But it is scarcely conceivable that events such as engendering and birth were ritually enacted. It is more likely that we are dealing with an ex post facto sacramental interpretation of these events.

The cycle of scenes depicting the birth of the king is followed by a cycle depicting the coronation and the assumption of the throne. This is the actual event to which the birth scenes refer, in the sense of a prelude. The king's assumption of the throne was *set in the light of a mythic prelude*, just as the myth of the heavenly cow set the present condition of the world in the light of a prelude. In the latter, we are told how the rebellion of humankind led to the separation of sky and earth, a story whose meaning is that we live in a divided cosmos that has forfeited its original unity. Here, in the myth of the divine birth of the king, we are told that the coronation of the king fulfills the will of the god who engendered the child and "socialized" it into the divine realm to rule as king of the world in peace and fear of the god. The assumption of the throne is traced back to a divine intervention, and this intervention is dated to before the engenderment, to the spiritual "conception" of the king in the will of the god. This is a legitimizing myth. Its purpose is not only to explain a present situation by means of a story that occurred in the past, to make the present situation "readable" by filling it with meaning, but first and foremost, and unmistakably so, to provide a mythic basis for a given pretender's claim to the right to rule.

The story of the divine descent of the royal child was first told of the three kings who began Dynasty 5, the dynasty that contented itself with more modest pyramids but added sun temples to them (see chapter 3.2.1) and included the title "Son of Re" in the official royal titulary. The story is not preserved in the form of an official cycle of reliefs, however, but rather in a folk tale, in a context of wondrous legends. This fact suggests rather clearly that we are not dealing exclusively with a piece of official royal ideology, but with a concept that was related in the form of a story in various contexts and which must thus have had a certain general influence and popularity in ancient Egypt. The story is also familiar to us today and is still told in a variant that differs in only *one* respect from the Egyptian version: the kingdom of Christian tradition is not of this world. But Egyptian tradition prepared the way for even this transposition. At a specific point in Egyptian history, the myth changed its form and its point of reference. It became a festival drama that was enacted one or more times each year in all the larger temples in the land, and it referred, not to the birth of the king, but to that of the child god in the respective temple triads. Now it was the new god who came into the world and ascended the throne. In this version, the emphasis of the myth shifted from its legitimizing to its explanatory and meaning-imparting function. It made "readable" and tolerable a contemporary situation in which the kingship lay in doubtful hands, in that the well-being of the land was in the hands of divinity. The Late Period in Egypt was a time of changing foreign rule. In this period, the myth lost its legitimizing reference. Because welfare was no longer embodied in the king, a festival drama was enacted to relate—or, rather, celebrate—how a god had come to bring salvation into the world. Kingship was legitimated through worship of the child.

5.4. The Genealogy of the Cosmos and the Kingship

When it was used as a cycle of reliefs on the walls of temples, the myth of the engendering and birth of the royal child considered in the preceding section always referred to a specific monarch. It thus did not occur *in illo tempore*, in the primeval time when the foundations of present reality were laid, but rather in contemporary history, in which the god intervened in a miraculous way that spanned the gap between sky and earth. There is an older myth that legitimates not the historical person of a given king, but rather the institution of kingship. In the earliest attestations, we are given little more than a genealogical list: Atum, Shu and Tefnut, Geb and Nut, Osiris, Isis, Nephthys, Seth and Horus. To discern the meaning of this list, we must arrange its elements:

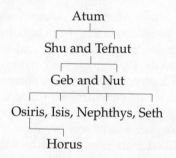

The upper portion of the list is a cosmogony. Atum is the god of pre-existence. His name means both "to be nothing" and "to be everything": he is the All in its condition of not-yet. In an act of self fertilization, he produces from himself the first divine couple: Shu (air) and Tefnut (fire). These then produce Geb and Nut, who are earth and sky. The Egyptians always connected this myth with Heliopolis. Heliopolis was the original city, the primeval mound on which Atum was able to gain a foothold in order to create—or better, secrete—Shu and Tefnut:

> You became high as the primeval mound,
> you arose as Benben

in the House of the Phoenix in Heliopolis.
You spat out as Shu,
you coughed up as Tefnut,
you placed your arms around them
as the arms of *ka*,
so that your *ka* might be in them.[7]

This is the oldest and "classic" cosmogonical text in Egypt, which was recited and recorded again and again over time. Here, the cosmogonical process has not yet developed into a story that could be told. Rather, it appears under the dominant aspect of a constellation: the embrace in which the father causes his creative life force to enter his children. In view of its concise form, we should speak of a "model" rather than of a myth.

The cosmogonic model of Heliopolis exerted an undiminished influence in Egyptian religion throughout the millennia of its history. The model's central concept is the "coming into being" of the cosmos, as opposed to its creation. The Egyptian word is *ḫpr*, written with the picture of a scarab-beetle, a verb meaning "to come into being, assume form," and its derived noun *ḫprw*, "emanation, embodiment, development" (see chapter 3.2.1). Atum is "the one who came into being by himself," and everything else came into being from him. The cosmos "emanated" from Atum, Atum "turned himself into" the cosmos. Atum was not the creator, but rather the origin: everything "came into being" from him. In the course of time, this concept was repeatedly elaborated on, and we deal with a series of these elaborations in Part II, for they belong in the context of explicit theology. In Egypt, theological discourse was sparked by the problem of creation. In its very first expressions in the royal ritual texts of the Old Kingdom, this concept is already at a surprisingly abstract level. Although we have scarcely more than names in these texts, the texts are filled with meaning of which the Egyptians themselves must always have been aware. From the very beginning, the two names Atum and Khepri/Kheprer designated one and the same divine being. Atum means "the finished," "the All" in the condition of nonexistence, and Khepri/Kheprer means "the Becoming One," which designates the changed aspect of the god in his spontaneous act of "coming into existence himself." At the same time, the two verbs from which these names are derived refer, in a manner that was quite transparent to the Egyptians, to the two aspects of time and eternity distinguished in the Egyptian language, *neheh*, "inexhaustible plenitude of time" of coming into being, and *djet*, the unchanging "continuation" of that which is completed. The Heliopolitan concept of the primeval creator god is less a mythology than the germ of a philosophy.

To this point, we have pursued only the cosmogonic reading of the list that served as our starting point. It took us as far as the third generation, Geb and Nut, earth and sky, but it cannot explain the deities who follow. There is another reading, however, that can be applied to the entire list, one that refers to succession to royal office. Atum ruled as the first king over the cosmos that emerged from him. As a consequence of the events related in the myth of the heavenly cow, Shu succeeded him on the throne. After Shu, Geb reigned; this change on the throne is the nucleus of a lengthy mythic tale that is preserved on a monument of the Late Period. Geb and Nut had five children, with Horus the child of the divine couple Osiris and Isis, who were already united in their mother's womb. After Geb, Osiris ruled first, and he was assassinated by Seth. The royal office thus fell to Horus, but only as a claim and a task: he was obliged to fight for it, wresting it away from Seth and avenging the death of his father. This "cratogonic" reading of the list is the actual mythological one: we can see how each change on the throne became a crystallization point of independent mythic discourse in a manner similar to the way in which theological discourse was kindled in the cosmogonic reading. In exact contrast to the cosmogony, however, the emphasis clearly lies at the end of the list:

	Cosmogony			Cratogony	
	Atum		Isis	Osiris	Seth
Shu	Tefnut			Horus	

We concern ourselves in the next section with the myths that crystallize around this end-constellation of the cosmo-cratogonic list from Heliopolis. Here, we consider only one point: the list begins and ends with a single god. Each of them stands in contrast with the deities who are grouped together: Atum as god of preexistence over against the deities who emerged from him, and Horus as the god who was incarnated, in each earthly, historical king, over against the deities who preceded him in the royal office in primeval times and who have now withdrawn to the sky. We thus have a threefold articulation in the temporal dimension:

Preexistence		Atum		
		Shu	Tefnut	
Primeval time		Geb	Nut	
	Isis	Osiris	Seth	Nephthys
Historical time		Horus		

Which reading, the cosmogonic or the political, was the originally authoritative one? The answer is that this entire constellation was connected with the concept of the Ennead, a group of nine, and that Horus did not belong to the group. He was the god who stood over against the other deities, and thus the point from which the entirety was conceived. The starting point was the king. He was the incarnation of the god Horus, the son who ever and again has to overcome the death of his father to gain his throne. The Ennead before whom he must prove that he is the rightful heir to the throne is both his family and the cosmos itself; read in descending order, his genealogy is a cosmogony. Therein lies the legitimacy of his office: it is the rule that the primeval god had exercised over those who emerged from him, the office of Atum, which had passed through the cosmogonic succession of the gods of air and earth to Osiris, the deceased father, and from him to the succession of historical kings in whom his son Horus was incarnate.

It seems to me that three features of this Heliopolitan cosmogony are worth stressing, because they are typical of Egyptian religion as a whole:

1. the "autogenesis" of the creator
2. the posteriority of evil
3. the continuity of cosmogony and history.

The decisive cosmogonic event was the appearance of the primeval god who "came into existence on his own." This act of original spontaneous genesis served as the model for every sunrise and every emergence of the land from the annual Nile flood, the actual "first moment," as the Egyptian concept of genesis was called. The second point has to do with the inevitability of the cosmogonic process. The maintenance of the cosmos, the work of the sun's course as a *creatio continua* in which the creator god who "came into being himself" caused a million forms to come into being from himself, had to be wrested through an ongoing defeat of the inimical forces of inertia and collapse into chaos. This antagonistic aspect was entirely absent, however, from the "first moment." Evil came into the cosmos only secondarily. We find indications of it already in connection with descriptions of the primeval condition in the Pyramid Texts:

> when sky and earth had not yet come into being,
> before the human race came into being and deities were born,
> before death came into being.[8]

> before that which was secure came into being,
> before strife came into being,
> before fear regarding the Eye of Horus came into being.[9]

The "strife" and the "fear regarding the Eye of Horus" are clear allusions to the conflict of Horus and Seth over the kingship. The origin of evil is evidently connected with the death of Osiris. From that time on, kingship and the preservation of the cosmos, of order and life, must be fought for and wrested from evil. The atrocity committed by Seth brought death and evil into the world. This is evidently the point at which cosmogonic primeval time turns into historical time. The Egyptians saw a break at this point and drew a clear boundary, so that we cannot speak of a "continuity of cosmogony and history." But the decisive point is that *the break is reversible*. Although it determines the present situation, it can be reversed. When Horus ascends the throne, the death of Osiris is overcome, his "wound" is "healed." Although the myth points to a gap between the present world and its original unity, it also points to the way back and maintains a link with its origin.

5.5. The Myth of Osiris

All three myths treated thus far have set a present situation in the light of a meaningful prelude. We may generalize by saying that myth ascribes a prelude to the present so as to explain it in a meaningful way (as in the myth of the heavenly cow), to authenticate it (as in the myth of the divine birth of the king), or to ground it existentially and politically legitimize it (as in the Heliopolitan cosmogony). Myth is rooted in the present and reaches back from it so as to represent it as what it has become. This is especially true of the myth of Osiris, which constitutes the final act in the overarching context of the Heliopolitan cosmogony and in its political reading as a myth of succession to the throne. It has to do with the present, with "the time in which we are," as stated explicitly in a text to which Erik Hornung has drawn attention:

> What is it: this time in which we are?
> It is the burial of Osiris
> and making his son Horus ruler.[10]

Here, we find a specification of the two poles between which this story extends: the burial of the father and the coronation of his son—in any event, to the extent that this is a story about a father and his son. The myth of Osiris comprises a number of stories or constellations: a story about a wife that is played out between Osiris and Isis, one or perhaps two (difficult to distinguish) stories about rival brothers played out between Osiris and Seth and between Horus and Seth, and a story about a mother and her child played out between Isis and Horus. It was actually Plutarch who first gathered all these stories into the single, comprehensive context of the "myth of Osiris." Here, too, we must distinguish between the story—or the cycle of stories—on the one hand, and on the other hand, the various forms in which it was told. If we do not begin with the Greek text of Plutarch, which is a reconstruction of the story, but rather with the forms in which the Egyptians expressed it, we see that it can clearly be grouped around the four or five aforementioned basic constellations of icons, each of which is a nucleus for the crystallization of texts that exist in highly diverse contexts: mortuary texts, magical texts, royal texts, and so forth.

No other myth (or cycle of myths) was even remotely as intensely woven into the cultural life of ancient Egypt, or in so many ways. This fact constitutes a striking difference between the religion of Egypt and other polytheistic religions. With regard to ancient Egypt, we can almost speak of a (distinct tendency toward) "monomyth," as the philosopher Odo Marquard of Giessen has called it. Polytheistic religions are also "polymythic." The Hindu, Sumero-Babylonian, Canaanite, and Greek religions offer ample demonstration of this statement. Egypt was an exception in this regard, and we may suspect that myth was more a political than a religious phenomenon and thus correlated with the expressly monarchic structure of the Egyptian state rather than with the polytheistic structure of Egyptian religion. To some extent, this point is correct. We must not forget, however, that the influence of the Osiris cycle was in no way confined to the official sphere. On the contrary, no other myth was more popular or played as great a role in healing spells, popular tales, and other private literary genres. Osiris was not a "state god" like Re and later Amun-Re. From the Middle Kingdom on, at the latest, he was generally recognized as the god of the dead, and his jurisdiction and worship extended to everything mortal. Along with the worship of Osiris, there was a distinct tendency to "democratize" exclusive forms of cult and belief. Nevertheless, it remained true that the myth of Osiris retained a distinctively political dimension of meaning, so that it can be designated, with complete justification, as the mythic articulation of the Egyptian concept of the state. It would perhaps not be surprising if Osiris had occupied the supreme position in the Egyptian pantheon, with the result that he played the principal role in nearly all the stories about deities. But that was in no way the case. Although Osiris was one of the most important deities, he was no "Supreme Being." In Egypt, such concepts were connected with the sun god, who was the antithesis of Osiris. Let us therefore set aside such hasty conclusions and allow the fact to remain that Osiris, without being the supreme deity or a state god, experienced a development in the mythic dimension that outshone all the other deities or even connected them to him.

The following treatment of the Osiris myth is oriented toward the sources, and it is therefore less concerned with the underlying story or stories as with the forms in which the myth found practical application and expression. It is therefore divided into the five nuclei around which such forms of expression crystallized.

5.5.1. SECTION ONE: DEATH, SEARCH FOR THE BODY, BURIAL, MOURNING

There is a spell from the Pyramid Texts that occurs in the Coffin Texts as part of a mortuary liturgy for the nocturnal wake for the deceased, and which probably already served a similar purpose in the Old Kingdom. It refers to what was most likely the starting point of the Osiris story in every Egyptian version of the myth (though not in Plutarch, who expanded it with a prelude):

> The *djed*-pillar of the *mandjet*-barque is loosened for its lord,
> The *djed*-pillar of the *mandjet*-barque is loosened for its protector,
> Isis comes, Nephthys comes,
> the one from the west,
> 5   the other from the east,
> the one as a screeching bird,
> the other as a mourning bird.
> They have found Osiris
> his brother Seth having thrown him onto the ground in Nedit.
> 10   When Osiris said, "Get off me,"
> his name Sokar came into existence.
>
> They prevent you from decaying,
> in accordance with this your name Anubis,
> they prevent your bodily fluids from dripping to the ground,
> 15   in this your name of Upper Egyptian Jackal,
> they prevent your body from smelling foul,
> in this your name of Horus of Chaty.
>
> They prevent Horus of the East from decaying,
> they prevent Horus, Lord of the Subjects from decaying,
> 20   they prevent Horus of the Netherworld from decaying,
> and they prevent Horus, Lord of the Two Lands from decaying.
>
> Truly, Seth will not be freed
> from carrying you, Osiris, in eternity.
> Awake for Horus,
> 25   stand up against Seth,
> Lift yourself, Osiris,
> first-born son of Geb,
> before whom the two Enneads tremble!
>
> The guardian rises before you,
> 30   the New Moon Festival is celebrated for you,

so that you may appear at the Month Festival.
Fare south over the sea,
cross the ocean,
for you are the one who stands unwearying,
35   who resides in Abydos.

You are radiant in Light-land,
you endure in the Land of Enduring.

Your hand will be taken by the *ba*s of Heliopolis,
your hand will be grasped by Re,
40   your head will be lifted by the two Enneads.
They set you, Osiris,
at the head of the two sanctuaries of the *ba*s of Heliopolis.
You live, you live,
lift yourself![11]

The text does not relate a story; rather, it explains cultic acts and their situative framework by an event in the divine realm, which is extended temporally into a prelude and a subsequent story and expanded into a construct of mythic actions. The cultic situation is the wake in the embalming hall (note the clear allusions to the context of embalming in verses 12–21) and the cultic appearance of the two mourning women in the roles of Isis and Nephthys, as known from many later mortuary texts and recitations in the Osiris cult. The focus of this (cultic) scene is the body of the deceased king, which is lying on the embalming table or in its coffin. This appearance is celebrated and explained as the discovery of the corpse of Osiris. The prelude to this event results from the logical presuppositions of this motif.

The discovery must be preceded by a search, as expressly noted in other spells from the Pyramid Texts:

To be spoken by Isis and Nephthys:
The screeching bird comes, the mourning bird comes,
it is Isis and Nephthys.
They have come in search of their brother Osiris,
in search of their brother, this King Pepy. . . .[12]

Lying down must be preceded by a felling, death by a killing:

You have come in search of your brother Osiris,
after his brother Seth felled him on his side,
on that side of Geheset.[13]

On the mythic level, the meaning of the cultic event, the appearance of the two mourning women beside the body of the king, is supplemented by a prelude: Isis and Nephthys, after traversing the land in search of their brother Osiris, find him in a place called Nedit or Geheset, murdered by his brother Seth. These events are the prelude in the divine realm, in whose light the present—the mourning and embalming of the king—are set. In this light, and this is evidently the sense of such an explanation, despair is overcome and action is possible. Seth, the embodiment of the cause of death, must be called to account for his evil deed. The death of Osiris will not thus be undone, but it will be integrated into the order of the world, which has been disturbed. Another Pyramid Texts spell, which had exactly the same history of adoption as spell 532 (cited at the outset of this section) and thus doubtless belongs to the same context of a funerary wake liturgy in the embalming hall, is explicit on this point:

The sky is in a turmoil,
the earth quakes.
Horus comes,
Thoth appears,
to prop Osiris up on his side
and cause him to appear before the two Enneads.

Remember, Seth,
take to heart
that word that Geb has spoken,
that reproach the gods have made against you
in the House of the Noble at Heliopolis,
because you have smitten Osiris.

When you said, Seth,
"I have not done this to him,"
that you might have power thereby,
because you were saved and gained power over Horus;

when you said, Seth,
"It was he who attacked me,"
and that name of his of Earth-attacker came into being;
when you said, Seth,
"It was he who struck me,"
and his name Orion came into being,
with long leg and broad stride,
at the head of Upper Egypt.

Lift yourself, Osiris,
for Seth lifted himself
when he heard the reproach of the gods

who spoke about the father of the gods.
(Give) Isis your arm, Osiris,

and Nephthys your hand,
that you may go between them.

The sky has been given to you,
the earth has been given to you,
the Field of Reeds,
the mounds of Horus and the mounds of Seth,
the cities have been given to you,
the nomes have been united for you by Atum;
the one who speaks about it is Geb.[14]

This spell, which refers to the appearance of two priests in the roles of Horus and Thoth (these are typical roles of the *sem*-priest and the chief lector priest) in the context of the same cultic situation that underlies spell 532, places not mourning but justification in the foreground. Both spells proceed from the situation of the deceased lying on his bier, and both set it in the light of a mythic situation or an event in the divine realm: the discovery of Osiris, who has been slain by his brother Seth. The mythic explanation facilitates action; in spell 532, the action of the mourning women, who bewail the deceased as Isis and Nephthys, embalm and awaken him, and in spell 477, cited here, the action of the priests, who as Horus and Thoth justify the deceased by putting his murderer on trial. Death is not an end, but the beginning of the funerary rites, and thus it is also the beginning of the story that explains these rites. If we wish to locate the story at the point where it becomes spoken, we must point to death as its starting point and its theme. The Osiris myth overcomes the experience of death by according this apparently catastrophic and hopeless situation an orientation in which it becomes meaningful to say to the deceased: "Arise!" "Stand up!" "Lift yourself!"—called out to the deceased as he lies stretched out, these exhortations constitute a common element shared by the two texts. They occur in a hundred other spells of the Pyramid Texts, and in later funerary literature, they are expanded into lengthy recitations and litanies that make a refrain of them, consistently addressing them to the deceased lying on the bier or to Osiris. The longest of these "raise yourself" litanies is in the Osiris sanctuary on the roof of the temple of Hathor at Dendara from the Roman Period. We can summarize all these recitations, from the Pyramid Texts through the latest Osirian mysteries, as a genre of "raise-yourself spells." The meaning and function of these spells become tangible in these injunctions, which constitute their common element and their focal point. Addressed to the deceased lying inert, the spells say, "Raise yourself!" on various mythic grounds. Their function is to raise the dead.

The history of the genre teaches us that the injunction "raise yourself" must be older than its reference to Osiris. In some texts it is addressed by a son to his father with no mythic role-playing, and scholars have correctly seen these as the survival of very ancient concepts. The attitude expressed in this injunction thus probably did not develop out of the Osiris myth; on the contrary, it was one of the sources of the myth. A hope handed down from prehistoric times, a belief in the non-finality of death, that it could be dealt with, and the practice of an original mortuary cult derived from this belief, created a mythic framework in which this act remained meaningful in a world that was becoming more complex. What was special about this mythic framework of action was that in it, both grief and hope had their place and their justification. Osiris was the object both of mourning that was directed backwards, that derived from the experience of loss, and of acts that looked forward, that sprung from a belief that a disturbed order could be restored. The myth extended the temporal horizon of the situation of the deceased both forward and backward, breaking the seal of death. All this took form in Osiris: he was the mourned and resurrected god who experienced and overcame death. It should not be said that the *form* of Osiris developed from the funerary rites and the attitude toward death expressed in them. I assert this genesis only for the *myth*, not for the form of the god. Osiris was an important deity who embod-' ied more than just the deceased father and husband in whom the funerary rites found their mythic archetype. Seth was another important deity, more than just the personification of the cause of death. But these are the roles the myth assigns to them. The myth is not theology, *it does not inquire after the essence of the gods; rather, it surrounds human actions with a story that invests them with meaning.* "Knowledge," wrote Nietzsche, "kills action. Action takes place in a veil of illusion." Myth creates this veil. This is an admittedly unkind formulation with regard to an "illusion" that sustained millennia. It is only in retrospect that we can determine what vision was veiled by the myth. For those concerned, however, it opened a veiled present.

5.5.2. SECTION TWO: CONCEPTION AND BIRTH OF THE CHILD

Osiris was the dying and rising god, the mythic precedent and guarantee that one could say to the deceased king, and later to every deceased person, "Stand up!" The fact that he had risen invested these words with meaning. As is well known, this role of Osiris has led to his being classified with a series of "dying and rising" vegetation gods from western Asia: Tammuz, Attis, Adonis. This might be true of him to a certain extent. Without doubt, Osiris had a relationship with the agricultural cycle and other processes of death and rebirth in nature. There are striking commonalities in ritual, such as the preparation of fast-blooming miniature beds in an eight-day festival cycle, which is also attested for Adonis. Perhaps these are traits in the essence of Osiris that predestined him for his role in myth. But his myth differs in essential respects from those of the vegetation gods of western Asia. The most important of these is that it encompasses two generations. Osiris rises in his son, but he himself abides in the netherworld as the deceased father whose royal rule has been passed on to his son. We shall return to this point below, in 5.5.5; what is important here is to be able to understand the meaning of the posthumous engendering of the son in the story as a whole. Osiris does not rise from death or return to this world. He is awakened from the sleep of death by the mourning, embalming, and transfiguration rituals only to the extent that Isis is able to conceive a son by him, one who will avenge his father's death and thus in a certain way "save" him.

The conception of Horus thus belongs to the funeral rites, so it is no surprise that it is principally mortuary texts that make reference to it. Pyramid Texts spell 632, the most important instance in that corpus, has already been cited in chapter 4.1 (see the text at note 7 there). Horus is the mythic role of the son and successor to the throne. He carries out the burial of his father, and his appearance in this ritual is accounted for by the myth of his posthumous engendering in precisely the sense of a legitimizing prelude, just as the myth of the birth of the king represented a legitimizing prelude to his coronation. The role of Horus accrues to the son and/or successor to the throne only at the death of the king, so that the latter is reborn as Horus by means of this death. The Coffin Texts preserve a lengthy text that must stem from a cult drama of the birth of Horus:

> Lightning flashes, the gods are in fear.
> Isis awakes, pregnant with the seed of her brother Osiris.
> The woman gets up quickly,
> her heart joyful because of the seed of her brother Osiris.
> She says, "O gods,
> I am Isis, the sister of Osiris,
> who mourns over the father of the gods;
> Osiris, who mediated the slaughter of the Two Lands,
> his seed is in my body.
> I have fashioned the form of a god in the egg
> as the son of him at the head of the Ennead,
> that he might assume rule over this land,
> the heir of his father Geb,
> who will put in a word on behalf of his father,
> who will kill Seth, the enemy of his father Osiris.
>
> Come, O gods,
> and protect him within my womb.
> Know in your hearts
> that he is your lord, this god in his egg,
> mighty in form, the lord of the gods,

greater and more beautiful than they,
adorned with two feathers of lapis-lazuli."

"Oho," says Atum,
"your heart is wise, O woman!
How do you know that this is the god,
the lord and heir of the Ennead,
whom you are making within the egg?"

"I am Isis, who is more effective
and more illustrious than all the gods!
It is a god in my womb,
he is the seed of Osiris."
Then Atum said, "If you are pregnant, you should hide, young woman,
that you may bear the one with whom you are pregnant against (i.e.,
    against the will of) the gods!

For truly, he is the seed of Osiris.
That enemy who killed his father shall not come!
Otherwise, he will destroy the egg in its infancy.
The one rich in magic (i.e., Seth) shall be in fear before him."[15]

The text continues, but the passage cited is sufficient to represent the mythic situation, the event in the divine realm, that is referred to here in the dramatic form of a dialogue. In the Coffin Texts, the spell was supposed to serve the deceased by enabling him to transform into a falcon, that is, to assume the characteristic form of Horus. But this is clearly a secondary use of this text, whose actual origin must be sought in a cultic drama similar to the drama of the divine birth, the same transformation of the myth of the royal birth that we encounter in the temples of the Graeco-Roman era.

5.5.3. SECTION THREE: THE BIRTH AND UPBRINGING OF THE CHILD

With the conception of the son, the first sequence of events in the divine realm comes to an end; at the same time, this event plants the seed of a new sequence in which Horus will play the principal role. The mortuary texts refer primarily to the first sequence, in which Osiris stands in the foreground of the action, for Osiris is the figure with whom the deceased is identified; the texts are supposed to permit the deceased to share in the mythic precedent of his salvation from death, making them magical texts for healing the deceased. The texts that fall into the third section are mostly magical healing texts in the strictest sense of the term. The Horus child was the figure with whom the sick were identified. Osiris is absent from the cycle of

episodes in the third section. In one of these spells, it is said once that
he had "gone out for a walk":

> Horus was a child in the nest.
> A fire befell his limbs,
> he did not know it, and it did not know him.
>
> His mother was not there to exorcise it,
> his father had gone out for a walk
> with Haphap and Amset.
>
> The son was small, the fire was strong,
> no one was there to save him from it.
>
> Isis came out from the workhouse
> at the time she loosened her thread.
>
> "Come, my sister Nephthys,
> with me, accompany me!
> I was numb, my thread was around me.
>
> Let me pass, that I may do what I can,
> that I may quench it with my milk
> and with the healthy water between my thighs!"[16]

Most of the texts in the third section of the Osiris myth are of this sort.
They deal with the upbringing of the child:

> I am Isis, who was pregnant with her nestling,
> who carried the divine Horus.
> I bore Horus, the son of Osiris
> in the falcon's nest in Khemmis.
> I rejoiced over it greatly,
> for I beheld the avenger of his father.
>
> I hid him, I sheltered him
> out of fear of that one (i.e., Seth),
> I wandered through Yamu begging
> out of fear of the evildoer.
> I spent the day seeking (nourishment for) the child,
> in order to care for him.
>
> I returned to embrace Horus,
> I found him, the beautiful Horus of gold,
> the helpless child, the fatherless,
> how he had moistened the bank with the water of his eyes
> and the spittle of his lips,
> his body was weak, his heart was faint,
> the vessels of his body did not beat.

I cried out, "It is I, I!"
but the child was too weak to answer.
My breasts were full, (his) body was empty,
(his) mouth longed for its nourishment.
The wells overflowed, yet the child was thirsty.
My heart leaped from its place in great fear.
The helpless child refused the jug, he had been alone too long.
I was afraid, for no one came to help me,
for my father was in the netherworld, my mother in the
    cemetery,
my older brother was in the coffin,
and the other one an enemy,
persevering in the aggressiveness of his heart toward me,
and my younger sister was in his house.[17]

Thus begins one of the longest magical healing texts against scorpion bites. There was much use of magic in Egyptian medicine, and such magical healing was a preferred occasion for the recitation of myth. Aside from certain works of popular literature from the Ramesside Period (we shall discuss one of these later in 5.5.4), such magical texts contain the most detailed mythic narratives preserved to us. Among these, the myth of Osiris plays a dominant role, and a nearly exclusive one in its third section. The helplessness of the Horus child was the archetype of all patients, and Isis' magical and maternal protective power was the archetype of medical help.

Instead of seeing just extracts from the myth of Osiris in these texts, we can regard them as an entirely independent cycle of myths, myths about mother and child with a meaning of their own, which neither presuppose the first and second sections as a prologue nor view sections four and five as an epilogue. These myths have their own characters— Isis and the Horus child—and above all their own stage, Khemmis. Khemmis was a mythic place in the delta, hidden and inaccessible, where Isis raised her child Horus in total seclusion. Mythic places are everywhere and nowhere, just like mythic times, which, according to the famous definition of Sallustius, "never happened, yet always are." Any temple in the land could represent this mythic place. Thus, for example, Queen Hatshepsut's Hathor sanctuary at Deir el-Bahari was understood as a representation of this mythical Khemmis, showing that the influence of this icon reached far beyond the magical texts. In the holy of holies of this Hathor chapel is a representation of a cow emerging from the papyrus thicket of Khemmis, with the royal child kneeling and nursing from her udder. The following speech is attributed to the cow:

(I) have come to you, (my) beloved daughter Hatshepsut,
    to kiss your hand and to lick your limbs,
    to permeate your majesty with life and well-being,

as (I) did for Horus
in the papyrus thicket of Khemmis.
(I) have suckled your majesty at (my) breast,
(I) have filled you with my effective power, with this my water of life
    and well-being. I am (your mother who has raised) your body,
(I) have created your beauty.
(I) have come to be your protection and to cause you to taste of my
    milk, that you might live and endure by means of it.[18]

Here, the icon of mother and child has been entirely removed from the context of the myth of Osiris. As mother of the Horus child, Isis, who in this instance has been merged with Hathor, is not only the great healing goddess, but also the bestower of legitimate kingship. Her milk not only heals illness, it makes the child a king, it "creates," as the Egyptian terminology puts it, "his beauty." Isis is the "kingmaker" par excellence. Even in the "Potter's Oracle" of the Ptolemaic Period, which has been preserved to us in Greek and serves to express political opposition, it is said of the prophesied savior-king that he will "come from the sun and be enthroned by the great goddess Isis." The king steps into the role of the royal child in the constellation of the mother-goddess Isis in order to incorporate the kingship of Horus into himself by means of her milk. In Egypt, the legitimate, salvation-bringing king was not the "anointed one," but the "suckled one." Many temple reliefs, particularly from the New Kingdom, represent him in this role, in the arms and at the breast of the mother-goddess Isis.

5.5.4. SECTION FOUR: THE CONTENDINGS OF HORUS AND SETH

If we have the impression that the narrative of the birth and upbringing of the Horus child in the third section of the Osiris myth consisted of relatively independent myths that did not derive their meaning from the overarching context, but rather from their underlying icon of the divine mother and her child, in the case of the fourth section, the independence of its myths of a contending must stand as demonstrated fact. In the fourth section, the following are almost inextricably intertwined:

1. The icon of the two fraternal antagonists in whose struggle and subsequent reconciliation the idea of the Egyptian realm as a "dual unity" or "united duality" was embodied
2. the "Hamlet" motif of the son who was obliged to avenge his uncle's murder of his father and thereby win the crown.

In both of these traditions, there is a conflict. In both, the rivals are Horus and Seth; in both, they are called "brothers," even though they are uncle and nephew in the second; and in both, rule over Egypt is at stake. In the first, however, Osiris is not mentioned, Seth is not a murderer, and Horus is not an avenger. Their conflict has no motive other than the antagonism of the south and the north, of Upper and Lower Egypt, which might have had a historical basis (Upper Egypt as a primarily nomadic society, Lower Egypt as a primarily agricultural, sedentary one), but perhaps merely springs from the oppositions typical of Egyptian thought. For this conflict, in which Seth rips out one of Horus' eyes and Horus rips off Seth's testicles, is again none other than a prelude that is supposed to explain the present condition: the globality of pharaonic rule and the (inner) peace of the governed spheres are expressed in this icon of conflicting and reconciled brothers as the result of a union and reconciliation. The conflict is always in the past, the present is characterized by the balance of the reconciled opposites and the united portions. Here, Seth is not actually conquered, let alone damned and banished. Rather, the opposition is transcended into a higher unity in which the two brothers in conflict find their justice and their place. In this evidently very old conception, Horus *and* Seth are incorporated in the king.

In the second tradition, the accent of the conflict of Horus and Seth is decisively shifted in connection with the myth of Osiris. Seth is a murderer, Horus an avenger; Seth is powerful but in the wrong, Horus is weak but has right on his side. There can be no balance, no reconciliation of right and wrong. Although physical confrontation also plays a certain role in the narratives belonging to this second tradition, this is simply because Seth is a violent god. But it is critical that here, the conflict assumes the character of a case at law that is conducted at Heliopolis, in the "Hall of Geb" or the "House of the Noble," before the two Enneads as a panel of magistrates with Geb (or Atum) as Chief Justice and Thoth as clerk of the court. The conflict aims for a result in which one of the "two lords" is definitively excluded from the rulership.

This neat separation of motifs and a division into two mythic cycles that were at least originally independent of one another is a theoretical construct. In reality, the texts mix these complexes of motifs in various ways. The change of meaning that the myth of the battle of Horus and Seth experienced in the framework of the myth of Osiris did not render the original constellation invalid. Both the "constellation of the uniting of the Two Lands" and the "constellation of avenging the death of the father" coexisted in Egyptian tradition and interpenetrated one another. Of all the basic icons or constellations in the myth of Osiris, those of the fourth section were the most widespread. Even this fact is connected with the two streams of tradition that flowed together. Horus and Seth's lawsuit over the succession to the throne became the archetype of the Judgment of the Dead and the "justification" by means of which every deceased person hoped to triumph over death. For this reason, there are many references to the fourth section in the mortuary texts:

> The earth is hacked up,
> after the two comrades (i.e., Horus and Seth) have battled,
> after their feet have dug up the divine pond in Heliopolis.
> Thoth comes, clothed in his dignity,
> after Atum has distinguished him before the two powers (i.e., Horus
>   and Seth), who are satisfied therewith,
> that the battle might cease and the strife come to an end,
> that the flame that blazed might be put out,
> that the redness might be calmed before the divine corporation
> when it sits to pronounce justice before Geb.

> Hail, you princes of the gods!
> NN is justified before you on this day,
> as Horus was justified against his enemy
> on that day of coronation.
> May he (i.e., NN) be happy among you,
> as Isis was happy
> on that beautiful day of singing
> when her son Horus took the Two Lands in triumph.

> Hail, O corporation of deities,
> which will dispense justice to Osiris NN
> because of that which he said when he did not (yet) know,
> when it was well with him, before he suffered pain!
> Go around him, stand behind him,
> so that Osiris NN might be justified before Geb, the crown prince of
>   the gods,
> by that god who will judge him according to his knowledge,
> after he has appeared, his feather on his head
> and his righteousness before him,
> while his enemies are in grief,
> and he triumphantly takes possession of all that is his.

> Hail, Thoth, in whom is the peace of the gods,
> and all the judges who are with you!
> Command that they come out to NN
> to hear all the good that he says on this day,
> for he is this feather that rises in the land of the god,
> which Osiris brought to his son Horus,
> that he might set it on his head as a sign
> of his justification over his enemies.
> It is he who crushed the testicles of Seth,
> he does not perish, he does not die . . .[19]

And so forth. In this text from a mortuary liturgy recorded in the Coffin Texts, the battle between the brothers Horus and Seth—in the sense of the first tradition—is linked—in the sense of the second tradition—with Horus' mythic suit over the succession to the throne, and the latter is then represented as the archetype of a judgment in which the deceased will "today"—probably on the very day of his death—prevail over his enemies and obtain "justification." This was the origin of the later concept of the Judgment of the Dead, in which every deceased person was obliged to answer before the tribunal of Osiris in the "Hall of the Two Truths."

But even in a royal mortuary text from Dynasty 19 (ca. 1200 B.C.E.), we meet with the mythic suit over the succession to the throne as precedent for the justification of the deceased:

> I (the goddess Neith) bring you Geb, that he might look after you,
> I grant that he says of you, "My eldest son,"
> that he says of you, "My office belongs to him!"
> "May the bad one fare badly, may the faulty one suffer fault!"
> (. . .) Geb speaks to Osiris in the presence of the Ennead and the two sanctuaries:
> "(. . .) Justification belongs to Osiris King Merneptah.
> He praises you (i.e., Osiris) as king of the gods.
> The netherworld and the west are in his hand,
> while the Two Lands belong to his son Horus."
> (. . .) Thoth writes it down for you,
> according to the statement of Re-Atum.[20]

This is no age-old mortuary text, but one written especially for King Merneptah at the end of the thirteenth century B.C.E. Even at this time, one and a half millennia after the age of the pyramids, the topos of the lawsuit between Horus and Seth in the "House of the Noble" at Heliopolis had not lost its explanatory power. The judgment pronounced on Horus in this suit—$mȝ^c$-$ḫrw$, "true of voice," that is, that he was right in his statement—was an obligatory addition to the name of every deceased person from the Middle Kingdom on. Just like Horus in his lawsuit with Seth, every deceased person was to emerge "justified" from the examination that decided his fate in the afterlife. The suit over the succession to the throne constituted the mythic prelude in whose light the present situation, the "now" of the deceased's arrival in the realm of the dead, was explained, notwithstanding the fact that it had been about rule over Egypt and not about eternal life.

The assumption of rule over Egypt at the moment a new king ascended the throne, is thus probably to be viewed as the this-worldly situation that received its meaning from the prelude of the myth of the legal proceeding between Horus and Seth. In fact, we find many allusions in royal inscriptions to the fact that the king has united the "two portions" in his hand, and thus that after the death of his predecessor, he has again united and assembled in its entirety an inheritance that had been disputed and divided among rival pretenders. A version of the myth that King Shabaka of Dynasty 25 (ca. 700 B.C.E.) had copied onto stone from a worm-eaten papyrus original likely also falls into this context of political function. Opinions differ by two millennia regarding the age of the original; some scholars have dated it to the beginning of Egyptian history, and others to the Old Kingdom, whereas more recently, some have dated it to the Ramesside Period or even the reign of Shabaka himself. The difficulty of dating the text speaks to the undiminished relevance of the myth. The passage that interests us here could just as well belong to the Old Kingdom as to the New Kingdom:

> (Geb, the crown prince of the gods, commanded)
> that the Ennead assemble.
> He separated Horus and Seth
> and forbade that they continue fighting,
> by placing Seth as king of Upper Egypt in the southland
> as far as the place where he was born, in *Sw*.
> And Geb placed Horus as Lower Egyptian king in the northland
> as far as the place where his father drowned, in *Psšt-t3wy*.
> So Horus stood over the one place and Seth over the other.
> They were reconciled regarding the Two Lands in *Ayan*;
> that is the boundary of the Two Lands.
> . . .
> But Geb regretted
> that the share of Horus was the same as the share of Seth.
> And so Geb gave his inheritance to Horus,
> for he was the son of his son, his first-born.
>
> Geb said to the Ennead, "I have decided on Horus—you—as the
>   heir to the
>   throne, who alone . . .
> Then Horus stood (as king) over the land.
> . . .
> It happened that rushes and papyrus were brought to the double
>   door of the temple of Ptah:
> that means Horus and Seth, who were at peace and allied with one
>   another—
> they swore friendship that they would no longer contend in any
>   [place] they [went].[21]

This version combines the two traditions, the battle between the brothers that ends in reconciliation and the case at law that ends in a judgment, in such a way that at first, the reconciled brothers rule jointly over the apportioned inheritance, and then Geb revises his decision and installs Horus as sole heir over the unified realm. But although the revised judgment excluded Seth from the rulership, the text concludes by again stressing the motif of reconciliation. For the Egyptians, these two aspects did not seem mutually exclusive, but rather, equally important: the aspect of *reconciled antagonism* represented by the first judgment, and the aspect of *undivided sole rule* proclaimed by the second judgment.

Scholars have tended to see this myth as containing historical reminiscences of the time of the unification of the Two Lands, when, after Upper and Lower Egypt had been opposed to one another as rival chieftainships, Upper Egypt first won the upper hand over the delta and then, with the establishment of a united realm with its seat at Memphis, the Lower Egyptian culture set the tone because of its higher level of civilization. But such a historical reference seems far too narrow. The historical reality of this myth surely lies not in the individual episodes of the action, but rather in the axiological system it founds with its narrative. Values such as the overcoming of antagonism, the balancing of opposites, the reconciliation and uniting of contending parties, integration of portions, the achievement of an overarching whole, the consolidation of rule in a *single* hand, and so forth, were a relevant evidence for Egyptians of all periods. All of Egyptian history is characterized by the ever-repeated effort to achieve and maintain the unity of the "dual kingdom" against its (as it were) natural tendency to collapse. The case at law between Horus and Seth was the mythic archetype of an ever-present historical reality, one that had assumed a special relevance in the period when the text was copied onto stone. The kings of Dynasty 25 stemmed from Napata at the Fourth Cataract, and they had left their home in Nubia and invaded Egypt with the goal of reuniting in a single hand the rulership that had fallen into a multiplicity of individual princedoms. Their policy was motivated by the same values of reconciliation, union, and centralization that are developed in the myth of the lawsuit between Horus and Seth.

Of all the myths in the Osiris cycle, the complex of myths about Horus and Seth was the most widespread. We have become acquainted with mortuary beliefs and official royal propaganda as the areas in which these stories were most often used. But we also find them in the everyday world, in magical spells used for healing purposes, in calendars that cite a mythic event for each day of the year and thus deem it to be a lucky or unlucky one, and finally in a work of popular literature from the Ramesside Period, Papyrus Chester Beatty I. This text, which is the complete antithesis of the archaizing, hieratic style of the Memphite Theology of Shabaka, tells the story, as its discoverer and editor Sir Alan Gardiner aptly remarked, "in the style of Offenbach."[22] The ups and downs of a legal proceeding unfold in a burlesque and even an apparently satirical manner in which the divine corporation, which is biased, unprincipled, and constantly changing its mind, is incapable of reaching a decision.

The first part of the text takes place before the court; both sides make their pleas, Horus' party for the right of the legitimate heir, Seth's party for the right of the stronger. The opinion of the goddess Neith and that of the Ram of Mendes, who are absent and not members of the Heliopolitan Ennead, are obtained in writing. When the opinion of the Ennead turns in favor of Seth, Isis protests, but Seth succeeds with his request to have a further session convened on an island and Isis excluded from participation. The second part relates how Isis gained access to the island by means of a ruse and, transformed into a beautiful maiden, caused the amorous Seth to pronounce his own judgment unwittingly. With that, the matter seems to be decided, and Horus is crowned with the White Crown. Seth does not accept the judgment, however—and the suit drags on, now in the form of a competition that is the topic of the third part. First, Horus and Seth battle one another in the form of hippopotami; Isis seizes a harpoon but is unable to kill Seth, because he addresses her as sister. Horus is furious at this act of mercy and decapitates Isis. He flees into the desert, where Seth finds him and rips his eyes out. But the wounds are immediately healed and the plot continues. The next competition in which Seth attempts to involve Horus is of a (homo)sexual nature. This episode is already attested on a papyrus from the Middle Kingdom. The loser is the one who is penetrated by the semen of the other. Once again, the tricky Isis succeeds in duping Seth. On her advice, Horus manages to catch Seth's semen in his hands, which Isis cuts off and replaces with new ones. She places the semen of Horus, which she obtains with the help of a lubricant, on lettuce belonging to Seth. When Seth then boasts of his rape of Horus to the Ennead, it turns out that he himself is the one who was impregnated. Yet again, for the umpteenth time, judgment is passed: Horus is in the right, Seth is in the wrong. And yet again, the verdict has no force, because Seth will not accept it. Finally, a boating competition is proposed. The victor is again Horus, who builds a boat of wood covered with plaster, whereas Seth builds a boat of stone that immediately sinks; and again this victory brings Horus no success. As an *ultima ratio*, a letter is sent to Osiris in the netherworld—as if there could have been the slightest doubt as to his opinion.

In fact, Osiris' reply marks the turning point. Osiris first appeals to the gratitude of the gods to him, for he created the grain of which their offerings consist. He has no success with this argument. In a second letter, he introduces a threat: his power as god of death, to which all the living, mortals and deities, are subject. This trump card immediately takes the trick. Even Seth is powerless against it and acknowledges that Horus is in the right. It is thus the right of the stronger that prevails in the end, or better: *sub specie mortis*, the rightful case proves to be the stronger. The claims of the physically stronger remained convincing only so long as the deities imagined themselves to be immortal. When they are reminded of their mortality, they, Seth included, immediately return to the principle of *Maat*, which alone makes it possible to overcome death. Only the legal title of Horus can withstand the argument of death. But Seth is compensated, in that the sun god takes him into his barque as his assistant in the daily battle against Apophis.

In this version from Papyrus Chester Beatty I, we encounter the myth of the contendings of Horus and Seth not as "holy writ," but as a piece of popular literature, just like the love lyrics on the verso of the same papyrus. The text clearly attempts to gather a number of episodes circulating in oral and in part also in written tradition into a continuous narrative. It is questionable whether and in what sense we are dealing with a religious phenomenon. The narrative makes use of mythic material in exactly the same way that other works of Ramesside popular literature make use of fabulous or historical motifs. In the history of religion and in ethnology, there is a distinction between "sacred" or "true stories" that may only be related under highly restricted circumstances and other stories that may be told anywhere and at any time. The text of Papyrus Chester Beatty I undoubtedly falls into the second category. But we must not forget that the same material was also told as sacred history, as in the Memphite Theology, and in a drama enacted on religious festivals at the temple of Edfu, and in a series of exorcism rites attested from the Late Period. Despite its secularization in the Ramesside Period, the myth of the contendings of Horus and Seth lost none of its religious influence or attraction; on the contrary, it seems to have become ever more predominant during the Late Period. In any event, its character was decisively altered in these later forms. In the older versions, there was always a consensus, with Seth agreeable and compensated at the end, whereas in the late versions, he was punished, annihilated, driven out, and explicitly condemned. Seth embodied that which was foreign, which in the course of centuries of foreign rule was represented ever more explicitly as evil. One of Seth's nicknames was "the Mede." With this change of meaning, the myth displays its continued vitality, whose reality is not to be sought in some single event in the distant past, but rather was fed by contemporary experiences and brought into conformity with an altered experience of the present.

5.5.5. SECTION FIVE: THE TRIUMPH OF HORUS

With its fifth section, the myth of Osiris opens up into the present and the future. The triumph of Horus signifies the end of strife and the beginning of a period of peace and well-being in which *Maat* will prevail on earth, a period to which every king laid claim, although presumably for the people it was often enough an object of hope rather than of experience. The triumph of Horus is the theme of innumerable hymns preserved in temple and mortuary texts, but whose actual *Sitz im Leben* was probably the festival of the royal coronation. Here is an abbreviated example from the occasion of the coronation of Ramesses IV:

> Oh, beautiful day! Sky and earth are in joy,
> you are the goodly lord of Egypt!
> Those who had fled have returned to their cities,
> those who hid themselves have come out;
> those who hungered are satisfied and happy,
> those who thirsted are drunk,
> those who were naked are clothed in fine linen,
> those who were dirty are radiant.
> Those who were imprisoned are set free,
> those who were bound rejoice,
> those in strife in this land
> are at peace.
> A high Nile has sprung from its source,
> to refresh the hearts of the people.
> (...)
> The son of Re, Ramesses IV, may he live, prosper, and be healthy,
> has assumed the office of his father.
> The entire double realm says to him:
> "Beautiful is Horus on the throne of his father Amun-Re,
> the god who sent him out,
> this ruler who conquers every land![23]

The coronation of a new king is explained in light of the myth of Osiris as a turning point leading to salvation. The suffering that broke out through the land at the death of the god is now at an end. In the light of a prelude that tells of assassination and murder, of grief and fear, salvation, joy, and abundance now make their appearance all the more gloriously to characterize the present. Papyrus Chester Beatty I also closes with such a hymn in praise of the present condition, placed in the mouth of Isis:

> Horus has arisen as ruler,
> the Ennead is in festival,
> the heavens are in joy.
> They garland themselves when they see how Horus,
> the son of Isis, has arisen
> as ruler—may he live, prosper, and be healthy—of Egypt.
> The Ennead, their heart is happy,
> the whole land is in jubilation,
> when they see how Horus, the son of Isis,

has been assigned the office of his father,
of Osiris, lord of Busiris.[24]

The temples of the Late Period in which deities, borrowing from
the myth of Horus, celebrated both a birth and a coronation festival,
are especially rich in these jubilant hymns. In particular, such hymns
were sung in the ritual of the Offering of the Garland of Victory (the
Garland of Justification):

Horus appears on the seat of his father,
the heart of Isis is broad.
Horus the mighty has conquered the Two Lands in triumph,
Horus has received the *wereret*-crown
from his father Osiris-Wennefer, justified.
Horus appears on the throne of Geb,
the sky above his head,
the earth under his feet,
the Nine Bows gathered under his sandals.
Let us be a protection for him!
A cry of joy rings out in the southern heavens,
joy reigns in the northern heavens,
the Ennead there is rejoicing,
the gods rejoice:
.Horus has emerged from his lawsuit
like Re when he rises in Light-land![25]

The same text is to be found more than a millennium earlier, in tombs
from the Ramesside Period (thirteenth century B.C.E.), tombs 183 and
184 at Thebes, thus showing that with the Offering of the Garland of
Justification, we are dealing with a rite that in earlier periods had
belonged to the mortuary cult and even to the cult of Osiris. From the
same period, we have the text of a high priest of Osiris at Abydos
named Wennefer (Louvre A 66.2), who says of himself

I brought the Garland of Justification
and transfigured the god with it.[26]

The theme of the triumph of Horus appears to be less an object of narrative than of festival activities—hymns and rituals—that had a perma-
nent place in the three areas of kingship, mortuary cult, and the cult of
Osiris. Joy was the basic theme of these festivals and their hymns. To
judge from the manner in which the triumph of Horus is dealt with in the
hymns, they aim to express "glad tidings." Most of the hymns begin with
the injunction, "Rejoice!" The triumph of Horus was the object of annunciation. What occurred in the House of the Noble at Heliopolis, the justification and coronation of the god, is to be announced to "all the people":

Rejoice, you women of Busiris,
　Horus has overcome his enemy.
Rejoice, you inhabitants of Edfu,
　Horus . . . has felled the enemy of his father Osiris.[27]

"Rejoice" is also directed to Osiris. It is said especially by deceased persons on the day of their death, when they descend from the realm of the living and introduce themselves to Osiris with a hymn. Coming from this world, the deceased are able to bring the god of the dead the "good news" of the kingship of the triumphant Horus:

Rejoice, you in the desert,
weary of heart, unite with joy:
your son Horus has been justified,
he has received the insignia of Re.
His mother Isis has come in peace,
her hands filled with life and dominion,
and stands guard over Wennefer.
The gods rejoice in the heavens,
the Enneads shout for joy,
when they see Horus, the son of Osiris,
sitting on the throne of his father.[28]

Or:

May your heart rejoice, you in the desert,
your heir abides on your throne!
The majesty of Horus lives as king,
prosperity and health with him.
Thoth makes his boundaries for him
and establishes his annals,
he hands him the lands as his possession
in the presence of the All-Lord.[29]

What the recently deceased person announces to the ruler of the dead is not a mythic event *in illo tempore*, but rather the present condition of Egypt, which in the light of the myth of Osiris assumes the character of a return of salvation. What was destroyed by the murder of Osiris has been restored by the king now ruling as Horus. Peace, abundance, justice, and piety toward the realm of the dead characterize the son's beneficent rule, which also restores the rights of his deceased father:

Rejoice, O lord of the gods,
may all broadness of heart be with you:
the cultivated land and the deserts are in peace

and pay their dues to your uraeus.
The temples are well founded in their places,
the cities and nomes
are founded in their names.
Offerings are brought to you,
and litanies in your name;
songs of praise are sung in your name,
and libations are made to your *ka*,
and mortuary offerings for the transfigured ones in your following.
Water is sprinkled on the offering loaves
for the *ba*s of the deceased in this land.
Effective is its entire condition,
like its original condition.[30]

The rejoicing over the triumph of Horus is the precise counterpart of the mourning over the death of Osiris. Both are extreme and all-encompassing. Just as the death plunges the entire world into the depths of despair, so the triumph transports it into the heights of rapture. The two emotions belong together as a pair at the beginning and the end of the story that transpires between them. The entire land participated in the story in an annual cycle of festivals, and all who took part in them experienced them. If we are somewhat reminded of the sorrow of Good Friday and the joy of Easter Sunday, it should again be stressed that in the myth of Osiris, we are dealing with two generations. The god who triumphs is a different one from the god who is killed. Osiris is not a resurrected god, but one who in death achieves a new form of existence in the beyond through the triumph and piety of his son, thus becoming the archetype of all deceased persons.

A certain Egyptian text, a hymn to Osiris, stems from approximately the middle of the second millennium B.C.E.; long before Plutarch, it presents a relatively coherent account of the myth. It demonstrates that the Egyptians themselves were conscious of the inner coherence of the episodes we have divided into five sections:

I   Isis, the powerful, the protector of her brother,
     who searched for him without wearying,
     who traversed this land in grief
     and did not rest until she had found him,

     who spread shadows with her feathers
     and created a breeze with her wings,
     who sent up a cry, the mourning-woman of her brother,
     who summoned the dancers for the weary of heart;

II   who received the semen and created an heir,
III who nursed the child in solitude, one knew not where;

IV   who introduced him, when his arm had grown strong,
into the hall of Geb—

the Ennead rejoiced:
"Welcome, son of Osiris,
Horus brave of heart, justified,
son of Isis, heir of Osiris!"
The judges of Maat were assembled for him,
the Ennead and the All-Lord himself,
the lords of Maat, who despise injustice, were gathered,
seated as a council in the hall of Geb
to give the office to the one to whom it belonged
and the kingship to the one entitled to it.
Horus was found justified,
the office of his father was given over to him.

V   He came out garlanded at the command of Geb
and assumed rule over the Two Banks,
the White Crown firm on his head;
he took possession of the entire land,
sky and earth were under his supervision.
Humankind were commended to him, *pat, rekhyt, henmemet,*
Egyptians and northerners,
what the sun encircles was subject to his will.

The north wind, the Nile, the inundation,
every plant, every vegetable,
the grain god gives all his ears,
the nourishment of the earth,
he creates repletion and grants it in all the lands.
The whole world rejoices, their hearts are glad,
their breasts are in rapture,
their faces rejoice, as each one worships his (i.e., Horus') beauty:
"How sweet is our love for him,
his charm penetrates (our) hearts.
Great is the love of him in every body

They have delivered his enemy to the son of Isis,
fallen through his own violence;
evil has befallen the rowdy one,
he who committed violence, judgment overtook him.
The son of Isis, he has avenged his father,
he who sanctified his name and made it splendid.
The worthies, they have taken their place,
reverence is established according to their laws.
The road is free, the ways are open,
how fortunate are the Two Banks!
The disaster is gone, the slanderer has fled,

the land is in peace under its lord,
Maat is firmly established for her lord,
one has turned one's back on injustice.
Rejoice, Wennefer!
The son of Isis has received the crown,
the office of his father was awarded to him
in the hall of Geb.
Re, he has pronounced it,
Thoth, he has written it,
the corporation is pleased with it.
your father Geb has issued a command in your favor,
and one has done as he said.[31]

CHAPTER 6

On the Meaning of the Three Dimensions: Concluding Remarks

To survey the most salient points in a concise manner, it was necessary to exclude two questions from the discussion of the implicit theology of Egyptian religion that was attempted in the preceding chapters. One has to do with the historicity, the other with the systematology of what we called the "dimensions of presence." We should like to treat these issues briefly, at least, at the conclusion of the present part of this book.

6.1. The (A-)Historicity of Implicit Theology

To this point, our treatment of Egyptian religion has been ahistorical or phenomenological. To illustrate certain points, we have drawn on sources from the Pyramid Texts down to the Graeco-Roman temple inscriptions, and even beyond, into the Hermetic corpus and other sources from (late) classical antiquity. This approach would have been entirely erroneous had our topic been "Egyptian religion." Obviously, during the three millennia from which our texts were drawn, Egyptian religion was subject to many changes, and sometimes to fundamental ones. Yet despite these changes, it is appropriate to speak of "the" religion of ancient Egypt, in the singular. None of these changes was sufficiently radical to modify the identity of this religion in a decisive manner. During these millennia, there was never a breach so great that what had gone before was no longer recognizable as simply the past. Akhenaten's religious revolution at Amarna could have signified such a breach, yet it remained but an episode. Even in the final centuries of this religion, people recognized the familiar in the very oldest texts, even while sometimes thoroughly misunderstanding them. The later periods are characterized by an emphatic conviction of cultural identity that embraced all of Egyptian history.

This self-understanding of Egyptian culture related above all to the unity of everything we draw together under the rubric "religion." Notwithstanding any and all historical change, there must have been enough continuity of basic elements and structures to guarantee the unity, indeed the sameness, of the phenomenon of Egyptian religion. In discussing the topic of implicit theology, we have attempted to catch a glimpse of precisely this fundamental continuity. These basic religious structures were implicit in that they reached down into deep layers of the culture that in part eluded the conscious grasp of its bearers. Only by becoming explicit did these structures become accessible to modification and theological elaboration.

The (relative) ahistoricity of implicit theology stands in contrast to the historicity of explicit theology. Together, the two determine the reality of a religion. The historical deficit of Part I of our treatment is therefore made up by the primarily historical orientation of Part II.

In any event, the materials discussed in Part I could also have been treated from a distinctly historical point of view. We could have inquired into the conditions under which the concepts and institutions connected with the individual dimensions came into existence, into their periods of flowering, and perhaps also into crises and periods of decline. Thus, for instance, the period of Egyptian history between 1000 and 700 B.C.E., known as the Third Intermediate Period and thus as a time of decline, could also count as a golden age of the "local" dimension of divine presence. At Thebes, a theocratic state was already established as early as the eleventh century, one that was ruled by oracular decisions of the god Amun himself and administered by his high priest. The latter, who wrote his name in a royal cartouche, held all the reins of ecclesiastical, civil, and military power. This theocratic model, which accorded all power to the temples, with the result that the local dimension of divine presence loomed large in the foreground, gained acceptance at other places as well during the centuries that followed. City gods soon ruled in Herakleopolis, Mendes, Athribis, and so forth, represented by high priests who were also civil and military leaders. In this period, the foundation was laid for the religious "feudalism" of the Late Period, and even that of the Christian era, when episcopal sees were established in the religious, not the administrative centers.

What stands out with special clarity in the theocratic forms of rulership of the Third Intermediate Period is the political importance of the cultic dimension. The rule that the local deity exercised over city and nome served to legitimate the high priest's de facto rule as mayor and commandant: the authority of the temporal power was derived from its cultic function. The theocratic model afforded the provincial governors the possibility of freeing themselves from subordination to the sovereignty of the Egyptian kingship, which had faded into mere theory. The decisive step toward feudalism and the collapse of central royal authority was taken at that moment when the military commandant of a given city assumed control over temple construction work and over the cult and its offerings. By the same token, this step was reversed and the central authority of pharaonic rule reestablished when Pharaoh alone was represented in these roles in all the temples in the provinces. The concept of the earthly rule of the deities of the nomes and cities bound up with the cultic dimension legitimized de facto rule, whether exercised by "nomarchs" or monarchs.

The political component of the local and cultic dimension, the indissoluble unity of cult and rulership, made the concept of the residence of a deity in a specific locale into an eminently historical phenomenon. We must thus suspect that the same was not unconditionally true of the other two dimensions. Concepts of the sacredness of the cosmos, of the manifestation of deities in celestial and natural phenomena, must have remained essentially unchanged, just like the consciousness of the radiant power of speech, of the sacred word, which made the divine manifest in this-worldly processes and phenomena and enabled the present to be explained in terms of the eternal. In essence, we know too little to be able to make out more than the basic structures that remained constant. Because the oral tradition has been lost to us, we cannot tell, for example, whether myths developed in conjunction with texts that became more explicit in the course of time, or whether, from the beginning on, a rich array of myths developed gradually in the context of statements that were recorded in writing.

6.2. On the Systematology of the Dimensions

To be sure, no grammar can be found in a library for many languages in this world. But it is equally sure that no language exists that has no grammar. The concept of grammar is implicit in the concept of language, just as the practice or "performance" of any language presupposes a mastery of the rules it entails ("competence"); whether the rules are encoded in printed form in a grammar book is irrelevant. What stands out in language as the paradigmatic instance of communicative act is true *mutatis mutandis* of all other forms as well. There is no communicative performance without the corresponding competence, no practice without theory. Further steps are needed to make this theory, already inherent in all action, into the object of conscious reflection, to explicate, elaborate, and rationalize it. The appearance and development of such metatheoretical discourse is as dependent on historical circumstances as is the question of when and whether a language becomes the object of an explicit grammatical description.

Theory that is always already implicit thus underlies every communicative act, quite independent of the appearance of explicit theory, and the theory underlying religion, that is, contact with the divine, as a category of communicative action, is the theme of what we have called "implicit theology." It is the "grammar" of religious activity, that store of rules and meanings that organized the Egyptians' contact with the divine.

There is thus no question of whether Egyptian religion implied a theology, but only a question of what constituted this theology. We have attempted to answer this with the analytical tool of the three "dimensions." To repeat, this theology had to do with the theory that underlay religious practice, contact with the divine. Practice came first: surely one did not first encounter the divine and then cultivate contact with it. We must therefore assume that in the Egyptian religion we encounter in the sources, many forms of contact with the sacred had extended from prehistory down into the historical period and were enriched over time by new content and new concepts that enhanced their meaning. Implicit theology was thus confined entirely to the sphere of practice. Its object was not the essence of the divine but rather contact with it, the forms in which it could be experienced and approached in the world, the forms of its manifestation and representation. Because this theory has to do with imparting meaning to communicative acts, the dimensions refer to the area of communication between the human and the divine, to divine presence and human encounter.

In the light of an inquiry that commences with explicit theology and then focuses on the essence of divinity beyond all religious practice, these dimensions assume a somewhat figurative status. Against the absolute transcendence of divinity, its sacredness and its hierophanic quality become relative. Deities did not dwell in temples—only their images. The sun, the air, and the Nile were not gods—the cosmic phenomena were only manifestations of a divinity that remained hidden. The divine was neither recorded nor tangible in names or in stories that circulated in writing or from mouth to mouth. Such issues were also raised in ancient Egypt; we shall encounter them in Part II, which is devoted to explicit theology. The total reality of religion thus far exceeds the realm we have described in Part I in the light of its dimensions. That discussion was not concerned with the dimensions of divinity itself, but only of contact with it. Beyond the three dimensions, there was always transcendence.

How, then, are we to understand this triad of dimensions? Should we assume that only these three can exist in any given religion, and that what is characteristic of historical religions is bound to be expressed in such a way that, according to the dominance of one of the three dimensions, we can divide them into cultic, cosmic, or language-related religions? Or should we instead assume that there is a certain quantity of possible dimensions of divine presence and religious experience of the divine, some of which are realized in dominant form in any given historical religion? Obviously, this question can only be answered by a broader discipline, such as comparative religion, for it is too much for a specialized discipline like Egyptology. Nevertheless, I venture some conjectures here. I am personally inclined toward the second alternative, and I assume that there is a multiplicity of dimensions, of which the three treated here were realized in dominant fashion in ancient Egyptian religion. This religion would thus be better understood if a comprehensive theory of religion were available, one that could, on the basis of a comparison of as many religions as possible, determine the totality of possible dimensions of divine presence. Only from the point of view of such a comprehensive theory would we be in a position to state what dimensions Egyptian religion ignored in placing the three identified here in the foreground. So long as there is no such theory, remarks like the following are lacking in a systematic basis. Even so, I believe that the question of the dimensions that were *not* realized in a significant manner in Egyptian religion should not be passed over.

There are at least three dimensions of religious experience whose overall absence or only rudimentary realization in Egypt seem to me to be significant for the essence of its religion:

1. intoxication, trance, ecstasy, "shamanism"
2. mysticism, meditation, contemplation
3. history and personal destiny.

The reader is referred to the investigations of Mircea Eliade into shamanism for examples of dominant expressions of the first of these dimensions of religious experience. Hindu religion and Judaism are probably the most distinctive examples of the second and third, respectively. All three dimensions are almost entirely absent from Egyptian religion, with the possible exception of the third, which in the Ramesside Period began to play a role that completely changed the traditional structure of the religion. We shall deal with this later. In any event, all such observations stand under the basic reservation that the sources, which are preserved to us by accident, reflect only a tiny excerpt from the ancient reality.

6.2.1. INTOXICATION AND ECSTASY

Reading the works of Mircea Eliade, one could arrive at the impression that shamanism is a universal phenomenon. In Egypt, however, one searches in vain for the relevant phenomena. The facts are easily obscured, for the Greeks rendered the Egyptian priestly title *ḥm-nṯr*, "servant of the god," as *prophetes*, and this rendering has also become established in more modern treatments of Egyptian religion. The Greek rendering is connected with the nature of oracles in the later periods of Egyptian history, and with the role of the priests as interpreters of indications of divine will. As already indicated, deities expressed themselves through a language of movement. Priests were obliged to explain the oracle and evidently also to record it, and they were admonished to do so with the utmost conscientiousness. This has nothing at all to do with prophecy. There is no indication that access to "another reality" was gained with the aid of any form of ecstatic technique. The concept of another reality was definitely present, and we have associated it with the Egyptian concept *akh*, "radiant power," in the context of the verbal dimension of divine presence. There are many indications that knowledge of this *akh*-sphere was connected with special forms of induction or initiation. The authorized speaker was able to actualize this sphere with his words. But there was nothing of trances or ecstasy in this connection. In Wenamun's report of his travels in the eleventh century B.C.E., the appearance of a Syrian ecstatic is described with all the trappings of the exotic. It is only in the Graeco-Roman era that divination spells furnish positive indications with their mention of qualified mediums (especially boys); but here, it is no longer a matter of Egyptian religion in the sense of the cultural identity discussed earlier.

To be sure, there were magicians in the earlier culture of Egypt, and in any case, we have magical texts from the Middle Kingdom on, spells that promised great efficacy if recited by authorized mouths and with adherence to the instructions. This seems to be a matter of the privatization of the cultic concept of the radiant power (*akhu*) of speech. The divine magicians Isis and Thoth possessed this radiant power in a paradigmatic manner. Typical uses of magic in the private domain were healing spells and spells that protected against demons, enemies, serpents, and the like, and less often, love charms. There is thus no lack of texts and rituals that we are clearly obliged to classify as magical. But what of the magicians for whose use these materials were intended? No magicians existed in the sense of a specialized profession, let alone in the sense of social outsiders (e.g., witches). Spells could probably be used at home by anyone who could read them and who observed the necessary prescriptions for purity. Naturally, healing spells were in the charge of physicians, who also exercised a religious function as priests of Sakhmet, goddess of sickness. We also encounter the magician as a type in literature, where he usually bears the title "chief lector priest." Egyptian magicians even make an appearance in the Bible bearing this title (in the abbreviated form *ḥarṭummîm* from *ḥry-tp*, "chief"). Papyrus Westcar from the

Second Intermediate Period (seventeenth to sixteenth centuries B.C.E.) contains stories about appearances of such magicians before monarchs of the Old Kingdom. One created a wax crocodile that swallowed an adulterer, another parted the waters of a lake by placing one half of the water on top of the other half so that a piece of jewelry that had fallen to the bottom could be recovered, and the third was able to reattach the severed head of a goose and predict the future. The magic of these men consisted of nothing other than the extracultic application of arts and practices that were also used in the cult: in the latter for the benefit of all, in magic for the benefit of the individual. Magic thus in no way transcended the three-dimensional space of divine presence and religious experience.

Intoxication played a certain role, specifically in the cult of the goddess Hathor of Dendara. This cult had a "Festival of Drunkenness," with drinking, music, and dance. Associated with the name of Hathor, and with the names of Sakhmet, Bastet, and Tefnut, who are scarcely to be separated from her, was the concept of a two-faced goddess who could be dreadful, deadly, and furious, as well as charming, gracious, and gentle. Drink and music had the function of calming the goddess. In the Myth of the Heavenly Cow, this goddess appears as the annihilator of the human race and is calmed with a "sleeping potion" of beer colored blood-red before she can complete her work of destruction. In the later periods, the goddess had a "Festival of Homecoming" (Egyptian *in.tw.s*, "she is brought") that had an expressly drunken character. What was celebrated was the "homecoming" of the goddess who—as related in the myth behind this festival—went to Nubia in a rage (over what is not clear) and then, calmed by Shu and Thoth, was brought home to Egypt. All the temples of Egypt greeted the returning goddess with ecstatic jubilation, general drunkenness, music, and dance. Although we must affirm that intoxication and ecstasy were strikingly absent from the general picture of Egyptian religion, the cult of Hathor constituted an important exception.

6.2.2. MYSTICISM

As paths to the divine, mysticism and ecstasy run in opposite directions: the path of ecstasy leads outwards, and that of mystic contemplation inwards. Both presuppose a certain transcendence and obliteration of one's own individuality and identity. The concept of self-obliteration seems deeply contrary to Egyptian thought, and perhaps this is why the mystical path was as little realized in Egypt as the ecstatic. There is evidence, though, that gives an impression of mysticism if considered superficially. If we understand mysticism as the obliteration of one's identity with the goal of becoming one with the divine, something of this sort seems to occur when a priest declares, in cult or in magic, "It is not I who says this to you, it is the deity NN who speaks (through me) to you," or when spells and rituals promise individuals that their knowledge or recitation or performance will make them into a deity:

The one who knows this spell
will be like the sun god in the east (see chapter 3.2.2., text at note 23)
The one who executes this pattern
is like the Great God himself.

Do we not have here a sort of mysticism aimed at divinization of the self?[1]

I have tried to explain how such statements are to be understood in chapter 4.3, in connection with the verbal dimension. To repeat, Egyptian cult is not to be understood as communication between the human and divine realms, but as an act of communication that took place purely in the divine realm, with priests playing the roles of deities in the framework of set constellations. The priests did not, however, act on their own initiative as individuals, but under a commission from society. Their own individuality was of no interest in this connection, and they thus in no way had to shed or obliterate it to be able to play divine roles in the cult. What mattered was ritual purity, not self-obliteration. Whether induction into priestly office entailed an initiation that as such implied concepts of death and rebirth must remain an open question. That no sources mentioning initiation are preserved need not mean that such a thing never existed.

It is in any event striking that the funeral rites are often presented as an induction into priestly office. The funeral ritual had the function of imparting to deceased persons the new identity of an *akh* ("radiant transfigured one"), thus enabling them to have contact with the divine. Like the priests, the deceased had to make their appearance as deities to associate with the gods and goddesses. Purity was insufficient for this purpose, even when it was extended to moral purity, that is, freedom from sin, as in the "justification" of the Judgment of the Dead. The deceased were obliged to submit to a hearing and undergo examination before they could finally stand face to face with the divine. These concepts and formulations, which are quite common in Egyptian mortuary texts, are highly reminiscent of the language and the conceptual realm of the Hellenistic mysteries. It would be reasonable to think that such factors had correspondences in the realm of the living. For now, however, this cannot be proved, given the state of our sources to this point. It is thus more prudent to understand all these phenomena that remind us of mysticism and mysteries, for the moment, as phenomena that were confined exclusively to the cult of the dead.

There is an entirely different manifestation in the history of Egyptian religion that we could at least remotely connect with the concept of mysticism. If we understand that mysticism entails an "interior path," the discovery and adoration of the divine in one's own heart, we may think of the Egyptian idea of "placing the god in one's heart," which was a central concept in personal piety. The latter was a movement that unquestionably transcended the traditional structure of the three-dimensional communicative sphere of divine presence and religious experience and represented something new and revolutionary in the framework of the traditional conceptual structure of Egyptian religion. We discuss this in detail later. We could at best call this movement "mysticism" if placing the god in one's heart corresponded to a sort of surrender of the self. The self-designation of the pious person as a "truly silent one" seems important in this connection. This "silence" seems to have been understood as a form of self-diminishment and abasement that silenced the voice of the self so that the voice and the guidance of the divine could be heeded. We thus cannot entirely deny that personal piety might have had a certain similarity to mystical concepts, but we can scarcely call it mysticism, for it was more a matter of action than of contemplation or meditation. The pious person who "placed the god in his heart" displayed his convictions through his deeds, by "acting on the water of the god." He did not withdraw from the world.

6.2.3. HISTORY AND DESTINY

A thesis that history as a dimension of religious experience and divine presence was unknown to Egyptian religion would meet with staunch objections. Two rather obvious, contrary examples impose themselves on anyone with even a superficial knowledge of pharaonic culture: oracles, and the concept of a "state god" under whose command the king exercised rulership as his son and representative. If Egyptian religion knew the institution of oracles, then the concept of the intervention of the divine in the destiny of the land, of the manifestation of divine will in history in the sense of individual and collective experience, cannot have been entirely foreign to it. In fact, this concept was not entirely foreign to Egyptian religion. It first appears in a work of belles lettres from Dynasty 12 (ca. 1950 B.C.E.) in reference to individual destiny. Sinuhe sees the will of a god he cannot name in his fate of flight and exile. Still earlier, a certain Ankhtifi of Moalla states in an inscription in his tomb that he was brought to the Horus-Throne nome by Horus, the god of Edfu. Half a millennium later, Hatshepsut and Tuthmosis III credited their throne to oracular decisions by the state god Amun and conducted wars "under his command." Two centuries later, we meet with explicit concepts of a theology of history in Ramesside inscriptions. Ramesses II experienced the helping hand of his father Amun in the battle of Qadesh. Merneptah extolled his victory over the Libyans with the words "Re turned back to Egypt." If a god intervened personally in battle or manifested his presence in its success, then we cannot avoid according history the status of a dimension of religious experience and divine presence.

I would raise two points in response to this undoubtedly justified objection. First, as in the case of personal piety (with which the theme of history is intimately connected), we are not dealing with a basic structure, but rather with a later development that intervened and altered the traditional structure. Oracles were entirely foreign to the Old and Middle Kingdoms, and even in the New Kingdom, we observe at first only a gradual spread of the relevant phenomena. Second, the concept of history that developed into a dimension of divine presence during the course of the New Kingdom remained a rudimentary one. Compared with Israelite religion, which has been aptly designated "history as revelation," Egyptian theology of history is lacking in the category of the past. Yahweh was the god who led Israel out of Egypt. No Egyptian deity was ever identified on the basis of an event that had occurred in the past. Amun was never called "the god who rescued King Ramesses at Qadesh." Moreover, aside from some seminal beginnings, Egyptian historiography did not make reference to the past. The Ramesside concept of history did indeed distance itself considerably from the traditional view of history, which Erik Hornung has aptly called "history as religious celebration," developing new forms of the experience of contingency and the openness of the future. We shall delve into these matters later. But the basic structure was never entirely outgrown; "history as religious celebration" was tantamount to lack of history. If history was the quasi-ritual reproduction of basic mythic patterns, then we are dealing with the typical and oft-described historical blindness of mythic thought. Mythic thought conceives of reality, to cite the well-known formulation of Sallustius, as referring to "that which never happened but always is." The meaning-imparting illumination of mythic archetypes sheds light on any contemporary contingency, and even if mythic thought faded in the New Kingdom, permitting a glimpse of the importance of historical events (we may cite in particular the documentation of the battle of Qadesh), it was not outgrown. Thus, in the course of the history of Egyptian religion, history became a dimension of divine presence and religious experience alongside the other three, but without gaining a dominance that decisively altered the total picture of the religion.

6.3. The Three Dimensions as Totality

In the preceding section, we have maintained the view that Egyptians developed the three major dimensions that dominated their religious experience at the cost of other dimensions that either did not appear in it or developed only to a rudimentary extent. Egyptian religion thus appeared to be a fragment lacking in essential elements of the religious. On the contrary, we must make it clear that the three dimensions that dominated in Egypt were not an arbitrarily selected portion of possible dimensions, but rather were fitted together into a meaningful totality. This can most easily be demonstrated by the role of the king. His task was threefold and corresponded exactly to the three dimensions:

1. The king had charge of the cult, offerings, and the building of temples. He made the gods and goddesses at home on earth in the temples and provided for their care and their maintenance.
2. The king kept the cosmos—that is, the course of the sun—in motion and fostered an abundant Nile inundation through offerings and prayer.
3. The king played the role of Horus, that is, he enacted *the* central myth that sustained the Egyptian state. His filial piety toward his "deceased father" Osiris, who had withdrawn into the afterlife, and toward the entire ensemble of deities, who bore a parental relationship to him, held together the community of deities, humans, and transfigured dead.

Seen from the point of view of the king, the triad of dimensions proves to be systematic and exhaustive. Fulfilling these tasks, the king could not also be a shaman, a mystic, and a history-explaining prophet.

It seems important to me that the Egyptians encountered the divine in all three dimensions of its presence explicitly as a *plurality*. *The implicit theology of Egyptian religion was polytheistic*, and I wish to emphasize this once again by way of a conclusion. In the cultic dimension, we have a multitude of temples that were not only the homes of various individual deities, but in which they were always venerated in conjunction with a community of other deities. Just as the respective local Enneads represented the divine realm as a whole, the combined assemblage of local deities and their territories constituted the political totality of the Egyptian state. In the cosmic dimension, the plurality of deities appear as the many powers whose cooperation and conflict keep the cosmos going and create reality. *The divine character of the nature of the cosmos is revealed in their plurality*. The cosmos is maintained by differentiated divine powers. This basic polytheistic principle of Egyptian religion was undermined by the revolution of Akhenaten of Amarna, but also confirmed as such by it. The whole theological argument of the hymns from Amarna is directed against the cosmic plurality of the divine and the divine life of the world of creation. In the verbal or mythic dimension, the polytheistic principle of differentiated multiplicity is expressed in constellations. The anthropomorphization of the gods meant more than just that they assumed human form; it expressed itself in particular in the fact that they were persons. A deity was a person first and foremost as one who acted, and that meant, in respect to other deities. The personality of the deities consisted of interactive relationships, that is, within divine constellations. *A deity was a person by virtue of social involvement in a "sphere of belonging."* The unity of the divine was inconceivable in all three dimensions—the cultic, the cosmic, and the mythic—and any reflection tending in this direction necessarily transcended the polytheistic dimensionality of implicit theology.

Part Two

EXPLICIT THEOLOGY:
THE DEVELOPMENT
OF THEOLOGICAL
DISCOURSE

CHAPTER 7

The Unity of Discourse

The treatment of ancient Egyptian religion in this book rests on the distinction between implicit and explicit theology. I have explained my understanding of this distinction in chapter 1. Implicit theology has to do with the ideas, symbols, and concepts embedded in the religious acts of a culture, and in its texts as well, whereas explicit theology operates on a metalevel at a reflective distance from religious activity. The latter has freed itself from action and created a context of its own. Borrowing a concept from Michel Foucault, I call this context "discourse." I understand by this a form of speaking in which statements refer to a common object as well as to *one another*, and thus a form of "intertextuality." Intertextuality arises when language has freed itself from its "empractic" embedding sufficiently to attain a form of its own as a "text," which is usually set down in writing. "Empractic" and "sympractic" texts—the concepts are drawn from K. Bühler[1]—are simply the verbal substrate, and as such a part, of a superordinate unity of meaning that deserves to be called "text" in the sense of an autonomous unity of meaning only as the combination of speech and act. Discourse unfolds only in the form of texts that make reference to one another, in the give and take of dialogue. It represents a sort of "work" on its assigned theme. *Every discourse thus has a history.* This fact distinguishes discourse from empractic speech, for instance, from mythology. Discourse occurs in positions that are achieved, defended, and given up, and that are always firmly anchored in society and time. Every discourse is a process. It thus has a history in a way different from mythology, which is not a process, at least not as long as it does not become a "work on myth" (H. Blumenberg) at the end of its history of transmission.

In Part II, I shall therefore not simply single out individual texts that I classify as "explicit theology" according to certain criteria; rather, I shall reconstruct the process in which these texts participated. I shall plead my case and attempt to substantiate, on the basis of selected examples, that a number of texts widely dispersed through time, and in part through a variety of genres, stand in an intertextual context of reference to one another and to a common underlying problematic. I shall maintain, and I hope to be able to demonstrate, that in the Middle Kingdom, in the course of assimilating the serious disruptions that occurred in Egyptian culture after the collapse of the Old Kingdom, a process of discourse began that then developed during the New Kingdom and altered the entire religion by formulating a new concept of divinity. Not only did this discourse have a history, it *made* history by moving ever more into the center of cultural significance and intervening in the life of society. This discourse became the context not only of texts, but also of changes and events that it caused, of which I need only cite the religious upheaval of Akhenaten as the most important.

Explicit theology, which speaks in the form of discourse, is thus a historical phenomenon that requires explanation, quite unlike implicit theology, which is self-evident if nothing more than contact with the divine is taking place, just as the grammar of a language is self-evident. The occurrence of an explicit theological discourse is not self-evident. We can certainly think of religions that get along without explicit theology, and in ancient Egypt, the beginnings of theological discourse were relatively late. We must therefore attempt to set forth the historical conditions of its appearance and development. The following factors seem to me to be especially important: (1) the specifics of the historical situation of the Middle Kingdom as an overcoming of a far-reaching cultural crisis; (2) the continuity of a problem whose treatment gave direction to the process of discourse, namely, the problem of thinking of "god" (in the singular) in the framework of a polytheistic religion; (3) an important factor for the development of discourse, the institutionalization of discourse through the appearance of a professional group to conduct it; and connected with the last, (4) the development of hymns as the typical vehicle for explicit theology.

The Middle Kingdom (ca. 2000–1800 B.C.E.) can be understood in general terms as a period of explication. The characteristic instance, it seems to me, is the appearance of the "Königsnovelle" as a literary form in which royal actions are fully justified. On the level of royal speech acts, things are no longer simply decided and commanded; rather, justification, argumentation, and convincing occur. The texts expand the representation of royal acts at the metalevel of a rhetoric of motives. These acts are clearly no longer self-evident, but are in need of justification. The collapse of central royal authority at the end of the Old Kingdom was accompanied by the experience of alternative forms of political organization that the attempt to restore the centralized state around 2000 B.C.E. was obliged to oppose through propaganda. A significant portion of the belles lettres, which were "beautiful" in an entirely new sense, in that these works were not anchored in the framework of a concise context of usage, served as a medium for royal propaganda that was intended to convince. The works represent conditions during the First Intermediate Period as a chaos and thus justify the restored central authority as a cosmos. Royal inscriptions themselves breathe this new spirit of argumentative, explicative rhetoric. One text justifies royal building activity entirely on the level of principles, another develops a political theory of aggressiveness, of terror through strength, in connection with the establishment of a boundary, and a third deduces the reestablishment of the festival of Abydos in a highly abstract manner from the principle of reciprocity.

This need to justify the king's monopoly on action, which had been called into question, as a restoration of universal norms, and to legitimate it through consensus, is manifest everywhere. The king rules as orator, as enjoined on him by the Instruction for Merikare:

> Be artful in speech, that you may overcome,
> [for] the strong arm [of a king] is (his) tongue.
> Words are stronger than any fighting.[2]

The power of speech that created agreement proved itself in this period of general lack of orientation. The king was supposed to overcome the general disorder not by force, but by speech. Speech alone created consensus, certainty, and reality. This was true in a comprehensive sense that went far beyond politics. With the collapse of the Old Kingdom, not only did the central royal authority come to an end, but, inextricably bound up with this development, the culture's entire canon of norms and values was called into question. Just as comprehensive was the need for a fresh orientation, for consensus and certainty—that is, for language, for texts that could outline a new horizon of reality through fresh questions and fresh answers. This is probably the explanation of the origin of this literature, of which we have significant remnants, with its philosophical reflection on existence and on explication of action. Equally comprehensive therefore is what is expressed and made explicit in these texts: prophecies and laments, dialogues, instructions, and stories. Theology was a part of this literature. Its explicitness stands in the context of a general and comprehensive explication of reality, which was accomplished through the new medium of literary discourse that was evidently developed for this purpose. The hallmark of this discourse is the lack of conciseness of its functional grounding. This is also true of the fragments of explicit theology treated in chapter 8.

The general Zeitgeist of the New Kingdom was basically different. Reality had solidified; it was no longer in question, and it was thus no longer the theme of basic literary reflection. We no longer encounter theological discourse disseminated by inserting explicit theology into texts with other themes, but in religious writing *stricto sensu*, in

hymns and eulogies composed by professional priests and not by phi-
losophizing civil servants. These professional priests were a new class
that had not existed in earlier periods. Priests had existed in Egypt
since the beginnings of state formation, but not in the sense of a differentiated professional group. Priestly offices had been held by
administrators who also had other tasks and offices. They performed
part-time service in the temple; divided into "phyles," they served in
rotation. At most, the "chief lector priests," whom we met earlier as
magicians, were full-time professional priests. The situation changed
in the New Kingdom. The individual branches of the administration—temples, state and royal lands, civil and military administration—became more distinct from one another, with the result that a
given official would be occupied in only one of these departments at
any given time. The professionalization of theological discourse
surely cannot be separated from this sociological fact. It was only with
the New Kingdom that there arose a social class capable of carrying
out such a discourse.

To be sure, the scope of the texts is correspondingly narrower;
focused on the essential, their explicative range is less grandiose. It is
for these reasons that these texts were not scattered throughout the
history of Egyptian religion, but rather are confined in time (the centuries of the New Kingdom, the sixteenth through the thirteenth centuries B.C.E.), though dispersed in space (Upper and Lower Egypt)
and through the various strata of society. Though the theological discourse was anchored in the new class of professional priests, we can
tell from the origin of the sources that in the course of the New
Kingdom, interest in such texts spread through the entire upper class,
and perhaps further still. During these centuries, hymns, and especially solar hymns, experienced a unique golden age. Theological discourse, which had been only a sporadic manifestation in the
intellectual culture of the land in the Middle Kingdom, became the
center of general interest in the New Kingdom.

It was not readers who had need of explicit theology in hymnic
form. Rather, these texts stood in a very special, perhaps unique communicative context. In the overwhelming majority of instances, they
were tomb inscriptions. The concept of the tomb changed in the New
Kingdom. The tomb became a place where the deceased had contact
not only with posterity, but also with the divine, and the latter aspect
gained ever more significance. The most important deity was the god
of light, for proximity to him meant overcoming the realm of death
and returning to the world above. Tomb owners would therefore have
themselves represented accompanied by a hymn to the sun at the
entrance of their tombs. We owe the large quantity of preserved materials to this need for texts. This phenomenon had little to do with
explicit theology. If it had only been a matter of a change in the con-

cept of the tomb and corresponding innovations in its decorative program, the need could have been satisfied by always recording the same text, or one of a small group of standard texts, at the tomb entrance. In fact, some texts were often drawn on for this purpose, but an astonishingly large number of texts were evidently fresh compositions. If we compare the texts, it emerges that without exception, the standard texts reproduce a constellative theology of the sun's *course*, whereas among the texts that are attested once or only a few times, a large number of them develop a nonconstellative theology of the sun *god*. These are the hymns in which the theological discourse of those centuries is preserved. Not the need for texts, but the need for *new* texts demonstrates the central position of theological knowledge and reflection in New Kingdom society.

In these many texts, the historical dimension of religious ideas manifests itself in a density and a differentiation that were unique for Egypt. The texts take clear positions in a process of developing the problematic and the tension inherent in the concept of the divine, creating new, ever more precise and suitable formulations and models. We have already touched on this problematic several times. It has to do with the tension between a concept of "god" in the singular as the creator and ruler who sustains and maintains all, and the polytheistic, constellative concept of "gods" as the vehicles of actions that constitute the cosmos. During the New Kingdom, this tension seems to have intensified into a cognitive dissonance that exploded into a revolution from above in the upheaval precipitated by Akhenaten of Amarna. Nothing shows more clearly than the Amarna Period the explosive nature of the questions dealt with in the theological discourse of the New Kingdom. Amarna signified not only a new religion, but also a new art, a new literary language that was closer to the spoken language, new policies, a new elite, and so forth. Probably no area of culture was unaffected by these radical changes. And yet Akhenaten's revolution was essentially theological in its core. Only theological discourse produces the context in which this crisis can be understood. The theology of Amarna religion as developed in this king's hymns can be located precisely in the history of this discourse. Amarna marks the point at which this discourse, as it became ever more important and central, intervened radically in the life of Egyptian culture and society.

The process of theological discourse in the New Kingdom was divided into three phases: pre-Amarna, Amarna, and post-Amarna. Each of these phases took a new position in the debate about the essence of god (in the singular), though only Amarna religion proclaimed its concept of the divine as a new god and a new religion. It is for this reason that the chapter describing the three phases of the development of theological discourse in the New Kingdom is entitled

"The New Gods," referring to the salient concept of a supreme being in each of these three respective phases. All three were new in that they could not be reconciled with the traditional, constellative world view with its three dimensions of experience of divine presence; all three ruptured the framework of the traditional polytheistic structures and led to a fundamental change in the polytheistic world-view.

At the end, a new, fourth dimension connected with the new concept of "personal piety" emerged. The human "heart" and individual history now made their appearance as a new dimension of experiencing divine presence, along with cult statues, cosmos, and speech. The divine was at work in the life of the individual, and the individual lived in direct contact with the divine; moreover, this concept assisted in the breakthrough of the notion of the divine that had been aimed at from the very beginning. The polytheistic constellations in which deities acted only in relation to one another and in set roles paled into insignificance in comparison with this new dimension of "divine immediacy." Instead of the mythic-polytheistic concept of action—of the cosmos as the actions of the gods—there was now a concept of action that was oriented toward the idea of a supreme being: the world as god's (in the singular) action. The unity of the theological discourse can be paraphrased with this formulation. The apparently heterogeneous phenomena of Amun-Re theology at the beginning, before Amarna, the theology of Amarna, and the "personal piety" of the Ramesside Period prove on this level to be phases of a single process of development that began in the Middle Kingdom.

CHAPTER 8

Theodicy and Theology
in the Middle Kingdom

8.1. Theodicy and Theology

Theodicy inquires as to the justness of the divine. It has its origin in the painful experience of injustice that has prevailed or righteousness that has foundered and is suffering. Ancient Mesopotamian and Israelite literature gave form to this problem in the type of the "righteous sufferer" (the composition *Ludlul bêl nemeqi* and the Book of Job). Egyptian literature took entirely different directions with its debate on this very issue, as is only to be expected in a culture that had developed such a uniquely sophisticated, distinctive, and original conceptualization of the problem of the reciprocal relationship between meaning and action, doing and faring, with its principle of *maat* (truth, justice, harmony, solidarity). But it is striking that the debate assumed the form of sapiential literature in all three cultures (Egypt, Babylonia, Israel). We should not allow ourselves to be deceived by the canonized transmission of the Book of Job. This is not just a matter of "world literature" in the Goethian sense of general human significance, but of "wisdom literature" within the specific context of ancient Israelite culture, in precisely the same sense as the Mesopotamian and Egyptian texts are understood as wisdom literature. In contrast to the diversity of the various religions and theologies of these cultures, wisdom was an international phenomenon that was common to the Mediterranean and Near Eastern world. This already points to a crucial distinction between theodicy and theology.

Literature, in the narrower sense of belles lettres (among which we must classify wisdom literature),[1] functions without a secure practical mooring in specific contexts of use. Because of the openness of its thematic scope, it operates in a much broader area than traditional religious discourse; like all functionally determined genres, the latter is embedded in actions ("empractic") and bound to a defined, more or less exclusive community of understanding.[2] The radical, total challenge that the problem of theodicy poses to the traditional conceptual world is conceivable only in the enlarged arena won by literature emancipated from established traditions of practice and understanding.

The inclusion of theodicy obliges us to forsake the narrower thematic framework that we have constructed for ourselves in our treatment of Egyptian religion, at least for this single chapter. We are compelled to broaden our scope if we otherwise wish to understand the development of theological discourse in the New Kingdom. To understand the origin and development of explicit theology in Egypt, in the context of Egyptian religion in the narrower sense of "contact with the divine," it seems to me to be of crucial importance that the impetus came from without. Literature represents a decided "outside" in relation to the narrower realm original to religion as we defined it in chapter 1. Its contribution and—to the extent that a functional definition of literature is possible—its task is to constitute such an outside, in the sense of a meta- or interdiscourse in relation to all narrower cultural subsystems and realms of discourse. Explicit theology and the discourse in which its debate unfolds in speech and writing belong within the framework of contact with the divine, of religion in the narrower sense, notwithstanding the fact that they take up the broadest philosophical problems, and that they relate only reflectively and "metapractically" to this area of human practice. In this sense, explicit theology belongs in the New Kingdom. But we shall see that its impetus and its beginnings not only reach back into the Middle Kingdom, but also extend beyond the narrower realm of religion. The contrast between explicit and implicit theology thus becomes clear. Had explicit theology been endogenous, had its origin been in the context of religion as an explication of the conceptual realm put into practice in contact with the divine, then its content would doubtless have been as constellative as, for instance, the knowledge put into practice in the solar cult, as codified in the form of the cosmographies or the Books of the Netherworld. Explicit theology's origin in wisdom literature and the problem of theodicy, however, clarifies its nonconstellative reference to divinity per se.

The problem of theodicy did not emerge on the level of contact with the gods, but on a much more general and comprehensive level of contact with the world, and specifically in the context of the general conceptual crisis that was touched off by the collapse of the Old Kingdom and that called into question the possibility of realizing *maat*, the Egyptian definition of religion in its most comprehensive sense. On this level, and in a situation of collapse, a question was suddenly raised, not of the gods (in the plural), and not of a specific one among them, but of "god" (in the singular), of the single divinity responsible for the creation and continued existence of the cosmos and its deities.[3] This question of god (in the singular) was posed—and this is the decisive point—not in the horizon of cult, but in that of wisdom, of debate with traditional knowledge of the order of the world and the possibility of living in harmony with it. It was posed in a revolutionary situation in which all order was called into question, in which all harmony appeared to be destroyed, and which the texts describe as chaos and catastrophe.[4] The discourse of wisdom was expressed in new sorts of texts that were later handed down and canonized as literature.

8.2. The Reproach of Divinity

One of these novel works of literature, known by its (modern) title of "The Admonitions of an Egyptian Sage" or "The Admonitions of Ipuwer," contains bitter laments over the sorry state of humankind and the collapse of order.[5] It contains a section representing a reproach of the creator god: he who created humankind, he who (as the sun) "spends the day tending to them," should not allow that they kill one another, but rather ought to concern himself with the continued existence of his "herd."[6] That was a virtue demanded in Egypt not only of cowherds, but—on higher and higher social levels—of all leaders of groups, such as expedition leaders and military officers. "There was no loss among my troops," they affirm, for this was the most important and positive result they could report regarding the successful outcome of their undertakings. All the harsher is the reproach raised in this text against the divine herdsman: "his herd is small." The god brought humankind into existence, but he does not tend to them. "Where is he today? Is he asleep? His power is not seen!" The violent slay the timorous, and the god's herd is decimated.

Unfortunately, the text is so damaged that we cannot determine whether these bitter reproaches and questions found an answer in this work. In any event, there remains the astonishing fact that they were raised at all.

8.3. The Goodly Herdsman: The Instruction for Merikare

The so-called Instruction for Merikare is a royal instruction in the form of a testament, for this literary fiction is an instruction of the king by his deceased father.[7] It ends—we might say, culminates—in a sort of hymn to the creator god as the goodly herdsman and sustainer of his beneficent creation that is unique in Egyptian literature.[8] We wish first to clarify its context. The structure of the instruction, as I understand it, is as follows:

I. The king's responsibilities in the realization of *maat*
   A. actions against certain types of creators of disorder
   B. speech and knowledge: royal rhetoric

    C. *maat* and the Judgment of the Dead as the basis for dispens-
      ing justice
 II. Historical section: the deeds of the father and political advice
III. Reciprocity as the principle that imparts meaning to action
    A. the confession of the father, who had destroyed the cemetery
      at Abydos during the wars with the south
    B. the relationship between *maat* and eternity; the god as lord
      of reciprocity
    C. the beneficent organization of the world as divine act

The hymn to the beneficent rule of god (in the singular) thus occurs in the
context of the theme of reciprocity and immediately follows a maxim
dealing with humankind's (or the king's) deeds for the god, thereby doing
right. In the framework of the principle of reciprocity, action on behalf of
the god pays off, for the god "does not forget the one who acts for him."[9]

    This *do ut des* maxim, at first so seemingly trivial, is placed in an
entirely different context by the hymn that follows. Before any action on
behalf of the god, the god has always already acted on behalf of
humankind. Typically interpreted by the Egyptians as a process—the
course of the sun—the cosmos is here represented as divine action that
is intended for humankind. We have already cited the text in connection
with the cosmic dimension of divine presence in chapter 3 (text at note
4). Here, I see the following strikingly salient structure in the formulation of the hymn:

Action		*Anthropocentric reference*
1. creation:	sky and earth	"for them"
2.	the sea	
3.	the air	"that their noses would live"
4. the sun's course		"for them"
5. creation:	plants, animals, fish, birds	"that they might eat"
6. slaughter	enemies, children	—
7. effect:	light	"for them"
8.	the sun's course	"to see them"
9. erection of a chapel		(to hear them)
10. creation of rulers and superiors		"to strengthen the back of the weak"
11. creation of magic		"to ward off the blow of events"
12. slaughter		—

Twelve deeds of the god are cited, and with only two exceptions ("slaughter," numbers 6 and 12), each one of them is expressly related to humankind as its basis and its goal. The world was created, and it is continually maintained, for the sake of humankind. The god concerns himself with humankind, he beholds and hears them. He protects the weak through the institution of rulership (an astonishing justification of the state!) and gives them magic to ward off disaster (a no less astonishing justification of magic!). These sentences are framed by two statements, clearly relating to one another, about the god as a goodly herdsman: "Well provided is humankind, the herd of the god," and "watching over them night and day." With its insistent repetition of the phrase "for them," this passage has a rather apologetic emphasis. These two statements, which lack the element "for them," fall jarringly outside this impressively closed framework. The same is true of numbers 6 and 12, which mark the middle and the end of the passage:

> He slew his enemies and took action against his own children,
> for they plotted rebellion.

> He slew the refractory of heart among them,
> as a man smites his son for the sake of his brother.

The reference to the reproach of the god, "his herd is small," in the Admonitions of Ipuwer is unmistakable. Both texts assume that "losses" have occurred, and the two are related to one another as are a prosecution and a defense. But there is a paradox, in that the prosecution charges negligence, whereas the defense pleads homicide. The prosecution reproaches the goodly herdsman for insufficient attention ("is he asleep?"). In the hymn, however, the god himself is made responsible for the losses. The concept of a father who smites his children is less unbearable than the idea of a sleeping or indifferent god who allows people to slay one another. In the first case, the god must be thinking, for he acts, but not in the second case. *The god's thoughtlessness, however, robs the world of its meaningful context.* To save the meaningfulness of the world, divine will must extend even to catastrophe, which itself must be conceivable as an act of the god.

The meaning of the god's conduct is to be seen in the punishment of evil. Indeed, the Admonitions complain *expressis verbis* that the god beheld the violence of evil without doing anything. We might wonder whether the smitten ones bewailed in the Admonitions are in fact identical with the rebels and the refractory ones who, according to the Instructions, have fallen victim to the righteous justice of the god. In any case, this justice occurred for the good of humankind: "as a man smites his son for the sake of his brother." This is a peculiar statement, and we hear nothing further about it in Egyptian tradition. The meaning is that even this has happened "for their sake," for love of the good among his creatures. With that, the hymn affirms precisely the godly involvement whose lack is bemoaned in the Admonitions.

Of all the fragments of theology in the wisdom literature of the Middle Kingdom, this text is the most explicit. It points the way out of the spiritual crisis by tracing all that happens back to divine will. Instead of the world as the action of the gods and goddesses in the constellations of the polytheistic religion, it posits reality as the action of the creator god, which springs from his creative will to maintain, and which is directed at humankind as his children, his herd. *The vanished evidence for the meaningfulness of human existence is shifted to the transcendence of the inscrutable will of a hidden god.* Looking ahead to the New Kingdom, to which this text was well known, it is maintained here that it is precisely this idea that stood at the center of the theological discourse that developed at a later date and would change the religion and even the world view of Egyptian culture.

8.4. The Apology of the Creator God: Coffin Texts 1130

A third text belonging to this context of the question of the meaning of suffering and divine justice is handed down in an entirely different environment from that of the first two, namely, not in a literary manuscript but on coffins of the Middle Kingdom; it is thus a piece of mortuary literature (Coffin Text 1130).[10] The American Egyptologist James Henry Breasted performed the great service of recognizing its significance more than ninety years ago. When we look more closely at the context of its transmission, we see that like the hymn in the Instruction for Merikare, this text is the crowning conclusion of a book; in this case, the Book of the Two Ways, a guide to the afterlife for the soul's journey after death. In a sort of self-portrayal, the sun god manifests himself to the deceased person who has reached his goal, the innermost circle surrounded by a ring of fire, in the immediate presence of the god:

> To be spoken by the Hidden-of-Names.
> The All-lord said, when anger had to be stilled among the crew of
> the barque,
> Be well and in peace!
> I shall tell you the four good deeds
> that my own heart did for me in the *ouroboros*-serpent,
> in order to silence evil.
>
> (1) I performed four good deeds in the threshold of Light-land:
> I made the four winds,
> so that everyone could breathe in his time.
> That is one of the deeds.

(2) I made the great flood,
so that the poor man would have use of it like the rich man.
That is one of the deeds.

(3) I made each one like his fellow
and forbade that they do evil.
But their hearts resisted what I had said.
That is one of the deeds.

(4) I caused that their hearts cease forgetting the West,
so that offerings would be made to the deities of the nomes.
That is one of the deeds.[11]

This speech of the creator god divides the totality of the world into
four clearly articulated areas:

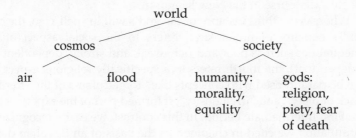

This speech also has an unmistakably apologetic character, as appears to
be explicitly stated in the first strophe. The speech is made only to "still
the anger" and "silence evil," and thus is a response to an uprising and
a reproach. It has often been assumed that this text is the response to the
reproach addressed to the god in the Admonitions of Ipuwer.

The reproach against which the creator god defends himself here
must have referred to the inequality of human beings. Social inequality
in the human realm is here represented as an alienation for which
humans themselves are responsible, one that not only was not built into
the order of creation as willed by the god, but was explicitly barred. The
god created the cosmic realm for the provisioning of humankind, and
not only "for them," as it is put in the Instruction for Merikare, but—and
this is important—so that each would have an equal share in it. Nature,
as the god created it for humankind, afforded no basis for social inequality; its gifts were there equally for all. And not only nature: the god also
created humans alike, "each one like his fellow," and he "forbade evil."
In this context, the "evil" can only be the abolition of the original, natural equality of all human beings. This is the answer to the reproach that
the god made humans different, some "timorous" and some "powerful," but not to the reproach of indifference. He forbade evil, but he does

not say that he punishes it, as stressed in the Instruction for Merikare. However, later in the same spell (which we cannot cite *in extenso* here because of its length), we read

> I judge the poor and the rich,
> I proceed equally against those who do evil.
> Life belongs to me, I am its lord.
> The scepter of rulership will not be wrested from my hand.[12]

This is the response to a reproach of the god's indifference. The creator god does not content himself with a benevolence that is cosmic and, as such, ethically indifferent. As "lord of life," he is the ethical authority who watches over justice and before whom social distinction ("poor and rich") pales into insignificance. These are leitmotifs that would have a determining influence on the development of theological discourse in the New Kingdom.

Whereas the third instance of the god's will in spell 1130, the creaturely equality of humankind, refers to the social aspect of evil (inequalities such as poor and rich, weak and strong, dependent and independent), the fourth refers to a specifically religious aspect that can be paraphrased with concepts like "forgetfulness of the afterlife," "lack of piety," and "irreligiosity"; it formed part of the experiences of the First Intermediate Period. In this contrast, we easily recognize the formulation we cited in chapter 1 as the basis of an Egyptian definition of justice (or morality) and religion in the narrower sense:

> speaking justice for humankind
> and satisfying the gods.[13]

The god defends himself against the reproach (to judge from his response) that he created impious creatures in human beings by stressing that he planted religion in their hearts by making it impossible to forget death. The connection between consciousness of death and piety is immediately comprehensible, but also astonishing, for it occurs nowhere else in Egyptian literature with such clarity. In the Instruction for Merikare, it is once stated, "trust not in the length of years,"[14] that is, be ever mindful of your mortality. A great many declarations in biographies amount to the statement "I led a righteous life, for I had my eye on the realm of the dead." The connection between morality and fear of death is well-attested, but not fear of death as the basis of religion. According to this text, humankind's forgetting of the afterlife represents a deviation from their creaturely concept. To be mindful of the West belongs to their nature, to forget it is their sinful alienation. The connection between the three texts seems evident to me. It is a typical phenomenon of intertextuality:

they refer to one another and to a common problem. The problem is the righteousness of the divine, which has been called into question; or, otherwise stated, how meaningfulness has become opaque in the realms of society and cosmos. It arises from the historical situation of a collapse that was experienced and treated as a crisis of meaning.

From these first manifestations of a sort of theological discourse, it is abundantly clear that—and in what sense—this is a question of "god" in the singular, not of the gods. It is also not a matter of a generic "god" as opposed to "man," but rather of the one specific god who created the world and is thus accountable for it, and before whom humankind, called to choose freely between working with or against him, must also be accountable. The problem of theodicy centers on the justification of "god" in the singular, not of the realm of the gods, on the justification of a single god who also cares for the other gods, for instance, by planting the fear of death, and thus religion, in the human heart.

> I created the gods from my sweat,
> while humankind are the tears of my eye,[15]

the All-Lord also states in the third text. This perspective, which posits a single god above and beyond the world and the other deities who belong to it, is not monotheistic. The existence of other deities is not contested. Nevertheless, it is clear that when "god" is spoken of, only *one* god is meant.

The texts belong to different genres. The Admonitions and the Instruction belong to the newly emergent (wisdom) literature in which moralistic discourse went beyond the bounds of literature composed for practical purposes and its traditional genres, especially the moralistic discourse of tomb biography, and reflected on the basic meaning of human existence in an unprecedentedly radical manner. Although the third text is handed down to us in the framework of mortuary literature, its unusually reflective ("metapractical") level reveals its origin in some other context that was closer to literature. The text we shall discuss next belongs more securely to the realm of the literature of religious practice, even if it is also presumably not handed down to us in its original context.

8.5. The Revelation of the God of Life: Coffin Texts 80

Spell 80 of the Coffin Texts has been handed down in the framework of a sequence of texts centering on Shu, the god of air, and the element of air as the *ba* of Shu. Its recitation as liturgy and its recording as mortuary literature were supposed to supply the deceased with air, which is the central wish of the deceased in many other texts. The details make clear that the scope of the text points well beyond this goal.[16]

We can treat this unusually lengthy text only summarily. It is another speech in which the All-Lord, the primeval creator god, reveals himself; this speech is embedded in a speech of the air god Shu or his *ba*, in whose form the deceased wishes to avail himself of air and the space it occupies—that is, to ascend to the sky. According to a later-attested theological concept, the *ba* of a deity was the characteristic cosmic manifestation in which he or she could be experienced by the senses. It is clear that this concept already underlies this text:

> I am this *ba* of Shu who is in the celestial cow,
> who ascends to the sky as he wishes,
> who descends to the earth as his heart desires.
> . . .
> The air of life is my garment,
> to emerge around me from the mouth of Atum.
> . . .
> I make light after the darkness,
> the air is my proper skin.
> . . .
> My efflux is the storm of the sky,
> my sweat is hailstorm and half-light.
> The length of the sky belongs to my strides,
> the breadth of the earth belongs to my foundations.[17]

The self-created primeval god himself now begins to speak. The connection to the whole is clear: he does not speak about himself, as in spell 1130, but about his children, the air god Shu and his sister Tefnut, whose cosmic form of manifestation (moisture?) is unclear. But that is not important; as we see, the theological thrust of this text goes in a direction quite different from the cosmic:

> Then Atum said: Tefnut is my living daughter,
> she is together with her brother Shu.
> "Life" is his name,
> "Maat" is her name.
> I shall live together with my two children,
> together with my twins,
> I being in the middle,
> one of them at my back, the other at my belly.
> As Life slept with my daughter Maat,
> I stood upon them, while their arms were around me.[18]

With a curious emphasis, the speech maintains three things:

- Shu and Tefnut are the children of Atum
- their (actual?) names are Life and Maat

- together with their father Atum, they constitute a distinct, mysterious, and intimate constellation.

The first of these points is a regular part of the framework of the traditional, constellative theology, and the next two go beyond it. Shu and Tefnut are depersonalized into Life and Maat in the sense of cosmogonic principles, and the description of their constellation with their father as "in front of" and "behind," as well as "within" and "without," makes it clear that they are not a group but a trinity, or better, that the two possibilities are paradoxically to be kept in mind at the same time: Atum, together with his children, Life and Maat—in another passage, the text explains the two children of Atum as *neheh*, "plenitude of time," and *djet*, "unchanging endurance"—as the two cosmogonic principles that dominate the All (= Atum):

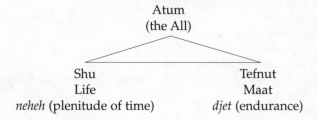

Atum
(the All)

Shu   Tefnut
Life   Maat
neheh (plenitude of time)   *djet* (endurance)

Sounding like a predecessor of Greek philosophical-mythic allegory, this passage makes clear its explicative distance from myth. Explicit theology is not mythological.

The speech describes the transition from preexistence to existence, which the Egyptians thought of not as a "big bang," but rather an awakening, a coming into conscious personhood of the primeval god who personified the All. United with the energies of Life and Maat (truth, order, justice, cosmic-social harmony), which filled and sustained him, he found the strength to stand up. The text centers on this mysterious moment when being (= life) was originally kindled, so as to clarify the inconceivable: that Shu and Tefnut were always already with Atum, and that this constellation of three deities did not exist *from*, but *before* the beginning:

when I was alone in Nun, inert . . .
they were already with me.

To paraphrase this basic concept of a preexisting triunity in more familiar language: *In the beginning were Life and Truth, and Life and Truth were with God, and Life and Truth were God.*

Nevertheless, notwithstanding this concept of a preexisting triunity, the preexistence of the primeval god is represented entirely in the sense of a constellative notion of person and act—as an *incapacity to act* (Egyptian *nniw*, "to extend inertly"):

> when I was alone in Nun, incapable of action—
> I found no place to stand,
> I found no place to sit,
> Heliopolis was not yet founded, that I might be in it,
> my chapels (?) had not been knotted together, that I might sit in them,
> I had not yet created Nut, that she might be at my head . . .
> the first generation of deities was not yet born,
> the primeval Ennead had not yet come into being—
> they were with me.[19]

Inability to act is an intolerable condition for a creator god. Atum therefore said to the primeval waters:

> I am swimming, very weary,
> my limbs (?) are inert.
> It is my son Life who lifts my heart.
> He will enliven my spirit, after he has bound together these limbs of mine,
> which are very weary.
> Then Nun said to Atum:
> Kiss your daughter Maat, place her at your nose![20]

Thus the cosmos came into being. What is described is an act of coming to one's self, a transition from a weariness that is incapable of action into consciousness, will, and act. In this concrete way of thinking, it is viewed as "lying" and "standing up." "It is your son Shu who will raise you up," says Nun to Atum.

In what follows, it is again Shu who speaks. In his first speech, he portrays his work in the created world, where every day at sunrise, he flows from the nostrils of the god who keeps creation going as the sun, for his own part enlivening the sun with breath—the sun, but also Isis and Osiris. He creates the light-filled space for the sun's journey by barque and "saves him from Apopis." In a second speech, he speaks as "Life, lord of time," created by Atum "when he was one and became three."[21] After this remarkably abstract and terse formulation of the peculiar triunity of Atum, Shu/Life, and Tefnut/Maat, the air god describes his role as god of life: as the "breath" in the throat of the All-Lord, and also as grain,

> when he sent me to this earth,
> the Isle of Fire,
> and when I became Osiris, the son of Geb.[22]

Again it turns out that the constellations of traditional theology dissolve in the abstractive power of this reflection. In this new identity of the god "Life," Shu and Osiris merge together!

In the novel perspective of this theology, it is not the identity of the god that is inquired after, but rather his essence. The distinction, as I see it, can perhaps be made clear in the following manner. The identity of the god is determined by his relationship to other deities, that is, his inclusion in constellations. That is the specific perspective of myth. From this perspective, for example, Shu appears in the Book of the Heavenly Cow as the son of the sun god, whom he succeeds in the office of ruler over the world of creation; or, in another of these succession myths, as the father of Geb, who is driven from rule by his rebellious son; or again as the brother of the lioness Tefnut, daughter of the sun, who leads the raging goddess home from Nubia. Here, however, he appears in a different perspective as the son of a god who developed into a trinity with him and his sister Tefnut, thus not only bringing himself into existence out of the preexistence of his solitude, but at the same stroke calling the cosmos into existence and beginning the process of creation. This trinity is no longer a constellation in the sense of constellative theology. The identities that make their appearance here do not constitute themselves through their distinction from one another, but rather through their unity of essence.

The texts themselves stress the originality of this theology, using negations to distance themselves from the conceptual realm of traditional, constellative theology:

I was not formed in my mother's womb,
I was not fashioned in the egg,
I was not conceived by conception,
I was not born in a birth.

He did not bear me with his mouth,
he did not conceive me with his fist.[23]

Explicit theology makes the constellative thought of implicit theology explicit by negating it. It manifests itself as an antithesis. It ruptures the constellation that portrayed the birth as a result of the onanism of the primeval god by stressing that this was not so. It counters the constellation positively, on the one hand, with the idea of a unity of essence that developed into a trinity, positing principles instead of the traditional names—the All, Life, and Truth. On the other hand, it is an inquiry into the essence of the divine, and here the answers are much less abstract and "allegorical." These negative statements are followed by

My father Atum spat me from his mouth
together with my sister Tefnut[24]

he blew me from his nose.[25]

This sounds scarcely less mythological than the birth through self-gratification that was so emphatically dismissed. But appearances can be deceiving. Let us look at other formulations of this theme:

> He created me in his heart,
> he made me out of his radiant power.[26]

> He was pregnant with me in his nose,
> I emerged from his nostrils.[27]

What these formulations are trying to express is that Shu is nothing other than the breath of the creator god. This is no mythological constellation. A god is not the breath of another god, any more than it would conform to mythological thought to conceive of a god as the "word" of another god. Here, the discourse begins to attain a higher plane on which—as in wisdom literature—we must speak of "god" (in the singular). The Egyptian language was not capable of expressing this distinction, but the texts hint at it when they avoid the names Re or Atum when they mean "god," speaking instead of "the one who came into existence by himself" (passim), or of the "creator of all" (spell 75) or the "All-Lord" (spell 1130).

Shu is not just the "breath of the god," but the air, as a cosmic element and as the "breath of life" of the world of creation. That is the decisive change in this new theological explication of the world, and it constitutes the conclusion of the lengthy text:

> Falcons live on birds,
> jackals on prowling,
> swine on the desert,
> hippopotami on reeds,
> humans on grain,
> crocodiles on fish,
> fish on the water in the Nile,
> as Atum has commanded.
>
> I lead them, I enliven them
> through this mouth of mine, as the life in their nostrils,
> I guide my breath into their throats,
> I tie on their heads through this powerful speech in my
>   mouth,
> which my father Atum gave me
> when (he) emerged from the eastern Light-land.
> I enliven the fish and the snakes on the back of the earth god,
> truly, I am the Life that is beneath the sky goddess.[28]

We have here two strophes, each consisting of eight verses. The first strophe describes the beneficent arrangement of the world created by Atum, in which the creatures are diverse and each is well provided for in its own specific way. The second describes the single, irreducible principle, unspecific to their number and diversity, that keeps all creatures alive, however different their requirements might otherwise be. Whether in the air or on the ground, in the desert or the swamp, whether they live on plants, animals, or water—they all live thanks to the "breath of life," the breath of the god, that fills the world as air and is at work in every living creature.

This is an inquiry into the unity behind the diversity of the world of appearances. And the answer is found in the single origin of all in the primeval, self-created unity; this is the answer of creation theology, and not just in this text, but in religious texts generally at the turn of the millennium around 2000 B.C.E. But this text goes a great deal further. Not in the sense of a mythological-polytheistic constellation, but in the sense of a theological development, it distinguishes an essential unity: "origin" (Atum), "harmony" (Tefnut, in the sense of an order that bestows harmony), and "life" (Shu as "air," "breath," and "plenitude of time"). The text constructs a theology of the "god of life" on this distinction. In the fourth, decisive section of this lengthy text, which is devoted to the development of this theology, the Egyptian word for "life" occurs no fewer than twelve times. This is a clear indication of what the concern is. An effort is being made (1) to characterize something as general, comprehensive, undifferentiated, and fundamental as "life" as the common unity behind the diversity; (2) to see this unity at work in the cosmos in the equally (or relatively) undifferentiated, comprehensive, and all-pervasive phenomena of air, light, time, and breath; (3) to explain them as the essence of a god; and (4) to declare that this god shares in the essence of the creator god from whose nose he streams as breath.

For centuries to come, Egyptian thought would be preoccupied by this theology of the god of life. It would be the basis of Akhenaten's religious revolution, the first attempt to found a religion known to history. But all "explicit theology" in Egypt drew its dynamic from this theology, down to the Corpus Hermeticum. The inquiry into the unity of the divine and the manifestation of that unity that we have seen here—life, *maat*, breath, plenitude of time—were both the starting point and the dominating theme of Egyptian theology.

8.6. Theology, Religion, and Language in the Middle Kingdom

Before we turn in the next chapter to the New Kingdom, the period that not only can be called the golden age of explicit theology, but whose history was essentially determined by the dominance of theological debates (we may think of Akhenaten's religious revolution and the establishment of the Theban theocracy), we must discuss the relative importance of theological discourse in the Middle Kingdom and the closely related issue of the choice of the texts treated, which might seem arbitrary to many who know the material. It should be made clear at the outset that the Middle Kingdom was no golden age of explicit theology. The texts treated here become meaningful only when they are viewed from the vantage point of a knowledge of the succeeding periods. They are the beginnings or predecessors of what would become a determining, history-making factor in Egyptian culture some centuries later. Considered in the context of the history of religion (note: not the history of literature) in the Middle Kingdom, the phenomena treated here are rather marginal. Two issues therefore seem to me to be sufficiently important to be mentioned briefly in this context:

1. the relationship of these presumably rather marginal beginnings or predecessors of explicit theology to that which we may view as the central religious phenomena or events of this period
2. the linguistic forms used by these earliest formulations of explicit theology and their relationship to the usual forms of religious and literary communication.

The central religious event of the Middle Kingdom was the spread of the Osiris cult—or better, religion—in Egyptian society, which is archaeologically tangible in the explosive expansion of an area at Abydos known as the Terrace of the Great God, where a thick cluster of tombs and cenotaphs (Egyptian *meahat*, "stela-place") began along the festival route traveled by the procession of Osiris from his temple to his tomb in U-Poqe; hundreds, perhaps thousands of stelae are preserved to us. Perhaps "spread" is not quite the right word. For it was not so much the cult of the god Osiris that spread through the entire land— although evidently, from early on, it belonged to the "program" of the Osiris religion, played a striking role in the texts, and then became a reality at the latest in the New Kingdom (into the Late Period, the Osiris religion represented a dominant phenomenon in this sense of a spread to the localities of Egypt). Rather, it was the other way around: the whole land made pilgrimages to Abydos. Thereafter, everyone strove to participate in the days-long festival dramas newly established by the kings of Dynasty 12 in honor of Osiris at Abydos, and also to enjoy this participation posthumously by means of a stela-chapel at the Terrace of the Great God. Abydos became *the* holy city of Egypt,

the isle to which one must make pilgrimage,
the walls determined by the All-Lord
(etc.; see chapter 2.1, text at note 15).[29]

From this time on, the pilgrimage to Abydos became a central component of the funeral ritual and tomb iconography. Abydos is perhaps the earliest example of a place of pilgrimage in the history of religion, and the festival of Osiris the earliest example of an associated festival. People made pilgrimage to Abydos and built tombs or stela-chapels there for the sole purpose of taking part in this festival.[30]

Wolfgang Helck has convincingly viewed the rites of this festival procession as the mythologization of the burial ritual of an early period in which Abydos was still a royal necropolis. In terms of our categories, this process can perhaps be understood as a mythic dimension: the anteriority of action to sacramental explanation, and the development in the Old Kingdom of a specifically divine realm of meaning that formed a semantic vault over acts that were, in part, of great antiquity. In any event, in my opinion, there is good reason to think that the rites of the great festival at Abydos go back to very old royal burial rituals. If so, the "spread" of the Osiris religion in the Middle Kingdom finds its simplest explanation. We must understand the phenomenon in the context of far-reaching changes in the mortuary cult and in beliefs regarding the afterlife. What spread at first, already at the end of the Old Kingdom, was the specifically royal concept of a life after death: that the king as "deceased father" became Osiris after death and assumed rule over the netherworld, and that the king possessed an immortal soul—called *ba* in Egyptian—that survived of its own accord independently of his integration into the community, ascending to the sky and entering the world of the gods. With only slight modifications, these beliefs became valid for all in the Middle Kingdom. Each person had a *ba* that survived death, left the body, and managed the posthumous journey into the divine realm. Each person became an Osiris and followed the mythic precedent of the god. Participation in the festival of Abydos was the concrete crystallization point of all these concepts, hopes, and myths. Because it was the burial of the god, because it was the god's precedent-setting transition to posthumous immortality, it imparted immortality to its participants.

That we could write a chapter about the theology of the Middle Kingdom without mentioning these complexes of concepts regarding Osiris and Abydos generally, which cast such a spell on the religious thought and practice of this period, sheds light on the unconventionality of our perspective. Theology and religion are two different things. What happened at Abydos, and what must be viewed as the central religious development in the history of the Middle Kingdom, could be treated entirely under the category of implicit theology, especially in the local-cultic and the mythic dimensions of divine presence. Abydos is not a source of explicit theology. There is a whole series of hymns to Osiris among the inscriptions on the stelae, but they stand outside the discourse of theology. Nothing was built on them, they did not stand at the beginning of an evolution of ideas. Rather, they were constantly copied. From a theological point of view, they were explicitly constellative:

> Greetings, Osiris, son of Nut,
> lord of horns, with tall Atef-crown,
> to whom were given the Wereret-crown
> and broadness of heart before the Ennead;
> whose majesty Atum has created
> in the hearts of humans, gods, transfigured ones, and dead.
>
> To whom rulership was given in Heliopolis,
> great of embodiments in Busiris,
> lord of fear in Yati,
> great of terror in Rasetau,
> lord of majesty in Herakleopolis,
> lord of might in Tjenenet,
> great of love in the land,
> lord of goodly remembrance in the god's palace,
> great of appearances at Abydos.
>
> To whom justice was given before the collected Ennead,
> for whom a bloodbath was staged
> in the great hall that is in Her-wer,
> before whom the greatest powers are in terror,
> before whom the oldest ones lift themselves from their mats,
> before whom Shu has instilled fear,
> whose majesty Tefnut has created,
> to whom the Two Chapels have come bowing,
> for the fear of him is so great, his majesty is so powerful.[31]

This is the beginning of the most popular hymn to Osiris from this period; it is a typical example of its genre, and it was handed down over the millennia. It does not refer to the god's essence, but rather to his status. We need only compare it with what Coffin Texts spell 80 has to say about the essence of Shu as god of the air—as life and plenitude of time, as the breath of the creator god and the breath of life in every nose—to gauge the difference. If we wish to draw explicit theology from their themes, as a reflection on the essence of a deity, then we must affirm that the Osiris hymns of the Middle Kingdom are unproductive. The Middle Kingdom Osiris religion was a fact of religious, not theological history.

Such few texts as we have singled out as theological "facts" from the large number of writings preserved to us from the Middle Kingdom are not marginal only from the quantitative point of view. They also belong to various genres and realms of discourse: the "reproach to the divine" belongs to a text complaining of political conditions, the figure of the "goodly herdsman" is from a royal instruction, and the other two texts form part of the mortuary literature. But something else seems crucial to me: that each of these texts that make theology explicit ruptures the framework of the genre to which it belongs. Political complaints do not otherwise reproach the divine, wisdom texts contain no other hymn to the creator and sustainer of all, and the mortuary literature knows no other theological determination of essence in the form of a divine self-description. I think this shows more clearly than anything else that these are expressions of a new theme for which no tradition of discourse had been developed.

The divine self-presentation is probably the most unusual form, and I feel that it is worth further consideration. The theodicy of the All-Lord in Coffin Texts spell 1130 and the theology of the god of air in spell 80 are preserved to us through their placement in the mouth of a deceased person, but their original function was probably different. In any case, they seem peculiar in the context of other cases of a deceased person representing himself in the role of a god. They were probably originally self-revelations of these gods in the form of monologues. This form seems significant to me. It might be that we draw too sharp a distinction between "revealed" religions and other types and accord too exclusive a sense to the concept of revelation. Do we not have here at least a related connection between the divine and speech? These texts break through or transcend the traditional relationships between deities and speech that we find in Egyptian religious texts, just as the explicit theology they express breaks through the framework of the theology of a religion grounded in cult. They are enclaves, so to speak, of revelation in the territory of a cult religion. Needless to say, Egyptian deities were not silent; quite the contrary, their verbal exchanges are perhaps the most important manifestation of their constellative relationships. The context of actions and roles in which they are included in the mythic dimension (which can therefore be called more generally the "verbal" dimension) is fulfilled first and foremost through speech. These revelatory monologues, however, are not constellative; rather, they are directed to all. This is an entirely different kind of speech from that normally used by deities. The difference between these monologues and the traditional speeches in the realm of the Egyptian deities that occur otherwise in religious texts should not be blurred if we insist on the distinction from the concept of revelation *stricto sensu* in revealed religions. From the Egyptian point of view, these monologues represent something new and unusual, and it seems to me that it is no accident that the theology enunciated in this novel manner runs counter to the basic structures of Egyptian religion.

CHAPTER 9

The New Gods

9.1. Amun-Re

9.1.1. NEW FORMS OF THEOLOGICAL DISCOURSE: ADDITIVE THEOLOGY

The New Kingdom was distinguished by the "professionalization" of theological discourse. We have the sociological fact of a professional priesthood on the one hand, and, on the other hand, the literary-historical (or better: discursive-historical) fact of a unique multitude of hymns to the sun and to Amun-Re. It is likely that the two facts are to be connected.

This theological "work"—this concept seems apposite, in view of the number of texts and the basic professionalization of theological discourse—was aimed at the concept of "god." A leading role, however, was played by the theology of a specific god, Amun-Re of Thebes; in Dynasty 18, the reflection on god (in the singular) that began in the Middle Kingdom became a theological explication of Amun-Re. As worked out in the texts, his role as supreme being not only places him in a new relationship to the other deities that ruptures all the constellations, but also relates him directly to the world of humankind, as had already emerged in texts of the Middle Kingdom. The form of the texts in which this theological work on the essence of Amun-Re (and at the same time the essence of god) occurs is itself instructive: it is a sort of divine titulary, an extension of the divine name Amun-Re by means of a string of epithets that follow a regular scheme and are drawn from a common stock of phrases.[1] Expanded into eulogies, these strings of epithets made their appearance in the form of theological insertions in texts with entirely different purposes, the so-called offering formulas that appear in the thousands in the repertoire of tomb inscriptions from all periods of Egyptian history. They have to do with the verbal performance of mortuary offerings. Following the stereotyped introductory formula, "an offering that the king gives," one or more divine names are mentioned, followed by requests on behalf of the deceased. Normally, explicit theology is not to be sought in this genre. No such eulogistic insertions are included in older offering prayers, and they are quite rare in later ones. They are characteristic, however, of the period of Hatshepsut and Tuthmosis III. We see clearly how, as it assumed professional form at this time, theological discourse made use of existing genres, modifying ancient traditions of composing and recording texts.

By way of an example, here is the eulogistic insertion from the offering prayer on the tomb stela of a man named Amenemhet (Theban Tomb 53):

> An offering prayer to Amun-Re, lord of Karnak,
> lord of eternity, lord of everlastingness,
> prince, lord of the great two-feathered crown.
>
> The sole one in the beginning, the greatest of the great,
> primeval god without his like,
> he is the great one who created men and gods
> . . .
> Living flame that arose from the primordial waters
> to illuminate those in the sky.
> Divine god who came into being by himself.
>
> He who speaks, and what is to happen comes about:
> a beautiful burial at his behest,
> a mooring in the western desert.[2]

Like all the eulogies in the offering prayers, this one is constructed according to a pattern that can be characterized as a fixed sequence of divine roles:

1. city god, for instance, "lord of Karnak," "lord of the great two-feathered crown"
2. ruler god, "lord over time and eternity"
3. primeval god, "the sole one at the beginning," "greatest of the great ones," "primeval god without his like"
4. creator god, "the great one who created men and gods"
5. sun god, "living flame that arose from the primeval waters to illuminate those in the sky"
6. ethical authority, "who speaks and it comes about."

With the exception of the category "city god," which represents a final link with the implicit theology of traditional religion, these roles or aspects have one thing in common: they are inseparably connected with the idea of divine unity. To be sure, Egyptian religion knew many royal gods, creator gods, primeval gods, sun gods, and ethical authorities. But this multiplicity results only from the perspective of an outside observer. Viewed from within, from the perspective of a participant, there could only be a single deity in whom these aspects were united. If a new god such as Amun appeared as creator and sun god, he did not compete with traditional creator gods or solar deities such as Atum and Re; rather, he incorporated their essence into himself.

Rationalizing such mergings of essence, that is, making them comprehensible through verbal formulations of a comprehensive concept of the divine, was probably the primary concern of Egyptian theology. The Theban theology of these decades can be interpreted as an attempt to fill the hyphenated formulation Amun-Re with theological content, that is, to develop a divine concept sufficiently comprehensive to include all the traditions concerning Amun and all those of Re as well. The pure Amun aspect of the city god and the pure Re aspect of the sun god are connected by the concept of the supreme being who had already emerged in the theological fragments of the Middle Kingdom in his aspects of primeval god, creator god, and god of life. I call this process "additive," for I have the impression that this new concept of a supreme being was arrived at primarily by accumulation and juxtaposition. All aspects of divine unity—preexistence, creator, sustainer—were combined and connected with one another by means of simple but well-ordered juxtapositions of sequences of predicates of Amun and Re. In this regard, Ramesside theology proceeded quite differently, namely hypotactically.

We would fundamentally misunderstand the sense of this theological work if we assumed that it was aimed solely at the Theban city god Amun, who had been promoted into a state god, and none other, so as to elevate him above all the other deities in the land, as befitted the traditional role of a state god. Rather, it was still directed at the concept of the divine, at the problem of thinking of "god" (in the singular), and not just "a god," in the framework of a polytheistic religion. This thesis requires substantiation, for nothing seems more obvious than such a religiopolitical explanation. Thebes was the city from which, after the second collapse of central rule in the Middle Kingdom, the third unification of Egypt had proceeded, this time in the form of a decades-long struggle for liberation, which resulted in the expulsion of the Hyksos, foreign interlopers who had ruled Egypt from the delta. Connected with these events was a far-reaching militarization of the political climate in Egypt. In the pursuit of the Hyksos into Palestine, the state extended itself far beyond its traditional boundaries and founded an international empire. The theme of rule over the world dominates the royal inscriptions. The career of the Theban royal house, from vassals of the Hyksos to international sovereigns, seems to be mirrored in the rise of the god of its city to the status of "supreme being." This parallel is doubtless anything but coincidental, and it finds its explanation in what we have said about the importance of the institution of state god for the political identity of the state in connection with the cultic-local dimension of divine presence. It certainly cannot be denied that changes in the concept of the state were expressed through changes in the concept of the state god.

Such an interpretation is not unjustified, but it does not go far enough. It eliminates entirely the intellectual context, which stretches back into the Middle Kingdom and forward into the Amarna and Ramesside Periods, and which we are reconstructing as theological discourse. To be sure, political history affords a context for events in the history of religion, one that cannot be ignored. But embedding phenomena horizontally in contemporary historical situations and processes must not lead to their being disembedded from their vertical or diachronic connections. My thesis thus rests on an attempt to understand the Amun-Re theology of Dynasty 18 on the one hand as a continuation of the beginnings of explicit theology in the Middle Kingdom and on the other hand as the starting point of the revolutionary changes that occurred in the religious history of the New Kingdom. From this perspective, this theology proves to be a position in the search for a new concept of the divine.

That this explanation does not entirely miss the mark can be shown by a single detail: the fact that the eulogies of Amun-Re could be transferred to other deities. One Theban eulogy appears on a monument from This with reference to the god Onuris,[3] and another one, referring to the goddess Nekhbet, in a tomb at el-Kab.[4] This phenomenon shows that we are not dealing purely with the theology of Amun-Re, but with formulations of a more general concept of the divine that—if the somewhat disrespectful comparison be permitted—could display the images of other deities like a clip-on picture frame. How, then—if not with the vying delimitation of competitive systems—are we to explain this compulsion for theological explication and the unmistakable propagandistic element in these texts? In fact, it was a matter of vying delimitation, but not (at least, not first and foremost) over against other deities, but over against older concepts. *Innovation, not competition, caused the pressure that led to theological explication.*

9.1.2. DIVINE WILL: THE BEGINNINGS OF THE FOURTH DIMENSION

Then: an oracle procession of his majesty (i.e., the god Amun)
without there having been a prior oracle on the "lord's stations" of
    the king.

The entire land fell silent.
"One knows not," said the king's nobles,
the great ones of the palace lowered their faces,
his (i.e., the god's) following said, "Why?"

The "full hearted" became "empty headed,"
their hearts trembled at his oracle.

The god arrived at the "Head of the River" and gave
a very great oracle at the double door of the palace,
which lay alongside the avenue of offering tables.

Then one turned north,
without knowing what he would do.
. . . Then the majesty of the All-Lord (i.e., Amun) inclined
his countenance toward the east and gave a very great oracle
at the western double door of the palace of the hall (named) "I Shall
    Not Leave Him,"
which lies beside "Head of the River."

The mistress of the Two Lands came out from inside the sanctity of
    her palace.
She went to meet the lord of the gods with praises.
Then she threw herself down before his majesty and said:
"How much greater is this than what is usual for your majesty,
O my father, who devises everything that exists,
what is it that you desire to happen?
I shall certainly act according to your plans."[5]

Thus begins the preserved portion of the account of her coronation that
Hatshepsut had recorded at Karnak and Deir el-Bahari. It reads like the
transcript of a novel religious experience. On the occasion of a festival
procession, the god went beyond the framework of "what was usual"
for him and began to "give a very great oracle," that is, to make his will
known through spontaneous movements. The divine will was aimed at
the choice and elevation of Hatshepsut to the kingship, a step that
doubtless also exceeded the framework of the usual in the political
sphere and could be justified only by a supernatural intervention. But
it would be incorrect to interpret the events as the staging of a legit-
imization of an unusual—female—succession to the throne. This is the
first but in no way the last time that we hear of oracles, of spontaneous
proclamations of divine will. Here we see the beginning of something
that was to become an ever more decisive factor in religious life, and
not just in Egypt. Such an effective form of religious experience was not
invented on an ad hoc basis. For it to attain such importance, it must
have had an indubitable reality for all, even for the beneficiaries of
these divine favors. We thus see no reason to cast doubt on the authen-
ticity of this experience. Rather, we must try to view both aspects of this
new reality and accord each its proper place: on the one hand, the experience of the "virulence" of a personal god who makes interventions,
"devises what exists" and asserts his will, and on the other hand, the

relationship between festival and propaganda, which would become a basic feature of the religious expression of politics in Egypt and would be used especially in the later periods of history by the Kushites, the Ptolemies, and the Romans to legitimize their (foreign) rule.

Amun was a new god, not because his name now appeared for the first time in the sources or because his cult was first founded at this time—both went back to the Old Kingdom at Thebes—but because he now showed himself from a new perspective, or in a new way, because novel religious experiences were now connected with his essence, experiences that did not fit in with the traditional dimensions of the experience of divine presence. The most striking feature of this new god was his will and the bewildering spontaneity and "virulence" with which he translated his will into deed and intervened in history. The *terminus technicus* for this new form of revealing his will was *biꜣt*, derived from a word for iron, a rare and strange substance that fell from the sky and thus embodied the unusual and supernatural, the unearthly and unheard of. Religious festivals were the only place where these new, unaccustomed experiences of divine intervention could be accommodated in the traditional institutions of religious life.

With this new institution of oracle processions, with the staging and at the same time the authentic experience of the supernatural, of the tangible, personal intervention of the god, festival occasions changed their character and assumed a tremendous new importance. From far and near, people flocked to Thebes to be present at the Opet festival and to take part in the new experience of a new divine presence. The festival became an occasion of pilgrimage and thus the locus of a great public gathering that united the land and served as an ideal stage for royal propaganda. From this time on, royal building activity was aimed first and foremost at the decoration of this stage: festival halls and processional ways, way stations and memorial chapels, pylons and hypostyle halls all served to embellish the route traversed by the god, lending institutional form to the new, fourth dimension of the experience of divine presence that was ever more powerfully emerging.

It is seldom that we can date things so accurately. This earliest preserved report of an oracle even states *expressis verbis* that no oracle had occurred previously and bears all the signs of an experience of something new and unheard of. And at precisely the same time, offering prayers in tomb inscriptions add eulogistic divine titularies to the name of Amun-Re, commencing the theological work on the essence of this god; and the custom began of adding hymns to Amun-Re on the thicknesses of the entrances to tombs and on statuettes representing persons in prayer. All these innovations are obviously related. Hatshepsut and Tuthmosis III founded and propagated not a new religion, but a new form of Amun religion that was enhanced by the fourth dimension. Religious consciousness had changed, and these monarchs, in particular Queen Hatshepsut, made themselves the champions of the new. It is certainly anything but a coincidence that this same Hatshepsut took up the myth of the "engendering of the son," which was related in the traditional categories of divine intervention in history, and placed her own destiny in the light of this traditional story (see chapter 5.3). All of this monarch's inscriptions are stamped with the same spirit of personal religious experience and of the confessional pathos of public sermons that later would characterize both the religion of Amarna and the "personal piety" of the Ramesside Period.

Like the cultic institutionalizing of this new dimension in the framework of the (pilgrimage) festival and the oracle procession, the theological determination of the essence of the "new" god centered on the idea of his will. In the brief words of praise with which she responds to the god's unprecedented revelation of his will, Hatshepsut herself reduces this theologumenon to the most concise formula imaginable: "who devises (thinks, plans) everything that exists."[6] The will of the god does not refer merely to this or that detail (e.g., that Hatshepsut is to ascend the throne), but to "everything that exists." This formulation defines the world as will and conception, and more specifically as the will and conception *of the god*. The world springs from the will of the god, and it owes its continuing reality to his thinking and planning intentionality. In terms of creation theology, the notion of creation through the word corresponds to this concept of the divine, and creative utterance now seems to become more commonly tangible in the texts for the first time. But it is usually not "everything that exists," all of reality, but in particular the divine realm that proceeds from the mouth of the god. The concept of creative utterance does not in the first instance interpret the relationship of "god" to the world, but of "god" to the other gods. These gods embody the hidden verbal order of the world, as it were, its conception, as it was devised and uttered by "god," the one who, as it is expressed in a contemporary hymn,

creates what is created,
who speaks, and the gods come into being.[7]

A similar formulation occurs in a longer text of fundamental importance for the theology of Amun in this period, Papyrus Boulaq 17 (Catalogue générale of the Cairo Museum 58038), which contains hymns to Amun-Re.[8] There are indications that this text predates the New Kingdom, for critical portions already occur on a statuette of Dynasty 17. It thus represents a sort of "missing link" between the theological discourse of the New Kingdom and the scattered attempts at explicit theology in the Middle Kingdom. The god of Hatshepsut and Tuthmosis III was thus in no way a new one, but he began to play a determining role in the religious life of the culture at the point when these monarchs allied themselves with him. I shall cite the formulation in its context, which makes it clear that we are dealing with more than creation theology:

> Greetings, Re, lord of *maat*,
> who hides his chapel, lord of the gods,
> Khepri in his barque,
> who commands and the gods come into existence,
> Atum, creator of humankind,
> who distinguishes their characteristics and creates their means of
>   subsistence,
> who distinguishes their skin color, one from the other.
>
> He who listens to the entreaty of one in distress,
> gracious to one who calls to him,
> who saves the timorous from the hand of the violent,
> who pronounces justice between the poor and the rich.
> Lord of cognition, on whose lips is creative word,
> for whose sake the Nile inundation comes;
> the lord of affection, the great of love,
> when he (i.e., the inundation) comes, humankind lives.
>
> He who grants a clear road to every eye
> that was created in Nun;
> whose radiance allows it to become light,
> over whose beauty the gods rejoice,
> at the sight of whom their hearts quicken.[9]

The god from whose will and commanding utterance the other deities emerge is none other than the "lord of *maat*," the ethical authority who "pronounces justice between the poor and the rich," "saves the timorous from the hand of the violent," and "listens to the entreaty of one in distress." We became acquainted with this concept of the god as the goodly herdsman who watches over justness in the Instruction for Merikare, where it is stated of him:

> He has erected a chapel behind them.
> When they weep, he hears.[10]

The hymn takes up this image with the phrase "who hides his chapel." The hidden chapel symbolizes the new dimension of the hidden omnipresence of the god and humankind's personal, direct access to him.

The entire hymn is addressed to Amun-Re, but the passage cited contains only the three names of the sun god, by which the traditional religion adored the morning (Khepri), midday (Re), and evening (Atum) sun. These traditional names are theologically explained as three aspects of the god: as *ethical authority*, the "lord of *maat*" with the hidden chapel, the *will* from whose commanding utterance the other deities originated, and the *creator of the individual*, who creates human beings in their individuality. It is clearly the role of *god of life* that is developed in these three aspects. The continuation makes it clear that inundation and light are important, along with *speech* as the form of the god's effectiveness as ethical authority. All three—speech, Nile inundation, and sunlight—are forms of his solicitous, sustaining maintenance of life. Speech is clearly a transformation of air, which we encountered in Coffin Texts spell 80 as the god of life's form of effectiveness par excellence. Amun theology built on these concepts and surpassed them with its idea of a god who sustains the world through his will and his word (which are one and the same), by thinking it and continually causing it to emerge from his consciousness. As god of life, Amun is a *god who speaks*, a god who speaks and hears what is right, who imparts instructions, who pronounces judgments, who discerns and decides, a god of consciousness/convictions and thus of ethics, a personal god and thus a god of personal devotion and decision.

In this sense, as a distinct, personal god of life defined by speech, will, and consciousness, and as ethical authority, Amun was a new god, and his worship was a new religion. In his greatness, he was not, like the other deities, undeniably always already present, capable of being experienced, and accessible to humankind in the three dimensions of traditional religion. Rather, individuals first had to become aware of his greatness, to make themselves conscious of him, to turn to him inwardly in an act of conscious decision and devotion: as the Egyptian formulation puts it, "to place him in their heart." In his mysterious omnipresence, this god was beyond the traditional dimensions of divine presence. In the *temples*, in the *cosmos*, and in the *texts*, he was a hidden god. He was not there for everyone like breath in the nose. He was omnipotent and omnipresent, but he was the personal god of life only for those who placed him in their heart:

Father and mother for the one who places him in his heart,
who turns away from him who passes heedlessly by his city.[11]

He grants life only to whom he wishes,
great old age to the one who places him in his heart,
the breath of his mouth to the one who stands in his favor.
The one who forever does not cease to gaze upon him.[12]

He who gives the breath of life to him to prays to him,
who makes lifetime excellent for him who "acts upon his waters."[13]

Amun's religion was a matter of conscious decision and heed. It did not suffice to feel close to this god in the temple, in the cosmos, and in sacred texts. It was imperative to make oneself conscious of him, to "place him in one's heart" and to act "on his water" at his bidding. His divine presence manifested itself in the course of a lifetime, in the personal history and piety of the individual. But this god also harbored the danger of being unrecognized by individuals. It was possible to "pass heedlessly by" him and not "act upon his water." Thus the necessity of theological work, of preaching and heeding. The human heart was the real temple of this god, who remained concealed in the three traditional "temples": the divine dwellings, the cosmos, and the sacred texts. He had to be preached to the human heart in the language of texts, love of him had to be spread through the land.

> I shall pray to you and make the gods hear
> and people know of your beauty, daily for all time.[14]

> I shall spread love of you through the land.[15]

> I shall tell all people of your power,
> for I have seen your power (?),
> I shall elevate you and lavish praise on you.[16]

This is a new language, expressing a new religion, or a new religious experience, or the experience of a new god. The difficulty of communicating this *movum* by means of traditional religion and its implicit theology should be obvious. It would not be long before there was open conflict.

9.2. The God of Amarna Religion

9.2.1. ORTHODOXY AND HERESY: THE NEGATION OF TRADITION

The religious upheaval of Akhenaten was without doubt *the* event in the religious history of the New Kingdom. Briefly put, it amounted to the replacement of the entire pantheon of traditional religion by a single and, as such, a new god. This new god is known by the name Aten, but he had a much longer name, one that itself represented a piece of explicit theology. What was important and decisive about this act, what distinguishes it as the central event in the history of the religion, notwithstanding the fact that it was an episode of perhaps twenty years' duration?

On the whole, and correctly, scholars have viewed the religion of Amarna as important because it was a monotheism that proclaimed the oneness of the divine. But it seems to me that it possessed a formal characteristic that was at least as important as the contentual one: that it was not a religion that had evolved naturally, but rather a founded religion, one that consciously opposed itself to tradition and manifested itself as a negation in the latent antithesis between implicit and explicit theology, between the constellative, polytheistic tradition and anticonstellative, monotheistic reflection. The religion of Amarna was the first of those great religions that represented a negation of the polytheistic religions that had evolved naturally. All these religions were founded—the Israelite religion of Moses, Buddhism, Christianity, Islam—and all of them operated with the emotionalism of negation and legitimized themselves as revelation. Tradition can only be overthrown by an incursion from outside. All these religions altered the religious consciousness of the societies in which they made their appearance. Opposing themselves with a gesture of orthodoxy to the (as it were) naturally evolved polytheistic cults, they displaced their adherents from the immanent sacredness of tradition and propelled them radically toward a transcendent salvation. Tradition was rejected as heresy, as lies and deception, and the experience of their negativity must have been a shock to their contemporaries.

This was especially true for Egypt. Whereas the founding of religions in antiquity occurred in a relatively modern religious and intellectual climate that was characterized by a plurality of competing religions and which had already abandoned the security of the individual and society in the unquestioned sanctity of evolved tradition, Akhenaten founded his religion in a world that—aside from the proponents of explicit theology—was solidly and unquestioningly rooted in its polytheistic tradition. What must have been shocking, and what we must on reflection appreciate as the real event in religious history, is less the proclamation of the oneness of the divine than the act of founding a new religion and the associated negation, abolition, and radical abrogation of so massive a reality as the polytheistic religion, which had evolved over thousands of years, which was present in the temples and cults, and which was woven in so many ways into the lives and the daily experience of society.

The founding of the religion must have been all the more shocking in that Akhenaten proceeded with unprecedented brutality. The new religion was not promoted, it was imposed. Tradition was not questioned, it was persecuted and forbidden. A police action was conducted against the very name of the god Amun as the embodiment of "heathendom," and it was hacked out of every monument throughout the land. This was of course just the sign that remains visible today of a general denunciation and persecution of the traditional cults. To appreciate the tremendous and consciousness-altering significance of these steps, we must bear in mind that this new religion did not make its appearance in a situation of competing doctrines of religious salvation or general lack of orientation, but rather set itself against plain reality and reduced it to an excluded alternative. Probably none of this would have been possible without the deep rupture that explicit theology had already effected in the Egyptian world view by means of its opposition to the constellative theology of the polytheistic religion. So long as the new ideas remained themes in a literary metadiscourse, as in the Middle Kingdom, their contrast with the implicit theology of the polytheistic cults was presumably scarcely evident.

With the professionalization of theological discourse in the New Kingdom, however, the explicit theology connected with Amun-Re of Thebes grew into a kind of movement and made the rupture visible in the context of the polytheistic view of the world. Implicit and explicit theology had already begun to distinguish themselves as the old and the new religion, and in this situation characterized by cognitive dissonance lay the significance of Akhenaten, in that he intensified the contradiction between the old and the new by radicalizing the new to the point of irreconcilability. Without this prior crisis in the polytheistic concept of the world, without the tension of cognitive dissonance in a society whose priestly elite had begun to distance themselves ever further from tradition in their theological work on the concept of the divine, Akhenaten's founding of a new religion would scarcely have been possible. These factors in the historical situation were of course nothing more than necessary, and in no way sufficient, conditions for what happened around 1360 B.C.E. Akhenaten's personal achievement as a theologian and the founder of a religion can in no way be diminished by this historical context of his deeds.

I thus submit that in the case of Amarna religion, it was *not* a case of an incursion from without, notwithstanding the fact that like all founded religions, it legitimized itself as such an incursion, such a revelation. *Rather, it was a radicalized position in the give and take of theological discourse.* To substantiate this thesis, I shall attempt to show that the negating force with which the religion of Amarna, like all founded religions, proceeded against the tradition it branded as false ran in two directions. First of all, as a proclamation of a single god, it opposed itself to polytheism, to plurality in the divine realm. In this respect, it did nothing other than to deepen and to radicalize the opposition that the explicit theology of theological discourse had already posed to the constellative theology of the polytheistic religion. It resolved the cognitive dissonance of what had become the problem of the relationship between unity and diversity by abolishing diversity. It thought the theological discourse through by drawing the logical consequence of its inherently anticonstellative tendency toward monotheism. *This* negating force of Amarna religion was thus an almost seamless continuation of the theological discourse. The other negating force directed itself squarely against the exponent of the theological discourse, against the god Amun-Re. Amarna religion in no way understood itself as a position in a debate, but as an absolutely new reality whose most dangerous opponent must have seemed to be Amun himself. The following treatment of the religion of Amarna is oriented toward this double direction of the negating force it directed at tradition.

9.2.2. THE NEW SOLAR THEOLOGY

Only since the early 1980s have newly discovered texts clarified the theological context of Amarna religion. Previously, scholars had mostly referred to the hymn to Amun-Re on papyrus Catalogue générale of the Cairo Museum 58038 (*ÄHG*, no. 87), which has already been cited here several times, as a precursor, and to the tomb stela of the architects Suti and Hor from the reign of Amenophis III (*ÄHG*, no. 89) as an early form of the religion of Amarna. Now, however, these allusions are more subtly differentiated. Along with the papyrus in Cairo, the hymns from Amarna demonstrate the affiliation of these new texts with the theological discourse, whose implicit monotheism they elevate to an explicit orthodoxy. The hymn of the two architects does not represent an early form of Amarna religion, though, but rather a theological movement that is now tangible in a whole series of other texts, and which I call the "New Solar Theology." These texts date to shortly before Amarna, and there is no doubt that Amarna religion sprang from this movement and represented a radical variant of the New Solar Theology.[17] But as the new texts demonstrate, this movement was in no way a variant or early form of Amarna religion, for if that were the case, it would have vanished along with Amarna. In fact, these texts pick up after the Amarna Period at exactly the point at which this new development had been interrupted by Akhenaten's upheaval and continue down until nearly the end of the history of Egyptian religion, side by side with texts expressing the rehabilitated constellative theology of the course of the sun.

The New Solar Theology can be defined as the explication and representation of the course of the sun in the nonconstellative categories of explicit theology. What it signified becomes clear if we bear in mind the central role that the course of the sun played in Egyptian polytheism and what an inexhaustible multitude of icons and constellations the constellative thought of the traditional religion had seen in these cosmic processes, which it explained as actions in a realm populated by deities. The New Solar Theology arose as a cognitive iconoclasm that rejected the entire mythic, pictorial world of polytheistic thought. It confined itself strictly to visible reality. All its basic principles can be understood as theological explications of cosmic phenomena, specifically the sun, its light, and its movement. Summarized briefly, they are

The Sun

1. *is alone in the sky, so that the sun god accomplishes his course in complete solitude:*

> You have placed yourself in the sky, you being alone.[18]

> You sole sun, whose rays are in the face![19]
> You sole sun—how many are your embodiments![20]

2. *is distant, so that the sun god is inaccessibly distant and unfathomable in his essence:*

> He has distanced himself on high, no one knows his form.[21]

> High one, whom no one can reach. . . .
> Hidden one, whose appearance is not known![22]

3. *is distant, but its light is on the earth:*

> who comes near the face, though he is afar,
> for every face faces him.
> One spends the day gazing upon him and cannot be satisfied.[23]

> You distant one in Light-land—
> your rays touch the faces.[24]

> Distant and (yet) near,
> whom one cannot discern![25]

> Very, very distant, too mysterious to reach,
> yet his rays penetrate the earth![26]

Light

4. *opens up the world, making it visible and useful to humankind:*

> Every road is filled with your light.[27]
> Light on every road.[28]
> Are you not the guide on all the roads?[29]

5. *fills the world with the incarnate visibility and "beauty" of the sun god:*

> No place is devoid of his light.[30]
> You bestow your beauty throughout the lands.[31]

Sky and earth are penetrated by your beauty.[32]
All lands are filled with love of him.[33]

6. *reveals the god who is hidden in it:*

> You cross the sky, and every face sees you,
> (though) your course is hidden from their face.[34]

> You are in view, though your course is hidden.[35]

7. *grants the ability to see to all eyes: all eyes see by means of you:*

> You are the eyes themselves,
> one sees by means of you![36]

8. *gives life to all creatures, who live on the sight of the god (on the light of the sun):*

> Every face lives on the sight of your beauty.[37]
> No eye lives that does not see you.[38]
> No one lives who does not see you.[39]

9. *is the gaze of the god, with which he beholds his creation:*

> Beautiful one, who descends from the sky
> to view what he has created on earth![40]

> You pass by over all that you alone have created
> and behold them, you being alone.[41]

> Who rises in the sky day after day
> to gaze on the lands he has created.[42]

Compare the Instruction for Merikare (see chapter 3.2.1, text at note 4):

> to gaze on them, he crosses (in the sky).[43]

Movement

10. *is the "work" of the god, which he accomplishes by rising and setting with miraculous constancy:*

> He accomplishes his tasks daily
> and does not hesitate to do what he did yesterday,
> who strives without wearying.[44]

11. *is—considering both space and time—miraculously swift:*

> The day is young, the course is broad,
> millions and hundreds of thousands of miles.
> You have accomplished it in a brief moment.[45]

12. *in the periodicity of his movement, the god ever again creates himself as a new and yet the same being:*

> You are newer today than yesterday,
> while you spend the night, you are already (set) for the day.[46]

> God of yesterday,
> who is born today.[47]

13. *creates time with its cyclical, rhythmic regularity:*

> Who creates plenitude of time and produces lastingness,
> who divides night and day.[48]

> Who creates the years and brings forth the months,
> who makes the days and fixes the hours,
> lord of lifetime by means of whom it is calculated.[49]

> Who creates the years and binds the months,
> days, nights, and hours, corresponding to his course.[50]

14. *and along with time, creates transitoriness:*

> each day under you is a moment,
> it passes when you set.[51]

15. *and along with time, creates the lifetime (ʿḥʿw) of every living creature, in whom individual existence and destiny can unfold:*

> You traverse the sky to create lifetime,
> to enliven men and gods.[52]

The New Solar Theology appears to be an inexhaustible source of such theological interpretations of cosmic phenomena. Radically rejecting the constellative mythology and iconography of the course of the sun, it replaces it with a religious phenomenology that proceeds from the visible appearance of divine actions, thus demythologizing solar theology and demythicizing the world view. The realm of images is rejected, leaving vision open to a new reality. The horizon that had been hemmed in by mythic images was opened up, setting free a veritable natural philosophy that nevertheless remained also a theological conception and interpretation of the cosmos. This was a cognitive revolution that cannot simply be equated with what would happen at Amarna. To be sure, Amarna would be inconceivable without this cognitive revolution. The reverse, however, was not true. Akhenaten's religious revolution was undone after his death. A cognitive revolution, however, cannot be undone, for breakthroughs at the cognitive level are irreversible. In the wake of newly won discoveries, one cannot go back again. Even after Amarna, the New Solar Theology remained a determining factor in theology and the religious world view.

The discovery, the cognitive breakthrough that revolutionized the Egyptian world view in a nearly Copernican manner, consisted of an inexhaustible multitude of phenomena it connected with the motion and the radiant light of the sun, and which the New Solar Theology generalized into the proposition that all life, indeed all existence and all reality in general, was a creation of the sun, one that was continually created anew each day. Light was not only considered to be the "sight" (9) and the "incarnation" of the sun god—his "beauty" (5) and "love"—but even the breath of life that the sun beamed to the embryo in its mother's womb. The hymn of the two architects lauds the sun god as "the Khnum and Amun of humankind."[53] Khnum was the god who formed the child in its mother's womb, and Amun the one who imparted the breath of life to it. The hymns to Amun from the Cairo papyrus already call him "the one who gives breath to the one in the egg."[54]

This tracing back of all reality to the single source of the sun god, who continually creates through his radiant light and his time-creating motion (which are thus the two fundamental cosmogonic energies), expresses a generalizing and universalizing attitude that must be viewed in the context of Egypt's general openness to the world during the New Kingdom. The old conception of Egypt as the cosmos, as an island in the midst of chaos, was obliged to yield to a new picture of the world that included the rapidly expanding Egyptian political horizon. Gifts, tribute, and trade goods were flowing in from all regions of the world: from Mycenae and Knossos, from the Hittites and the Assyrians, from Mitanni and Babylon, Libya, Nubia, and distant Punt. Often and convincingly, the universalism of Amarna religion has been connected with the historical processes of the New Kingdom, with Egypt's rise to the status of a world power in the international arena, which was ordered by international law. I wish to emphasize this connection, but also to state more precisely that this was not something specific to the religion of Amarna, but rather that it was the Zeitgeist of the era, a cognitive revolution that had found theological expression before Amarna and came to dominate the entire religion of the New Kingdom. The general political situation of the time constituted the historical context of the New Solar Theology, and this in its turn constituted the specific theological context of Amarna religion.

To what extent this last statement is valid can easily be shown with the help of the texts. For the fifteen categories we used to characterize the New Solar Theology, precisely corresponding formulations can be adduced for nearly all of them from the texts at Amarna. I need not make such an attempt in detail here, for any reader can easily be convinced by consulting, for instance, the collection of translations made by Schlögl (1983, pp. 71–88). Here I shall cite only some formulations in which the Amarna texts are especially apposite and precise, and perhaps go even further than the New Solar Theology. I shall follow the same ordering of the categories.

1. *uniqueness:*

You living sun, besides whom there is no other.[55]

3. *distance and closeness:*

He is in the sky and also on earth.[56]
You are distant, but your rays are on earth.[57]

4. *accessibility of the world:*

Every road is open by means of your shining.[58]

5. *parousia, "beauty," "love":* passim.

6. *manifestness and hiddenness:*

He is in our sight, but we do not know his body.[59]
You are in their sight, but no one can know your passage.[60]

7. *"all eyes see by means of you":* passim, for instance:

The one who makes eyes for all that he has created.[61]
You are father and mother for those whose eyes you have created.
When you rise, they see by means of you.[62]

8. *seeing = living:* passim
   And note, in addition to the usual phraseology, the theologically sophisticated formulation of the Short Hymn to the Aten:

Millions of lives are in you, to enliven them,
the breath of life for the nose is the sight of your rays.[63]

9. the god beholds the world:

> You have made the sky distant so as to ascend to it,
> to behold everything you have created, you unique one.[64]

10. work, constancy:

> Constant in rising and setting,
> day after day, without cease.[65]

13–15. *creation of time as a cosmic dimension and as individual lifetime:*

> Who binds the years and creates the months,
> who makes the days and reckons the hours,
> lord of lifetime, through whom they can be reckoned.[66]

> You set each one in his place and create their sustenance,
> each one has his nourishment, and his lifetime is reckoned.[67]

> The earth comes into being at your nod, as you have created it,
> you rise, and they live,
> you set, and they die,
> you are lifetime itself: one lives through you.[68]

The last passage in particular, which is from the Great Hymn to the Aten, demonstrates impressively the clarity and logic with which Akhenaten thought through and reformulated the postulates of the New Solar Theology.

The content of the theological position of Amarna religion had already been almost entirely arrived at by the New Solar Theology. Summarizing this position, we must stress in particular the consistent "heliomorphism" of this divine concept. In this theology, all statements about the divine are derived from the figure of the sun. The god is none other than the sun, and his effectiveness consists in light and motion. The polytheistic concept of the cosmos had explained the sun's course not as an action, but as a network of interrelated actions in which the sun god played both active and passive, transitive and intransitive roles in various constellations in the divine realm as his "sphere of belonging." This is the form in which a constellative theology conceives of a god as a person and of divine effectiveness as action. To think of the sun as a deity meant to unfold him into the constellations of a "sphere of belonging." This personal unfolding was reversed in the New Solar Theology. The demythologizing of the sun's course led to the concept of a single, solitary god who did not precede the world as a primeval god, as in the preexistence and creation theology of the Middle Kingdom, but who eternally confronted it in the distant sky across which he coursed. Instead of the god's implication in the world in the form of his constellative inclusion in the realm of the divine, there was a distant confrontation of god and world; this was no longer a constellation, for there could be no other constellations beyond it. Instead of the interrelated actions of his active and passive self-unfolding, there was the *single*, one-sided active action in which he turned to the world, enlivening it through the "work" of his course, with the world correspondingly passive and reduced to the status of an object of his creative and life-giving action. Instead of the "life" of the sun god, there was the work of endowing the world with life, and instead of the complex web of his personal, constellative implication in the world, there was the simple confrontation of god and world, with the divine realm demythologized into the world (or better, "nature"), into the mere object and vessel of his life-endowing action.

The extent to which this last position had already been attained in the New Solar Theology remains an open question. It is certain that the sun god worked alone and "heliomorphically" in nothing other than his radiant light and his motion. But it is difficult to decide whether this work was already seen as the only effective agency in the world, capable of explaining everything. The New Solar Theology stood, and understood itself, in the context of the other deities. By way of an example, the frame of the stela of the two architects contains offering prayers to, among others, Hathor, Khons, Mut, Amun-Re, Anubis, and the God's Wife Ahmes-Nefertari. Though other deities no longer participated in the course of the sun, they were nevertheless there, and their mere existence stood in the way of a total demythologizing and disenchantment of the world. The question is the extent to which a theological concept, however central it might be, was capable of altering the traditional structure of the experience of divine presence in the three dimensions of cult, cosmos, and myth. Amarna religion, however, proved capable of doing precisely that. Akhenaten's feat was to make a religion out of the New Solar Theology, a religion with cult, iconography, and conceptual dimensioning of divine presence, that is, of religious experience and contact with the divine. The principal difference between the New Solar Theology and the religion of Amarna has to do with the difference between theology and religion.

9.2.3. AMARNA RELIGION

Though the theology of the hymns at Amarna generally corresponds to the position of the New Solar Theology, Egyptian culture was fundamentally altered by the introduction of Amarna religion. We need only put together all the ways in which the Amarna Period differed from tradition to get an idea of what religion meant in this stage of the culture.

Amarna meant a new artistic style, a new iconography, new temple architecture, a new cult with new rituals and festivals, and also a new written language, to name only the most salient features. It is quite clear that this religion also effected an entirely new position on the sacred in the world and a different dimensioning of the possibility of religious communication. These facts are already clear in the iconography.

The religion of Amarna knew no cult statues. The god was worshiped only as the sun, his sole form of manifestation. The principle of symbolic mediation and representation ("indwelling") that defined traditional cult was replaced by the principle of "identitary" incarnation. There were thus no representations of the god in the form of statues. Instead, representations were two-dimensional, all of them included in scenes in sunk relief. This last point strikes me as especially interesting, for it confirms yet again the connection between "icon" and "constellation." Even Amarna religion, which had abolished all the constellations of traditional religion and constellative thought generally, and, in a consistent continuation of the New Solar Theology, had set the sun god vis-à-vis the earth in his uniqueness and his solitude, could represent the god only in action—and that means, in a constellation. The god could not be represented "in himself," in the uniqueness of his celestial existence, as expressly stated:

Who builds himself with his own arms,
artists do not know him.[69]

The god could be represented only in a constellation with the royal couple, in connection with an act that was itself embedded in a great context that embraced sky and earth. But it was the king (usually accompanied by the queen) who performed this act.

In these representations (see Figure 6), the god is pictured as a round disk with a distinctly convex bulge, and thus probably a sphere. Amarna religion evidently conceived of the sun as a globe, unlike the disk of traditional Egyptian belief. Below the sun rears a uraeus-serpent, from which hangs a hieroglyph signifying "life." Rays emanate downward from the sun, ending in hands, the sole vestige of anthropomorphism. The hands extend hieroglyphs for "life" to the noses of the king and queen, who were no mere mortals, or lie in blessing (or acceptance?) on the offerings and other earthly objects. This representational concept had no precursor in Egyptian art. Traditionally, the sun disk with its outstretched wings had always hovered over scenes inactively, like an emblem. There are verbal precursors, however, as in a passage from the hymn to Amun in Cairo; as one of the most explicit representatives of theological discourse, it develops an anticonstellative concept of the god of life standing over against the world in unique solitude with the following formulation:

Greetings, you who accomplish all this,
single sole one with many arms![70]

Precursors also exist in the writing system: the pictorial concept of the radiant Aten is clearly derived from a hieroglyph that means "light" (though not "sun"). To judge from the iconography, the god of Amarna religion was conceived of not just as a sun god, but also as the god of light. It might have been thought that this "personal union" was obvious and lay in the nature of things. This is perhaps physically but not historically correct. Like many people who have lived close to nature, the Egyptians did not originally make a causal connection between daylight and the light of the sun. In the Coffin Texts, it is Shu, god of the air, who "makes it light after the darkness." The word *shu* originally meant "light-filled air," and although it served as a divine name designating the god of air, its meaning as a lexeme changed in favor of "light." Evidently hidden behind Amarna religion was a physical concept that perceived the connection between daylight and the sun while retaining the connection between light and air. The god of this religion was the sun, which filled and penetrated the earth in the form of air replete with light.

This representation is always accompanied by an explanatory caption—the lengthy name of the new god, which on the analogy of the royal titulary was written in two cartouches:

(Re-Harakhty, who rejoices in Light-land)
(in his name Light, which is in the sun).

This formulation, which still contained the divine name Re-Harakhty and that of the air god Shu, which was homonymous with the word for "light," was later changed to

(Ruler of the horizon, who rejoices in Light-land)
(in his name as Light which comes from the sun).

However we are to understand this complex formulation, it is clear that we are dealing with an item of explicit theology. With it, a theology that has congealed into an orthodoxy is attempting a precise definition of the essence of the god, one that excludes any misunderstanding or error of interpretation, which we understand only when we know what it was directed against. The affirmative content of the formulation can be reconstructed only by reading it as a negation. What is negated here are the dimensions of divine presence that had been integrated into the world view of traditional religion. The new god did not take the place of individual deities such as Amun or the sun god, but rather of the divine realm as a whole, and he was obliged to make a fresh definition of his immanence, his accessibility, his capability of being experienced.

"Who rejoices in Light-land" refers to the cultic-local dimension, to the idea of the earthly residence of the divine. Light-land is normally the celestial, cosmic locale of the deity, but here, it also refers to the city of Amarna, whose ancient Egyptian name was "Light-land of Aten (i.e., the sun)." "In his name as Light . . ." refers to the verbal dimension of divine presence. What is meant is that the god has Light as his name, not in the sense that he is called light, but in the sense that light embraces all that can be said about this god. His essence is manifest in light, not in myths and genealogies. With that, the three dimensions of divine presence are reduced to the single dimension of the cosmic. *There is no divine presence other than light.* For this reason, the temples consisted of open courts, and mythology and speculation were discarded in favor of a theology that exhausted itself in a theological interpretation of sunlight.

The hymns in which this theology of light is developed constitute the apogee of religious poetry in Egypt. Their unique beauty is explained on the one hand by their theologically grounded confinement to a nature flooded by light and to visibility as the sole dimension of divine presence, and on the other hand by the unique explicative pressure under which this new religion placed itself. In these hymns, which were doubtless written by the king himself, a new teaching had to be developed in an obligatory form and propagated among the people. Thus emerged texts of unprecedented clarity and explicitness. By way of an example, the notion of endowing the embryo in the womb with life, which had been touched on in older texts with brief turns of expression ("who gives breath to the one in the egg," "Khnum and Amun of humankind"), was now expanded into an embryological tractate of no fewer than eighteen verses. Confinement to the visible precluded any theological speculation about creation, for the creative power of the god had to be demonstrated in the visible present. It was thus that embryology replaced creation theology, along with another theme that I call the "beneficent order of the world." The creator discloses himself to the beholding eye in the plenitude and the demonstrable order of his works. The Great Hymn to the Aten develops this theme in thirty verses that twice culminate in an astonished cry:

How many are your works,
which are hidden from view,
you sole god, whose like does not exist![71]

How effective are your plans,
O lord of the plenitude of time![72]

This hymn praises the diversity of creatures, the many forms of life, the various races and languages of humankind, and the varied living requirements of these people. While the Egyptians lived on the Nile, the god had "placed a Nile in the sky" in the form of rain. Plenitude and order—precisely that which is also wonderingly praised in Psalm 104:

> O Lord, how manifold are your works!
> You have created them all in wisdom.

Verses 20 through 30 of Psalm 104 go back to the Great Hymn to the Aten. Its theme—the demonstration of the life-endowing, creative effectiveness of the god in a world demythologized into "nature"— made the text theologically acceptable, and its unique clarity and explicitness were capable of being translated. This relationship was recognized by scholars at an early date, after which it was cast into doubt. But the evaluation of night as the absence of the divine is decisive. In the Amarna hymn, we read

> When you set in the western Light-land,
> the earth is in darkness,
> in the condition of death. . . .
> Every beast of prey comes out of its den,
> every worm bites.[73]

In Psalm 104, we find

> You create darkness, and it is night.
> Then all the beasts of the forest rise.
> The young lions roar for prey,
> begging their food from God.
> When the sun rises, they withdraw
> and lie down in their dens.

This negative valuation of night as the suspension of the divine, life-endowing light is specific to Amarna religion. The psalmist could not have derived the inspiration for his verses from any later Egyptian text. In the alternation of day and night, the god gives life to the world and takes it away:

> When you rise, they live,
> when you set, they die.[74]

The psalm expresses the idea, stripped of its specifically solar form, thus:

> When you hide your face, they are in terror.
> When you take (your) breath away, they perish and return to dust.
> When you send forth your breath, they are created, and you renew
>   the form of the earth.

This very motif already occurs in one of the Amarna Letters (no. 147), in a verse cited by Abimilki of Tyre in his letter to the Egyptian king; it is most likely translated from Egyptian and in any case is of Egyptian inspiration:

Who gives life through his sweet breath
and diminishes (it) through his might.[75]

In this single instance, we have a connecting link between Egyptian, Canaanite, and biblical poetry. Yet Moran, basing his work on an article by Grave,[76] renders these verses as

qui accorde la vie par son doux souffle
et revient avec son vent du nord.[77]

It seems evident to me, however, that the idea of the god's intermittent injection of life into the world is common both to the Psalm and to the Egyptian hymn. The "sweet breath" that appears in the Bible as *ruach* is a common Egyptian metaphor both for time and light. "The sight of your rays," we read in the Shorter Hymn, "is the breath of life in their noses."[78] Naturally, this does not mean that biblical monotheism goes back to Amarna, as Sigmund Freud in particular affirmed in his influential *Moses and Monotheism*. The theological connection consists simply in a certain relationship of the respective concepts of nature: in the concept of a nature that has been demythologized but is nevertheless creaturely and intimately connected to the creator, so that its very existence is itself a great hymn to the deity who created it.

In the tradition of the theological discourse, Akhenaten's god represents the idea of the "god of life" in its purest form of expression. In this regard, he most nearly resembles the god Shu in the Middle Kingdom theological concept treated in chapter 8.5, in which the air god Shu is explained as "life" and as "plenitude of time." These are the two central concepts of Aten theology. Where he is not called by his lengthy theological name, he is regularly styled "the living sun," and the word *neheh*, "plenitude of time," is used as if it were another personal name of the god. Eliminating all other aspects of uniqueness that the "additive" Amun theology of Dynasty 18 had heaped on its god—primeval god, creator god, and especially ethical authority (this aspect is discussed in the next section)—Amarna theology concentrated on the single aspect of god of life, and with its uniquely explicit and penetrating description of visible reality, it strove to trace everything back to a single source of life: the sun. We stand here at the threshold less of the monotheistic universal religions than of natural philosophy, and had this religion won out, we might have expected a Thales rather than a Moses. The sun continually created reality through light and motion, that is, through visibility and temporality. The inexhaustible living energy of the sun—"millions of lives are in you, to give them life"[79]—radiated into his creatures through the rays of the sun, considered as the breath of life, and the world, made visible and accessible and ordered by his light, emerged from the god as his embodiment:

> You create millions of embodiments from yourself, alone:
> cities and towns,
> fields, roads, and river.[80]

Through its movement, the sun also created time, in which the world, formed and endowed with life, could unfold daily: "You are lifetime itself—one lives through you."[81]

9.2.4. REPRESENTATIVE THEOCRACY — CONCEPTUALIZATION OF DIVINE ACT

Notwithstanding all his "cosmosizing" and "heliomorphosizing" of the concept of the divine, Akhenaten still clung to the explanation of cosmic processes as action, as made clear by the text passages already cited. The New Solar Theology had already replaced the network of actions of the traditional world view, in which the sun god was entangled as both an agent and one acted on, actively and passively, transitively and intransitively, with a single, transitive action of a single god; replaced constellated interaction with action; and replaced life and rulership with the animation and domination of the world by the god. The world had thus already been demoted to the status of object of divine action, notwithstanding the fact that the other deities still had a place in it. Akhenaten pursued this path to its logical conclusion by dispensing with the other deities. The polytheistic world view, which conceived of the relationship between the sun god and the world as interaction and as a differentiated, constellative involvement of the god in a realm populated by deities, had granted the world a differentiated, divine life of its own. The new world view, which set the distant sun over against the world, had undifferentiated it. Akhenaten did away with its divine status.

This tradition of a solar understanding of nature—the "reading" of nature from both the manifest and the hidden effects of the sun's light and movement—has already been traced back to the implicit theology of wall reliefs of Old Kingdom date in connection with the cosmic dimension of divine presence. In this regard, Akhenaten effected a breakthrough in an area that had presumably concerned Egyptian religion from the very beginning without ever dominating it: the cosmic dimension. We must now inquire as to the manner in which this dimension can be reconciled with the category of action that is con-

nected to the concept of the creator god as a person and thus to the
third dimension of speech and semantics, of sociality and communication. In other words, in a world devoid of other deities, who is the
partner of this god? For whom does this god act when he rises in the
sky? The Instruction for Merikare had already supplied an unequivocal response to this question: "for them," for humankind, the "cattle
of the god," his "images that have emerged from his body." This "for
them" occurs often enough in the hymns at Amarna: "They live when
you rise for them."[82] At Amarna, however—and this is new—this
anthropocentric reference that understood the course of the sun as
"work," as the god's service to humanity as a herdsman, was overlaid
by another reference, namely, to the king. The god rises in the sky to
endow his creatures with life, but he does this for the king, his son:

> The rising one, he makes all that exists grow for his son;
> haste has been in every foot since you founded the earth.
> You direct them for your son, who emerged from your body,
> ... Akhenaten.[83]

The god's life-endowing effect relates to the creatures, but his rule-
endowing effect relates to the king:

> Your rays embrace the lands to the end of your entire creation,
> as Re, you reach their boundaries
> and subject them to your beloved son.[84]

Light and time, the two forms of divine act, have a double explanation. Not only do they repeatedly endow the world with new life,
existence, and reality, but in doing so, they maintain it in an equally
perfect state of dependence.

> At your nod, the earth comes into being as you created it:
> you rise, and they live,
> you set, and they die.[85]

This dependency is explained as the god's rulership over the world. As
the sole source of life, the sun is lord over life and death. The god subjects the world and makes it obligated to him by means of his rays, and
the task of the king is to administer it for the god and to make offerings
to him of what the god had obligated to himself through his rays.

> What is under the sky, to its end,
> all that your rays behold,
> belongs to your son as you created it,
> that he may gladden your heart with it.[86]

Life and rulership, these two age-old categories in the religious explanation of the course of the sun (see *ÄHG*, pp. 35–63), transitively restated as enlivening and mastery, now became the central conceptual categories of divine action. The theme of domination is what was expressed by writing the god's name in cartouches. The god's rule over the world was realized as a theocracy. It was not, however, an "identitary" theocracy (borrowing from the terminology of political science), but rather a "representative" one. The god exercised his rule with and through his son. This was the only real constellation left in Amarna theology. It was constructed in the form of a triad, for it included the queen as well as the king. The official proclamation of this divine rule reads

> Live the king and father (Re-Harakhty, who rejoices in Light-land)
> (in his name Light, which is in the sun), who gives life forever and
> ever; the lord of the Two Lands (Akhenaten), great of lifetime; the
> mistress of the Two Lands (Nefertiti), who lives forever.[87]

Structurally, this constellation is identical to that developed in Coffin Texts spell 80, a text we classified as "theological discourse" and thus as belonging to the tradition of explicit theology. Akhenaten, who stood in that tradition, must have known this text, or at least the theological concept that lies behind it:

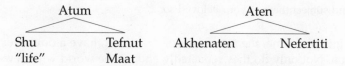

This is the triad of Amarna as it was represented on the stelae of household altars (Figure 6). This triad was the object of household cults and private devotion, and it was the only form in which the new god was accessible to the piety of the individual. The rich constructed small sanctuaries with three altars for this triad in the gardens of their villas. The king and the queen prayed to the god, and the people prayed to the triad. It was only in this triad that the cosmic life force of the sun manifested itself as a god in act and was accessible to the prayerful devotion of humankind. In the religion of Amarna, piety was a relationship between the god and the king (father and son) on the one hand, and between the king and the people on the other hand. Direct human piety toward the god was excluded, for outside the theocratic constellation, the god was nothing other than the sun, than life-giving power. Piety is an act of turning toward that presupposes the possibility of turning away, and thus presupposes conscious decision. Piety means to place a deity "in one's heart." In Amarna religion,

FIGURE 6. Akhenaten and Nefertiti. Berlin Egyptian Museum 14145.
From *Nofretete · Echnaton* (Berlin, 1976), no. 78.

it was just this form of personal piety that was reserved for the king,
as the only one who had placed the god in his heart and as the only
one to whom the individual could make a pious decision to turn.

> I am your son, who is beneficial to you
> and who elevates your name;
> your power and your might are fast in my heart,[88]

says Akhenaten in the Short Hymn to the Aten, whereas in the Great
Hymn, we read

> When you are gone, and there is no longer an eye
> whose sight you have created,
> so that you must not see yourself alone,
> and that which you have created,
> even then you remain in my heart,
> for there is no other who knows you
> besides your son, Akhenaten.[89]

Amarna religion monopolized piety and knowledge of the god—in Egypt, the two were inseparable, for the heart was the seat of emotions and knowledge—in the institution of kingship. What that meant is made clear in the following section.

9.2.5. ATEN AND AMUN

I have already noted that of all the deities of the traditional pantheon, only Amun was systematically persecuted. His name was erased from every monument in the land with a thoroughness that serves us as a reliable criterion for dating: where the name is not destroyed, the monument was built at a later date. This persecution directed specifically at Amun must have had a special meaning. What was expressed was a rejection, a negating force that cannot be comprehended with the categories discussed thus far.

There is a somewhat superficial explanation of this phenomenon that perhaps nevertheless contains a kernel of truth. It has to do with considerations of economic politics. Because of huge donations from the Tuthmosid conquerors, the Theban state god Amun had grown into an economic power that gradually threatened to become dangerous to the kingship. It is doubtless correct that in the local dimension of divine presence, Amun was by far the wealthiest deity, far surpassing all the others. When it became a matter of initiating and endowing the cult of a new god, it was first and foremost Amun whose possessions must have been drawn on for this purpose. The new god also appeared in Amun's role as state god before he was proclaimed to be the only one. This exacerbated the situation. As the symbolic personification of the state and the "father" of the king, Amun was his only rival. But it was surely not as an economic power that Amun was dangerous to the kingship. The donations made to temples were in no way inaccessible to the king. Wars had only to be waged "by command of Amun" to be financed from the temple treasury. Rather, Amun was dangerous to the kingship through that other form of his presence which we have proposed to designate the "fourth dimension." Amun was the speaking god, the divine will that intervened in history, the god who was capable of being immediately experienced by individuals, and to whom the individual could directly turn, the god who in many ways threatened to shrink the king's "monopoly on action." In the god Amun and the fourth dimension of divine presence that he embodied, history, a more far-reaching change in the "structure" of piety in Egyptian religion was heralded than Amarna religion itself meant. In the persecution of Amun, there emerged that other negating force of Amarna religion, one that had a distinctly conservative character and was directed less against the past than against the future. A comparison of the two gods is thus informative with regard to both, and it will help us better to understand not only the religion of Amarna, but also the development that followed it. I shall make this comparison on the basis of certain points that all derive from the confrontation of cosmos as the second dimension of the experience of divine presence, which was absolutized at Amarna, and history as the fourth dimension, which was repressed by Amarna.

Amun, the God Who Went out in Procession

In the context of the cult of Amun, festival processions had gained new importance as occasions for making the god's will known. The whole land would travel to Thebes, which developed into a place of pilgrimage, a holy city of a new sort. Temple architecture took this into account and expanded into urban dimensions. What corresponded to this at Amarna? The concept of a procession could not be associated with a purely cosmic, "heliomorphic" god. The sun's only movement was its course in the sky. At Amarna, the king was the god who went out in procession. Architectonically—and thus evidently also ideologically—the concept of procession played an even greater role at Amarna than at Thebes. The layout of the great Aten temple is practically a caricature of the principle of a processional way. The king's procession is the most popular theme in Amarna iconography. The many kiosks and windows for royal public appearances took the place of the way stations at Thebes. In the framework of Amarna religion, the public appearances of the royal family had a hierophanic quality; they were manifestations of the god who, as the sun, was inaccessible to the personal devotion of the people. The divine was personally present to the people only in the ceremonial processions of the king.

Amun, the Speaking God

Amun was the god who "devised what exists," from whose verbally articulated will reality arose, although he did not express himself in speech, but rather through the code of his barque's movements in processional oracles. With him was connected a new form of dialogue between king and god, lengthy exchanges in which the king praised the god and the god proclaimed his will and his pleasure in speeches that were in part highly poetical. There was nothing of that at Amarna. At Amarna, we have superb royal hymns, but not a single fragment of divine response. The god's "expression" was confined entirely to light. In the Great Hymn to the Aten, while Akhenaten says, "You cause him (i.e., the king) to know your plans and your might,"[90] this is not a verbal revelation, but rather an "enlightening" of the king, on whom the true meaning and the correct explanation of the divine light has dawned. Aten was a silent god. The concept of oracles, of miraculous signs, of unforeseeable interventions, was unthinkable at Amarna.

Amun, the Ethical Authority, the Judge and the Helper of the Needy

Nothing is more characteristic of the conservative tendency of Amarna religion than the complete elimination of this aspect from its concept of the divine. The function of divine judge, which had its origin in the problem of theodicy, was one of the central concepts in the explicit theology of the Middle Kingdom. The divine judge plays an important role in the Instruction for Merikare and the hymns to Amun on papyrus Cairo CG 58038,[91] two texts that were known in the Amarna Period. In both texts, the role is particularly connected with the sun god, and it was only when he was equated with Amun that the latter became an ethical authority. In view of the unmistakable similarity of the hymns at Amarna to these two texts, the omission of this important, ethical aspect of the god is doubly striking. It is in royal texts that we find the corresponding phraseology. The king is the one who "lives on Maat" and looks after the poor, the god of destiny whose will and grace decide the fortunes of the individual. At Amarna, the divine role of judge and helper, of "ethical authority," was thus one of the personal aspects of the deity that could be experienced by individuals only in connection with the king, and which the king thus made manifest as the representative of the god. As the sun, the god shone over the just and the unjust. His judging, punishing, and saving will was embodied in the king alone.

Amun, the God of the Individual

A Theban text says of Amun,

> Father and mother of the one who places him in his heart,
> but who turns away from the one who passes heedlessly by his city.[92]

At Amarna, the god is also called "mother and father" (and always in that order):

> You are mother and father for those whose eyes you have created;
> when you rise, they see by means of you.[93]

Such predicates are characteristic of the New Solar Theology as a whole:

> You are mother and father for all eyes,
> you rise for them daily, to create life for them.[94]

This sounds similar, and perhaps this is why scholars have not noticed what appears to me to be the decisive difference. At Amarna, the status of children of the god was a natural and given relationship that the individual shared indiscriminately with all other human beings, and indeed, with all creatures that had eyes. The individual always already stood in this relationship, regardless of whether it had consciously become his, and it could not be taken away from him. At Thebes, however, to be a child of the god had been a relationship in which the individual placed himself consciously, by "placing the god in his heart," and the god in no way granted it to all indiscriminately, but rather, with perfect reciprocity, only to those who devoted themselves to him.

Amun had confronted the individual with a claim to a decision and to conscious devotion, for he himself was a god of conscious devotion, the divine concept of a new, individualized stage of consciousness, will, and decision. In this respect, Amarna represented an attempt to reverse this thrust at individuation and to confine humanity, vis-à-vis the god, to the undifferentiated collective identity of creatureliness. Reciprocal devotion was restricted to the relationship between the god and the king, on the one hand, and on the other, the king and his officials.

All four aspects discussed here belong to the fourth dimension, and in all of them, it was not the god but the king who took the place of Amun. Considered from the standpoint of the king, the repression of the fourth dimension in Amarna theology has the character of a retaking of a lost or at least an endangered bastion. Religious activity was one of the most important monopolies of the Egyptian kingship. As the one in charge of offerings, cult, and temple architecture, the king was the sole person called and authorized to act before and on behalf of the divine. Although these functions and this authorization were largely delegated to the priesthood, he remained the only person who could have contact with deities in his own right. The possibility of direct contact with the divine on the part of individual human beings, of their acting before and on behalf of the divine, did not exist in the traditional three dimensions of divine presence. Rather, it made its appearance in a fourth dimension that altered the traditional structure in the same way that the god transcended the three-dimensional structure of implicit theology and began to intervene directly in the history of the human realm by means of spontaneous expressions of his will.

9.3. World-God and Helper of the Needy: The Transcendent God of the Ramesside Period and the Breakthrough of the Fourth Dimension

9.3.1. PRELUDE

Amarna religion was not a naturally evolved one; it was a founded religion, the first one we know of in the history of religion—and it did not outlast the lifetime of its founder. It was an episode of no more than twenty years' duration. But its consequences were so deep and so wide-ranging that they cannot be overestimated. They were felt in every area possible, with the result that on the whole, the transition from Dynasty 18 to Dynasty 19, to the Ramesside Period, represents the turn of an era, perhaps the most significant turning point in all of Egyptian intellectual history. We shall confine ourselves here to religious phenomena in the narrower sense, which constituted the center of events. We can justifiably speak of the religion of the Ramesside Period as a "new religion." It was neither founded, nor did it evolve naturally. It was the old religion, but—to use an image from natural history that imposes itself in this connection—it had altered its structure under the tremendous pressure of the Amarna Period. In this respect, the religion of Amarna was the prelude to Ramesside religion. It produced the specific climate from which the old religion could emerge altered into something new.

In what did this "climate," this "tremendous pressure" consist? In the banning and the persecution with which Amarna religion overran the old deities and their cults, in particular that of Thebes and its god Amun-Re. Amarna religion doubtless had more effect with the negative vision of its censorship than with the positive vision of its canon. We do not know how widespread the new religion was among the Egyptian population, but we would surely not be wrong in imagining that the number of its adherents was rather small. In an age in which there were no mass media, such a far-reaching and sudden change could only have affected the tiny elite whom the king reached with his "teaching." But all felt the force of the brutal persecution of the old religion. The cessation of the cults, the expulsion of the priests, the closing and destruction of the temples, the hacking out of representations and names that had fallen out of favor, took place for all to see. For a brief time (though for those concerned, a nightmarishly long one), traditional polytheism experienced the same fate that would finally be dealt it by Christianity fifteen hundred years later. The fact that we know so little about the repercussions of this early culture shock, that no sources provide insight into the details of what happened, into how it was experienced and coped with, should not lead us to believe that these were theological disputes that left the common man cold. Quite the opposite seems to have been the case. To be sure, the common man had little share in the official cult of the new god. Instead, he had an even greater share in the coercion of the state, which was vigilant lest he secretly practice some forbidden cult. In that way, religious questions probably affected him more than ever before.

It is in fact strange that so little thought has been given to this side of Amarna religion, though it must have constituted the greater part of its everyday reality. All too often, it is pictured as an era that was inspired by light, that rejoiced in nature, and was open to the world, and not as a time of religious intolerance, persecution, and police control. It is correct to orient oneself to the sources, but we must not forget that these sources preserve only the official picture. In this instance, little imagination is needed to conjure up the dark side of the picture. And once we think through this matter of persecution, we even find sources whose expressiveness has heretofore remained unappreciated.

The way is pointed by a text that evidently stems from the period of persecution itself. A *wab*-priest of Amun and functionary in the mortuary temple of Smenkhkare, Akhenaten's successor, recorded the text in a tomb from an older period, and thus in a relatively hidden spot:

My heart longs for the sight of you,
    O lord of the persea tree,
when your neck receives garlands!
You grant satiation without eating,
    and drunkenness without drinking.
My heart longs to see you,
    joy of my heart,
Amun, champion of the poor!
You are the father of the motherless,
    the husband of the widow.

How lovely it is to speak your name:
it is like the taste of life,
like a garment for the naked,
like the scent of a flowering twig
    at the time of summer's heat . . .
like a breath of air for him who was imprisoned.
. . .
Turn back to us, O lord of the plenitude of time!
You were here when nothing had come into being,
and you will be here when "they" are at an end.
You let me see darkness that you give—
shine for me, that I might see you!
. . .
Oh, how good it is to follow you,
Amun, O lord,
great to find for the one who seeks him!
Drive off fear, place joy
in the heart of humankind!
How happy is the face that beholds you, Amun:
it is in festival day after day.[95]

I take this poem to be a psalm of mourning that describes the situation during the period of persecution. If this interpretation is correct, the experience was characterized by an almost paradoxical antinomy of exterior and interior: external absence of the god and internal certainty of belief. On the one hand, the poem speaks in a mourning tone of longing for the sight of the god, who has turned away ("turn back to us") and of the "darkness" of the god's absence, and on the other hand, it speaks with praises of the inner experience of a divine presence that has become detached from all external signs: satiety without eating, intoxication without drinking, precise metaphors for the almost mystical experience of divine presence, even in the absence of the festival that had once caused the god to appear before the eyes of all but could now no longer be celebrated (the expression "when your neck receives garlands" alludes to the festival of Amun). Even in the darkness of persecution, with the god banished from the "visibility" of the three traditional dimensions of divine presence, a faithful heart could still conjure up the reality of the god. The mere mention of his name was inexpressibly "sweet," "like the breath of life for one who was imprisoned," and afterwards, as before, the "searcher" "found" the "greatness" of the hidden god.

These images are unquestionably mystical, though "mysticism" is an inappropriate and anachronistic concept in this connection. The mystic absolutizes the inner presence of the divine and takes satisfaction in it; here, however, we are dealing with an agonizing polarization of reality into an exterior and an interior, manifestness and secrecy. The author of this psalm of mourning was no mystic; for him, the interior and the exterior belonged inseparably together. The opposition unfolded in this poem rests on a dialectic: it is internal certainty of the god that causes the external reality from which the god has been banished to appear to be "darkness," and it is the external reality of persecution that creates the intensity and the reality of an exclusively internal experience of the presence of the god. My thesis is that it was precisely the experience of the period of persecution, as recorded in this dialectic, that determined the religious ambiance of the following era, the "age of personal piety," as Breasted aptly called it in 1912.

From the Ramesside Period, we have a multitude of psalms of mourning and faith like this poem from the period of persecution, in particular on votive stelae of private persons, but also in the form of pupils' exercises on ostraca and in manuscripts used in schools, as well as tomb inscriptions and even royal temple inscriptions. We have come to call these texts and their expression of an entirely personal relationship to the divine by the label "personal piety." It seems to me that this language and the experience it expresses were coined in the Amarna Period, which was the latent phase of what manifested itself in the Ramesside Period and determined the religious profile of that era. The psalm of mourning cited earlier must be understood as the single preserved remnant of a literature of dissidence that circulated clandestinely from mouth to mouth.

It is certainly no accident that it stems from Thebes. Thebes suffered the most during the Amarna Period, and it was the stronghold of dissidence. The most important texts expressing personal piety, insofar as it is recorded in private inscriptions, stem from Thebes. The splendor of these texts is often in inverse proportion to the modest rank of the persons who composed them. Scholars have even spoken of a "religion of the poor." But this phenomenon finds its explanation if we assume that the language of the dissident literature remained alive in the memory of the Thebans and influenced the style of both experience and expression at all levels of society in the period that followed.

I shall cite some extracts from one of these texts. It is from a votive stela set up by the artist Nebre on behalf of his son Nakhtamun:

I shall praise Amun,
I shall compose hymns in his name:
I shall praise him
to the height of the sky and the breadth of the earth,
I shall proclaim his power to him who sails upstream and him who
sails downstream:

Beware of him!
Proclaim him to son and daughter,
great and small!
Speak of him to children and to children of children who are not yet
born!
Speak of him to the fish in the river and the birds in the sky!
Proclaim him to the one who knows him and the one who knows
him not!
Beware of him!

You are Amun, lord of the silent,
who comes at the call of the poor.
I called to you when I was in sorrow,
and you came to save me.
You gave breath to the one who was imprisoned,
and saved me when I was in bonds.
You are Amun-Re, lord of Thebes,
you save the one in the netherworld.
You are the one who is gracious to him who calls on him,
you are the one who comes from afar![96]

The dialectic of exterior and interior underlies this text as well. It unfolds into the two themes that are typical of personal piety: confession and experience. The greatness of the god was experienced within, in the innermost horizon of private destiny, yet it was announced and confessed to all the world, great and small, contemporaries and descendants, even fish and fowl. The impressive pathos of this rhetorical confession is bound up with its rather artful form, in which annunciation is expressed chiastically using the imperative mood: beware, proclaim, speak of, speak of, proclaim, beware. We can easily imagine this poem, whose strictness of form is typical of oral poetry, in the mouths of dissidents from the period of persecution. The longing of the people had been vented in such poems during the "Babylonian Captivity" of Amun religion. Persecution and confession go hand in hand.

"Prison" and "bonds" are invoked in this text, as well. But these do not refer to the "exterior," to which the psalm of mourning from the Amarna Period opposes the freedom of the inner conceptualization of Amun's name, but rather the internal state of a person who has sinned against the god and thus seen the god turn away from him.

This concept of human consciousness of sinfulness vis-à-vis the divine can even be called the key experience of personal piety. In the present instance, Nebre felt "cast into bonds" on account of his son Nakhtamun,

> as he lay ill, on the brink of death,
> as he was in the power of Amun on account of that cow of his.[97]

Evidently, Nakhtamun had misappropriated a cow from the temple herd, and his subsequent illness was interpreted as a punishment visited by the incensed god. As a result, Nebre pledged a public proclamation of this experience of the power of the god "before all the land" and

> found the lord of the gods, come like the north wind, sweet breath
> before him; he saved Nakhtamun.[98]

The interior experience of the event, which is represented exteriorly as a rhetorical confession and proclamation of the greatness of the god to all the world, is determined by a consciousness of personal sin against the god:

> As the servant is known to commit sin,
> the lord is known to be merciful.[99]

It is this sin that casts the individual into "prison" and the "darkness" of divine absence. Thus, for example, other texts state

> I am the man who swore falsely
> to Ptah, the lord of Maat.
> He caused me to see darkness by day.
> I shall proclaim his might to him who knows him and to him who
> does not know him,

small and great:
beware of Ptah, the lord of Maat.[100]

Lo, you cause me to see the darkness that you make,
be gracious to me, that I might proclaim it![101]

Individuals felt a personal connection to the divine that was put at
risk by their transgressions. Only a complete externalization of the
damaged interior by a public confession of guilt and the experience of
the god's power could cleanse this personal tie between the god and
the individual. In this consciousness of sin, which was so characteristic of personal piety, the experience of Amarna was applied to the
individual. Akhenaten's deed became the paradigm of an act of sacri-
lege. The people must have viewed the persecution of the old gods as
the most fearful of sins. The official denial of the gods merely intensified their interior certainty of their reality. In the dialectic of the exterior and the interior, the banishment of the gods actually
demonstrated their power: their absence was experienced as a turning away, a darkness that hung over the land and the worshipers of
light, who were cast into the night.

The sun of him who does not recognize you sets, Amun,
but he who recognizes you says, "It has risen in the forecourt!"
He who attacks you is in darkness,
even when the whole land is in light,
but he who places you in his heart,
lo, his sun has risen![102]

Some have even wished to see a direct allusion to Akhenaten in these
verses. Whatever the case might be, it is certain that the Amarna Period
made clear for all eyes to see what it meant to deny or to confess the reality of the gods. The old religion emerged from its Babylonian Captivity
as a confessional religion. Thereafter, people knew of the absolute reality of the gods, but also that they shed light only on him who put them
in his heart and were "found" only by him who sought them.

Thoth, you sweet spring
for one who thirsts in the desert!
He is closed to the one who has found his mouth,
but open to the silent.
If the silent one comes, he finds the well,
if the heated one comes, you are closed.[103]

"Silent" and "poor" are the self-designations of the Ramesside understanding of existence, namely, that personal destiny was directly subject to divine will.

How beautiful it is to sit in the hand of Amun,
the protector of the silent, the savior of the poor,
who gives breath to the one he holds dear.[104]

We thus find ourselves before the paradoxical (if not entirely unfamiliar) historical situation that a failed revolution abetted the eventual breakthrough of that against whose beginnings it had been directed. Personal piety was nothing other than what we have defined, in the context of our theory, as the fourth dimension of divine presence, that new sphere of religious experience beyond cult, cosmos, and myth, whose horizon was the human heart and personal history, in which personal destiny could be interpreted directly as the personal will of a deity. We have traced the beginnings of this new dimension back into literary sources from the Middle Kingdom and assessed the spread of the new concepts in the New Kingdom, especially in connection with the cult of Amun at Thebes, where royal inscriptions record Amun's oracular interventions in the succession to the throne, while tomb inscriptions of officials know of the judgment of the god, who passed decision over good and evil in his capacity as ethical authority and whose grace was extended to the pious one who "put the god in his heart" and "acted on his water."

Amarna religion, which was conservative in this regard, had turned itself against these beginnings, proclaiming a concept of the divine that was inaccessible to the devotion of the individual. In its attempt to restore the royal monopoly on religious activity, it had declared the king himself to be the god of the individual and referred all individual piety to him as lord of grace and destiny. With this hybrid excess of its religious function, the kingship lost its credibility. Just as Akhenaten had usurped the personal piety of his subjects with his royal cult, so now, in reaction, the concept of the divine assumed many traditional aspects of the kingship. "The god is king": the emphatic proclamation of the kingship of the god became a central theme in post-Amarna hymns. And it is clear that no mythical divine monarchy was meant, in the traditional sense of the third, mythic dimension, but rather that in the sense of the new, fourth dimension, the god was recognized as the true, authentic king of the land, who directly determined the destiny of human affairs.

Amarna religion also assisted the breakthrough of the fourth dimension by banishing the deities of the old religion from the three traditional dimensions of divine presence. The temples were closed, the cults were discontinued: the gods and goddesses were absent and ineffective in the cultic and political dimension:

For when his majesty appeared as king,
the temples of the gods and goddesses

from Elephantine to the marshes of the delta
. . . were about to be forgotten,
and their holy places, in a condition of collapse,
became ruin heaps, overgrown with weeds,
their divine dwellings were as though they had never existed,
their temples were a footpath.
The land was in extreme distress,
the gods had turned from this land.
If an army was sent to Syria,
to expand the boundaries of Egypt,
it was not granted the slightest success.
If one turned to a god in prayer,
to ask counsel of him,
he did not draw nigh at all.
If one went to a goddess, likewise,
she did not draw nigh at all.
For their hearts had become weak in their bodies.
They (the Amarna monarchs?) had destroyed what had been created.[105]

Their cults disrupted, the deities terminated their residence in Egypt, leaving the land in political failure. In this retrospective of the Amarna Period from the Restoration Stela of Tutankhamun, we have an express statement of the unity of the cultic and political spheres that anticipates the Asclepius apocalypse (see chapter 3.3, text at note 45).

As for the cosmic dimension, we have already noted that it was claimed by the new god, stripped of its divinity, and demoted to the status of "nature." There was no remnant that the new teaching could not explain as the effect of light. In the end, there remained language, the collective memory of the culture as handed down in myths, names, genealogies, and the like: and here began a thorough *damnatio memoriae*, whose devastation we can still observe throughout the land. There commenced a regulation of language that eliminated from discourse not only the names of the deities, but also—with even greater consistency than the Old Testament—the plural form "gods." It is clear that even public confession of one's personal god had been forbidden to the individual during the Amarna Period when Aya, the successor of Tutankhamun, boasts,

I have removed the wretchedness,
each person can now pray to his god.[106]

The only resort was the internal. The gods and goddesses hibernated "in the hearts" of their adorants as objects of longing, mourning, and the injunction that circulated clandestinely: "Beware of him! Proclaim him to great and small!" The fourth dimension of divine presence and religious experience, previously perhaps the property of a small elite of the faithful in the context of the Theban cult of Amun, now became the common property of all concerned; the entire people had suffered under the persecution of the old gods. In the secrecy of the subculture, the new views regarding the divine immediacy of human existence, piety as placing one's god in one's heart, and acting before one's god achieved a dissemination throughout society that later became manifest in the literature of personal piety:

> Every face says, "We belong to you!",
>> strong and weak together,
> rich and poor with one mouth,
>> all things equally.
> Your loveliness is in all their hearts,
>> no consciousness is without your beauty.
> Do widows not say, "You are our husband"?
>> and little ones, "our father and our mother"?
> The rich boast of your goodness,
>> the poor direct their regard to you.
> The imprisoned one turns to you,
>> the sick one calls to you.
> Your name is an amulet for the solitary one,
>> well-being and health for the one on the water,
>> a rescuer from the crocodile,
>> good to think of in the hour of fear,
>> who saves from the mouth of the heated one.
> Everyone turns to you, beseeches you,
>> your ears are open to hear them and fulfill their wish.[107]

9.3.2. THE ANTINOMIES OF THE RAMESSIDE CONCEPT OF THE DIVINE

By way of a conclusion, I should like to return to the theological discourse to whose history this second part of our survey is devoted. The Ramesside Period was the zenith of this history. This was the period of the loftiest—that is, the most comprehensive, most explicit, and most complex and expressive—texts. Paradox served as the basic means of formulating this theology. The various aspects of divine unity were now no longer arranged paratactically, but rather opposed to one another with exaggerated, antithetical images whose paradoxical "as well as" points to the fact that the essence of the divine is transcendent and beyond any possibility of rational expression. This new concept of the divine is antinomically structured. In what follows, I shall treat, at the very least in passing, the most important of these antinomies.

Cosmos and History

Lord of *neheh*, who creates *djet*, . . .
Destiny and prosperity are in his hand.[108]

Such juxtapositions of divine efficacy, which can be experienced in the cosmos and in history, that is, in each personal, individual history, as exemplified in the temporal dimension in this text referring to the moon god Thoth, characterize the complexity of the Ramesside concept of the divine. It is significant that the new concepts regarding the direct influence of the divine on history make no distinction between the official, royal sphere and the private lot of commoners. The effectiveness of a deity in the fourth dimension, as helper of the needy, savior, deliverer, but also as judge, avenger, punisher—in brief, as subject of a personal will that expressed itself through wrath and grace—embraced all spheres of the *conditio humana*. In the Egyptian language, the technical term for manifestations of divine will in the human, historical sphere was *bau*, which had meanings such as "display of power," "punishing force," "wrath," and "intervention." In the language of our sources, this concept was now the designation of the fourth dimension, which joined the traditional triad of cult image, cosmic form of manifestation, and name. The concept "display of power" comprehends nearly everything that we have ascribed to the fourth dimension: the concept of a personal god whose will determines the fate of the land and of the individual, and the concept of the immediacy of the divine, which "displays its power" in the horizon of every individual existence. Texts expressing personal piety recount these displays of power, and "accounts of displays of power" could even serve as a designation of the genre.

"Beginning of the account of Ptah's display of power" are the opening words of a stela inscription from which we cited an extract earlier (see chapter 9.3.1, text at note 99). In these texts, individuals relate that they have "found" the god. This word seems like a *terminus technicus* for the personal and direct experience of divine presence. The most conspicuous account of such an experience is the poem in which Ramesses II had the Battle of Qadesh commemorated. It relates how the king, attacked by ambush and abandoned by his army, called to Amun for help and "found" the god, and how the latter extended his hand to the king and saved him from the midst of the enemy. This text also stands as proof that personal piety was not a religion of the lower classes, as has actually been maintained. Personal piety was rather a phenomenon in this history of consciousness, a "Zeitgeist" that was common to artisans, officials, and kings. "I begin to proclaim your greatness,"[109] commences a hymn to Amun by Ramesses III, which further reads

He who speaks your name,
you are a herdsman to him,
you place him on the water of your command.

He who fills his heart with you,
his heart is sweet,
for lo, you direct your eye at him,
day by day,
you protect the one who travels on your waters.

He who turns to gaze on you,
    whose eye lights up,
you cause him to be sated with your beauty
    that is in the sky.

Even kings made use of the fourth dimension to develop a new theology of history.

Divine will manifested itself in the political destiny of the land every bit as much as in the fate of the individual. "If an army was sent to Syria, it was unable to succeed": thus had Tutankhamun described the situation during the Amarna Period, when the gods "were damaged in their cults." "Re turned again to Egypt" is Merneptah's interpretation of his victory over the Libyans, and a hymn celebrates Ramesses VII's ascent to the throne with the words, "Amun turned again to Egypt." The blessings with which the gods rewarded the piety of kings were manifest in the political well-being of the land.

Wrath and Grace

The antinomy that defined the fourth dimension of the experience of divine presence was that of wrath and grace. The divine will that directed its multitude of blessings to the pious also punished the godless with its wrath:

Blessed is he who puts you in his heart!
Woe to him who attacks you!
For your display of might is so powerful,
your plans so effective, your grace so swift.[110]

This antinomic structure of the fourth dimension compelled the individual to make a decision. His existence was directly exposed to the divine, and his destiny lay in divine hands. But he himself decided, through his pious devotion or his obstinate indifference, whether he would meet with a "blessed is he" or a "woe to." During the Amarna Period, the possibility of godlessness had been a reality and a general experience. People had learned that life was not a cosmic force that was always already effective before any pious devotion to the divine, but rather that it was at the disposal of the gods and could only be enjoyed by those who did not stray from the path of righteousness. But even those who had strayed from the path of the gods could find grace by confessing and proclaiming the divine power they had experienced. A wrathful god was also capable of "turning to grace" in an instant:

> The lord of Thebes does not spend the day in wrath,
> when he rages, it is but for a moment,
> and nothing is left.
> The breeze has turned to us in grace,
> Amun has come, carried in his breath of life.[111]

Wrath and grace, these were the two aspects of divine will and of the "display of power" in which this will manifested itself, blessing or punishing, in the horizon of history.

Juxtaposed to this was the cosmic effect of the divine as "god of life," as in the following extract from a hymn of Dynasty 22 date:

> He is a Khnum, excellent potter,
> the breath of life,
> the breeze of the north wind;
> a high Nile, on whose *ka* one lives,
> who provides for gods and men.
> Sun of the daytime, moon of the night,
> who crosses the sky without wearying.
>
> Mighty in display of power, mightier than Sakhmet,
> like a fire raging;
> great of grace, who cares for the one who adores him,
> who turns to heal suffering.
> For he gazes on humankind, there is no one he does not know,
> and he heeds millions of them.
> Who can withstand your wrath,
> who can avert the rage of your might?[112]

Life-Bestowing Elements

Just as divine wrath and grace was manifest in history, so the god's guiding and sustaining power expressed itself in the three life-bestowing elements of air, water (the Nile inundation), and light (sun and moon). This must be understood quite literally, as a continuation of the philosophy of nature that, as a theology of the "god of life," derived all life in the world from the effects of a divine, elemental power: the air of the Shu theology of the Middle Kingdom (see chapter 8.5), the light of Amarna theology (see chapter 9.2), and now the triad of air, light, and water:

> Life belongs to you, there will be no other
>   who gives life to every visage.
> You are the light that drives off evil,
>   no eye lives that does not see you,
> you are the air that allows the throat to breathe,
>   no animal lives that does without you.
> You are the inundation that keeps humankind alive,
>   no "face" lives if you are not in it.[113]

This cosmic theology of a god of life now culminated in a lofty vision of a pantheistic deity whose body is the cosmos:

> His right eye is the day,
> his left eye is the night,
> it is he who guides the "faces" on all the ways.
> His body is the primeval water,
> his entrails are the inundation
> that creates everything that is and keeps all that exists alive.
> His breathing is the breath in every nose,
> his are destiny and fortune for everyone.[114]

The concept of an incarnate divine *parousia*, celebrated as the "beauty" and "love" of sunlight in the religion of Amarna, is now connected with the cosmos:

> Your skin is the light,
> your breath is the fire of life:
> all precious stones are joined in your body.
> Your limbs are the breath of life in every nose,
> one inhales you in order to live.
> Your taste is the Nile,
> one anoints oneself with the brilliance of your light-eye.
> . . .
> One walks upon your visage
> in your embodiment as earth god.[115]

Embodiment and Disposal

This concept of a god of life elevated into a "world-god," whose pantheistic consequences are discussed later, entailed more than just the cosmic; it also encompassed the antinomies of embodiment and disposal, cosmos and history. The god was "life" not only in the sense of the elemental, cosmic life forces that constituted his body—sun and moon, air and water—but also in the sense of destiny and fulfillment, prosperity and well-being, which he disposed of freely as he wished:

> You are life,
> blessings are under your control:
> abundance and lifetime,
> provision for the afterlife and burial.[116]

> Lord of life,
> who gives to the one he wishes;
> the circuit of the earth is under his authority.[117]

The Ramesside concept of the divine combined the two aspects that Amarna religion had apportioned to the god and to the king: the all-sustaining cosmic principle and the personal will, the ethical authority, that disposed of the assignment of life and death according to good or evil. Thus, for example, the antithesis of far and near, which at Amarna had been conceived of purely as cosmic ("you are in the sky, but your rays are on the earth"), was now interpreted as the mysterious, dual unity of "cosmicity" and personality:

> He is distant as the beholding one,
> near as the hearing one.[118]

The concept is of course already to be found in the Instruction for Merikare (see chapter 3.2.1 and chapter 9.2.2); what is new is simply the antithetic formulation, the programmatic uniting of the cosmic and the personal, which is to be understood as a reaction to the reductionistic one-sidedness of the concept of the divine in Amarna religion.

The god of Ramesside theology was the cosmos, in that he embodied it:

> Your two eyes are the sun and the moon,
> your head is the sky,
> your feet are the netherworld.[119]

> You are the sky,
> you are the earth,
> you are the netherworld,
> you are the water,
> you are the air between them.[120]

But he was also the cosmos in that he held it in his all-embracing consciousness:

The one who proclaims the future in millions of years,
eternity is before his countenance
like yesterday when it has passed.[121]

This comparison, which is familiar to us from verse 4 of Psalm 90
("before you, a thousand years are like yesterday when it has
passed"), has to do with the consciousness of the god, whose omniscience embraces the world in its spatial and temporal dimensions.
The concept of consciousness includes not only knowledge, "over-
sight," but also disposal. The same text goes on to state:

Destiny is with him,
the years are in his hand,
birth and prosperity are under his command.[122]

"The years are in his hand"—this concept stamped what can be called
the Ramesside experience of life, down to its most mundane expressions. Thus, for example, one might impart the following sort of information about one's circumstances in a letter:

It is well with me today.
The morning is in the god's hand.[123]

This attitude of a "truly silent one" accorded with the admonitions of
contemporary wisdom literature:

Think not of the morning before it has come.
Yesterday is not like today (i.e., one day is not like another) in the
hand of the god.[124]

This insight into the unavailability of the future and the changeability
of a reality that springs from the will of the divine found its most
explicit expression in the Instruction of Amenemope:

Do not say, "today is like tomorrow,"
for how will that end?

Morning comes, today passes:
the flood has become like the edge of the waters.
The crocodiles are exposed, the hippopotami are on dry land.
The fish are crowded together, the wolves are sated.
The birds are in festival, the fish nets are empty.
But all the silent ones in the temple
say, "Re is great of grace."
Fill yourself with silence, and you will find life,
and your body will be hale on earth.[125]

The unity of theology, attitude, and lifestyle that characterized the
Ramesside Period is clear in these texts. The all-encompassing reality
of "god" (in the singular)—and not "the gods"—was not the object
just of theological speculation, but of mundane knowledge as it was
lived.

Embodiment and Transcendence

The question is how to conceive the reality of the individual gods vis-à-
vis the all-encompassing reality of this singular god. There seem to be
only two solutions to this problem: the monotheistic one, which categorically denies the reality of the plurality of deities, and the pantheistic one,
which explains the various deities as aspects, names, forms of manifestation—in brief, as immanent refractions of the transcendent unity of the
single god. Amarna religion chose the first of these, and Ramesside theology the second. The relationship between "god" (in the singular) and
"the gods," perhaps the most critical of all antinomies, was treated as the
opposition between openness and hiddenness, immanence and transcendence. To clarify this point, the following text may stand for a multitude of sources:

> Mysterious of transformations, gleaming of forms of manifestation,
>   wondrous god, rich in forms!
> All gods boast of being his,
>   to magnify themselves with his beauty, as he is divine.
>
> Re himself is united with his body,
>   he is the great one in Heliopolis;
> one also says "Tanen" to him,
>   Amun, who emerged from the primeval waters to lead
>   the "faces."
>
> Another of his transformations is the "Eight,"
>   primeval god, begetter of the primeval deities who bore Re!
> He completes himself as Atum, one body with him.
>   he is the All-Lord, who began existence.
>
> His *ba*, one says, is that which is in the sky,
>   he is the one who is in the netherworld, who commands in the east.
> His *ba* is in the sky, his *body* is in the west,
>   his *image* is in "Southern Heliopolis" and wears his crowns.
>
> Unique is Amun, who is hidden before them,
>   who veils himself before the gods, so that his essence is not known.
> He is more distant than the sky,
>   he is deeper than the netherworld.

No god knows his true form,
  his image is *not* unfolded in the writings,
  one learns *nothing* certain about him.

He is too mysterious for his majesty to be revealed,
  he is too great to be discovered,
  too mighty to be known.
One falls down immediately out of terror,
  if one speaks his secret name, wittingly or unwittingly.
There is no god who can call him by it,
  the *ba* who hides his name according to his mysteriousness.[126]

The division of the text into two unequal halves ($2 \times 8 + 2 \times 7$ verses) rests, in a manner comparable to the internal form of a sonnet, on a conceptual antithesis, a change of aspect: the paradox of manifest diversity and hidden unity. Using all the possibilities of theological argumentation developed in the Ramesside Period, the first part aims to conceptualize the relationship between god (in the singular) and the gods and the forms of the immanent embodiment of this god in the polytheistic divine realm. The number three plays a special role here, as a *triad* to which the plurality of deities can be reduced, and as a *trinity* in which the transcendent unity of the god unfolds in this world. In the Ramesside Period, the institution of "state god" was replaced by a national triad composed of the gods of three sacred cities, Heliopolis (Re), Memphis (Ptah-Tanen), and Thebes (Amun). Another hymn from this same collection explains how the multitude of the realm of the Egyptian deities can be reduced to these three, because they embody the three traditional dimensions of divine presence:

All the gods are three:
Amun, Re, and Ptah, who have no equal.
His name is hidden as Amun,
he is Re in countenance,
his body is Ptah.[127]

Ptah stands for the cultic (body = cult statue) dimension of the divine realm, Re for the cosmic (visibility), and Amun for the verbal (name). The text interprets the national triad in the temporal dimension as three successive stages of the god's becoming the world:

1. preexistence: Amun and the eight primeval gods who embody chaos (water, endlessness, darkness, nothingness)
2. primeval hill: Ptah-Tanen, the creator
3. course of the sun: Re, the sustainer.

The second group of three is not triadic, but trinitarian: the *ba*, image, and body of the god as the three constituent elements of his person, in which his transcendent essence unfolds in the immanent world, thereby producing the three-tiered arrangement of the cosmos into sky, earth, and netherworld. This teaching occurs often in hymns of the Ramesside and later periods. Common to all these forms of theological argumentation is the principle of hypotaxis; the various aspects of the god are not juxtaposed additively, but rather develop outward from the idea of an articulated whole: *ba*, image, and body; sun, cult statue, and name; sky, earth, and netherworld; light, air, and water; Amun, Re, and Ptah; preexistence, primeval hill, and the course of the sun. These are not paratactic, but rather hypotactic series in the sense that their elements are constituents of a superordinate unity.

The second part of the text opposes this learned *theologia positiva* with a *theologia negativa* that reads like a retraction of all that was stated earlier. Amun is not three, but one: he does not manifest himself in the other deities, but rather conceals himself from them; he does not turn himself into the cosmos and fill it with his threefold essence, but rather stretches far beyond it. There can even be no teaching about him, because the very hiddenness of this *deus ineffabilis* surpasses all human and divine knowledge. He can be called by no name, not even the name Amun, whose name as good as means "the hidden one" in Egyptian.

We must allow this artificial paradox to have its effect before setting about a search for mediating categories. These are not lacking, however. We are probably to see the most decisive mediating category in the curious concept of "*ba*-ness," with which the text concludes ("*ba*, who veils himself according to his hiddenness").

Ba is an enigmatic concept. It designates as much the visible manifestation of a hidden power as the hidden power behind its visible manifestations. Thus, for instance, as a visible manifestation, the sun can be called the *ba* of the god (as twice in our text). But then, in the sense of the hidden power that manifests itself in the sensory realm, the god is called *ba* in the final verse. This is not the *ba* of a god, but simply *ba*, the hidden power that can be experienced, named, and conceived of in the plenitude of the polytheistic divine realm. Later hymns go so far as not to call this hidden god by any name, for all names, even Amun, can only refer to the this-worldly sphere of manifested diversity. Such hymns simply call the god "*ba*," for instance:

> *Ba* with hidden countenances and mighty majesty,
> who keeps his name hidden and his image mysterious![128]

The *ba* concept serves to mediate between the hidden god and the polytheistic divine realm, though this mediation is a mystery that surpasses human sensory perception and endeavor and is most suitably expressed as a paradox.

One and All

"One and All"—and thus in the ancient Greek form *hèn kaì pân*—was the motto of western Romantic pantheism. The origin of the Greek formulation has yet to be unambiguously explained, but the clearest traces lead to Egypt in late classical antiquity. *Hèn tò pân*, "all is one," accompanies the ancient Egyptian symbol of the *ouroboros*-serpent biting its own tail as the title vignette of a medieval manuscript dealing with alchemy. Similar formulations are frequent in the Corpus Hermeticum. In a Latin inscription, Isis is called *una quae es omnia*, "You one, who are all." In Egypt of late antiquity, Isis was the deity with whom the Ramesside concept of a supreme being as world-god and helper of the needy was linked. As a transcendent universal deity to whom even fate was subject, her influence extended far beyond Egypt's borders, throughout the late classical world. There is thus a whole series of important Greek-language hymns to Isis, as well as aretalogies—self-depictions of the deity written in the first person, like the examples from the Coffin Texts of the Middle Kingdom discussed above (see chapters 8.4 and 8.5)—which seem to continue the theological discourse of the New Kingdom, thus indicating that the Ramesside concept of the divine remained alive and unaltered. It is thus justified to inquire whether there is anything in Egyptian that corresponds to the formulation connected with this divine concept in Greek and Latin texts, *hèn tò pân*, *una quae es omnia*, *omnia unum esse et unum omnia*, and so forth.

There is in fact an Egyptian formulation that implies approximately the same thing; it first appears in the sources in the early Ramesside Period, after which it is attested continually down to the latest antiquity, and it is always connected with the concept of a universal deity. It is "the one who makes himself into millions," with many variations, such as "who becomes millions," "who creates millions," or even "whose body is the millions." The classical concept of the "all" and the "whole," *tò pân*, *tà pánta*, *omnia*, appears in Egyptian as "millions." It is not, however, connected with the concept of an all-embracing but closed totality, but rather with one of an endless, uncontainable plenitude. In Egyptian, "millions" also means "endless," and the word is etymologically connected with the concept of "eternity" as an endless plenitude of time. We meet here with the same "dynamic" concept of the cosmos that we deduced from our analysis of the concept of the sun's course in connection with the cosmic dimension. Not the "all" that once emerged from the preexisting unity, somewhat in the manner of a "big bang," but rather the plenitude of living beings that incessantly stream from the god's transcendent unity: that was the Egyptian version of the pantheistic antithesis of unity and omniformity.

From the very beginning, the dialectic of unity and diversity or omniformity determined the subject matter of theological discourse and the dynamic of its development. At first, in the theology of the Middle Kingdom, it was related to time in the concept of a preexisting unity that "became three" in its transition into existence. In the New Kingdom, as we first see in the Cairo hymns to Amun (which perhaps stem from the late Middle Kingdom), this dialectic developed into a heightened form of primacy theology; heightened, in that the relationship of the prime being was no longer expressed as a constellation involving a god and other deities, but rather an opposition of the single god and the world. The forms of this opposition were juxtaposed additively. Next, in the New Solar Theology, this paratactic agglomeration of roles was reduced to the *single* form of the sun god and the *single* role of the god of life. As a radical variant of this theology, Amarna religion then categorically denied the multiplicity of deities, thereby robbing the world of its differentiated divine existence. The world became "nature," deprived of its gods yet filled with the divine: a vessel, a creation or emanation of the light that made it visible.

It was only the Ramesside Period that arrived at the epoch-making solution that prevailed until the Christianization of the ancient world. It returned to polytheism, that is, to the concept of the divinity of the world, as an ineluctable reality, though with its pantheistic theology of transcendence, it developed an entirely new terminology that made it possible to conceive of the diversity of deities as the colorful reflection of a hidden unity. It worshiped the unity as the hidden god, the *deus absconditus et ineffabilis*, the "sacred *ba* of gods and men"[129] whose names, symbols, emanations, manifestations, shadows, and images were the various deities.

This epoch-making breakthrough to a transcendent concept of the divine marks the goal of the process we have designated as "theological discourse." But it also characterizes the general piety of the era. We must not separate this step toward a new, pantheistic concept of the divine from that other step that we have called the "breakthrough of the fourth dimension." It was the gods (in the plural) whose presence was felt in cult, cosmos, and verbal tradition; but it was the transcendent, hidden god (in the singular) on whom the individual (the "truly silent one," the "poor one") felt entirely dependent and in whose hands he placed his existence. This god transcended the world not only with respect to the mysterious hiddenness of his "*ba*-ness," in which no name could name him and no representation could depict him, but also with respect to the human heart, which was filled with him. He was the hidden god who "came from afar" yet was always present to the individual in the omniscience and omnipotence of his all-encompassing essence. He was not only the cosmos—in Egyptian, the totality of the "millions," and also *neheh* and *djet*, "plenitude of time" and "unalterable duration"—into which he unfolded himself, but also history:

> Your being is the endless plenitude of time,
> your image is unalterable duration,
> all that happens springs from your planning will (*ka*).[130]

This concept of the divine dominated Egyptian religion from the Ramesside Period on. Kings and commoners bowed to the "planning will" of this god. With regard to the kingship, we have noted Ramesses II's adventure at Qadesh, as well as the exceptional piety of Ramesses III, along with the theology of history in the Ramesside Period, which made the king entirely dependent on divine "grace" and the fate of the land on divine will, just like the destiny of the individual. It remains to be added that in Dynasty 21, the final step was taken and the god was installed *de jure* as king, not in the sense of a representative theocracy, as at Amarna, but in the "identitary" sense of a royal rule exercised personally by the god through oracular decisions. Thebes became the center of a theocratic state that united the nomes of Upper Egypt under the rule of Amun. This development is to be understood as the final consequence of the process we call the "breakthrough of the fourth dimension" of divine presence, of history and destiny. But other sources show with equal clarity that the worship of this hidden universal god expanded into a sort of popular religion. In the Ramesside Period and its aftermath, Egyptians were filled with a consciousness of the changeability of the world, the instability of human relations, and the risk of human existence. They emerged from the security of *maat* and viewed themselves as delivered up to an uncertain future that sprang from an inscrutable divine will. In this situation, they yearned for nothing so much as to find a new security "in the hands" of this god who stood above the other gods. In popular religion, magic is an infallible indication of such a sense of life and interpretation of existence. In magical papyri of the Ramesside Period, we find the first recorded hymns to the transcendent, universal god, hymns of a sort that would appear in cult contexts only hundreds of years later:

> Greetings, you sole one who makes himself into millions,
> who extends in length and breadth without bounds,
> equipped power that created itself,
> uraeus-serpent with huge flame,
> rich in magic, mysterious of form,
> hidden *ba* to whom reverence is shown!

King Amun-Re, may he live, prosper, and be healthy, the self-created,
Akhty, the eastern Horus,
The one who rises blazing with light,
the light that shines upon the gods.

You have hidden yourself as Amun, the great one,
you have distanced yourself in your embodiment as sun,
Tanen, who elevates himself above the gods:
the self-rejuvenating old one who traverses *neheh*,
Amun, who abides in all things,
this god who founded the earth through his decision.[131]

In the Greek magical papyri from late classical Egypt, it is the god
Agathos Daimon, Egyptian *Shai*, "Fate," who is addressed as the universal god over all the other deities:

You, whose unwearying eyes are the sun and the moon,
whose head is the sky,
whose body is the air,
whose feet are the earth,
while the water around you is Ocean:
Agathos Daimon,
who creates and nourishes and increases all good,
the entire populated earth and the whole cosmos![132]

In Egyptian sources of the later periods, we also encounter a bold
attempt to make pictorial representations of this "supergod" over the
other deities, who is hidden and as such incapable of representation, so
as to secure his omnipotent protective and healing power, in the form of
the so-called Bes Pantheos. This was a demon with seven different heads.
No one would have connected this evil-averting monster of popular
imagination with the idea of a supreme being, had the secret of the identity of this creature not been revealed by a caption to a vignette in a magical papyrus published in 1970:

The Bes with seven heads . . .
it embodies the *ba*s of Amun-Re,
. . . lord of the sky, the earth, the netherworld, the water, and the
    mountains.
who keeps his name mysterious before the gods,
the giant of a million cubits,
the mighty one who fastens the sky on his head,
[. . .] from whose nose the air emerges to give life to all noses,
who rises as the sun to brighten the earth,
from the effluxes of whose body the inundation flows to give life to
    every mouth.[133]

The demonic Bes, whose seven heads symbolize the totality of deities, is thus not himself identical to the pantheistic supergod of the gods; but for the magician alone, he embodied the plurality of deities who were explained as the *bas*, the manifestations of power, of the hidden, single god. This is entirely in the spirit of the Ramesside theology of transcendence and demonstrates not only that its concepts remained alive until the end of Egyptian paganism, but that they had penetrated to the lower levels of popular piety and religion in Egypt.

Abbreviations

ACF	*Annuaire Collège de France.*
ADAIK	Abhandlungen des Deutschen Archäologischen Instituts Kairo, Ägyptologische Reihe.
Äg. Abh.	Ägyptologische Abhandlungen.
AHAW	Abhandlungen der Heidelberger Akademie der Wissenschaften, Philosophisch-historische Klasse.
ÄHG	J. Assmann. *Ägyptische Hymnen und Gebete.*
An. Aeg.	Analecta Aegyptiaca.
AOAT	Alter Orient und Altes Testament.
APAW	Abhandlungen der Preussischen Akademie der Wissenschaften, Philosophisch-historische Klasse.
ASAE	*Annales du Service des Antiquités de l'Égypte.*
BACE	*Bulletin of the Australian Centre for Egyptology.*
BAe	Bibliotheca Aegyptiaca.
BD	Book of the Dead.
BEHE	Bibliothèque de l'École des Hautes Études, section des sciences religieuses.
BES	Brown Egyptological Studies.
Bibl. Aeg.	Bibliotheca Aegyptiaca.
Bibl. Beitr.	Biblische Beiträge.
Bibl. d'Ét.	Bibliothèque d'Étude.
BIFAO	*Bulletin de l'Institut Français d'Archéologie Orientale au Caire.*
BJRL	*Bulletin of the John Rylands Library Manchester.*
BM	British Museum.
BSFE	*Bulletin de la Société Français d'Égyptologie.*
CB	Coniectanea Biblica, Old Testament Series.
CG	Catalogue générale of the Cairo Museum.
CL	Collection Latomus.
CT	A. de Buck. *The Egyptian Coffin Texts.* 7 vols., OIP 34, 49, 64, 67, 73, 81, 87. Chicago, 1935–1961.
DÖAW	Denkschriften der Österreichischen Akademie der Wissenschaften, Philosophisch-historische Klasse.
DVLG	*Deutsche Vierteljahrsschrift für Literaturwissenschaft und Geistesgeschichte.*
EU	Egyptologische Uitgaven.
FIFAO	Fouilles de l'Institut Français d'Archéologie Orientale du Caire.
GM	*Göttinger Miszellen.*
GOF	Göttinger Orientforschungen, IV. Reihe: Ägypten.
HdO	Handbuch der Orientalistik.
HO	J. Černý and Sir A. Gardiner. *Hieratic Ostraca.* Oxford, 1957.
JEA	*Journal of Egyptian Archaeology.*
JNES	*Journal of Near Eastern Studies.*
LÄ	*Lexikon der Ägyptologie.*
LÄS	Leipziger ägyptologische Studien.

LL	J. Assmann. *Liturgische Lieder an den Sonnengott: Untersuchungen zur altägyptischen Hymnik*. Berlin, 1969.
MÄS	Münchner ägyptologische Studien.
MDAIK	*Mitteilungen des Deutschen Archäologischen Instituts Abteilung Kairo.*
MEOL	Mededelingen en verhandelingen van het Vooraziatisch-Egyptisch Genootschap "Ex Oriente Lux."
MF	*Mannheimer Forum.*
MIFAO	Mémoires de l'Institut Français d'Archéologie Orientale.
MKAW	Mededelingen der Koninklijke Nederlandse Akademie van Wetenschappen, afd. Letterkunde Nieuwe Reeks.
MMIFAO	Mémoires publiés par les membres de la Mission Archéologique Française au Caire.
NAWG	Nachrichten der Akademie der Wissenschaften in Göttingen, Philosophisch-historische Klasse.
OBO	Orbis Biblicus et Orientalis.
OIP	Oriental Institute Publications.
OLA	Orientalia Lovaniensia Analecta.
OMRO	Oudheikundige Mededelingen uit het Rijksmuseum van Oudheden te Leiden.
PdÄ	Probleme der Ägyptologie.
PMMA	Publications of the Metropolitan Museum of Art Egyptian Expedition.
Prob. Äg.	Probleme der Ägyptologie.
PT	Pyramid Texts (cited by spell number).
Pyr.	Pyramid Texts (cited by paragraph number).
RdE	*Revue d'Égyptologie.*
RdT	*Receuil de travaux relatifs à la philologie et à l'archéologie égyptiennes et assyriennes.*
RHR	*Revue de l'Historie des Religions.*
SAK	*Studien zur altägyptischen Kultur.*
SAOC	Studies in Ancient Oriental Civilization.
SHAW	Sitzungsberichte der Heidelberger Akademie der Wissenschaften, Philosophisch-historische Klasse.
SHR	Studies in the History of Religions.
SMBMÄS	Staatliche Museen zu Berlin, Mitteilungen aus der ägyptischen Sammlung.
SO	Sources Orientales.
SOR	Studies in Oriental Religions.
SSAW	Sitzungsberichte der Sächsische Akademie der Wissenschaften, Philologisch-historische Klasse.
STG	J. Assmann. *Sonnenhymnen in thebanischen Gräbern*, Theben 1. Mainz am Rhein, 1983.
SVR	Studien zum Verstehen fremder Religionen.
TT	Theban Tomb.
UGAAe	Untersuchungen zur Geschichte und Altertumskunde Aegyptens.
Urk. I	K. Sethe. *Urkunden des Alten Reichs*. Urkunden des aegyptischen Altertums, vol. 1. Leipzig, 1935.
Urk. IV	K. Sethe. *Urkunden der 18. Dynastie*. Urkunden des aegyptischen Altertums, vol. 4. Leipzig, 1927–1930.
VDAW	Veröffentlichungen der Deutschen Akademie der Wissenschaften, Institut für Orientforschung.
WA	*World Archaeology.*
WdO	*Welt des Orients.*
YES	Yale Egyptological Studies.
ZÄS	*Zeitschrift für ägyptische Sprache und Altertumskunde.*
ZDMG	*Zeitschrift der Deutschen Morgenländischen Gesellschaft.*

Notes

Chapter 1. Religion: Divine Presence and Transcendence

1. J. Assmann, *ÄHG* (Zurich, 1975), no. 20, ll. 31–37.
2. *ÄHG*, no. 213, ll. 2–3. Italics added.
3. *ÄHG*, no. 139, ll. 1–5; J. Assmann, *STG* (Mainz am Rhein, 1983), no. 37; M. Carmela Betrò, *I Testi solari del portale di Pascerientaisu* (Pisa, 1990). Italics added.
4. H. Cancik, "Augustin als 'constantinischer Theologe,'" in *Der Fürst dieser Welt*, ed. J. Taubes (Munich, 1983), pp. 136–138; R. Schröter, "Die varronische Etymologie," in *Varron: Entretiens sur l'antiquité classique* 9 (Vandeouvre and Geneva, 1963), pp. 79–100, esp. 98–99; A. Dihle, "Die Theologia tripartita bei Augustin," in *Geschichte - Tradition - Reflexion*, ed. H. Cancik et al. (Festschrift. Martin Hengel) (Tübingen, 1996), pp. 183–202.
5. J. Yoyotte. "Champollion et le panthéon égyptien," *BSFE* 95 (1982): 76–108.

Chapter 2. The Local or Cultic Dimension

1. Asclepius 24, *Corpus Hermeticum*, vol. 2, ed. A. D. Nock, trans. A. J. Festugière, Collection des universités de France, pub. sous le patronage de l'Association Guillaume Budé (Paris, 1945), p. 326. See also P. Derchain, *RHR* 161 (1962): 175–198; M. Krause, *XVII. Deutscher Orientalistentag*, ZDMG suppl. 1 (1969): 48–57.
2. On the Egyptian concept of city, see D. Franke, "Zur Bedeutung der Stadt in altägyptischen Texten," in *Städtische Formen und Macht: Veröffentlichung der interdisziplinären Arbeitsgemeinschaft Stadtkulturforschung*, vol. 1 (Aachen, 1994), pp. 29–51.
3. K. Sethe, *Urk.* I (Leipzig, 1935), p. 46, and often otherwise.
4. BD spell 183.
5. TT 216; B. Bruyère, *Rapport préliminaire Deir el Médineh (1923–1924)*, FIFAO 23 (Cairo, 1926), p. 43.
6. Turin 912.
7. Inscription of Harsiese, CG 42210; E. Otto, *Die biographischen Inschriften der ägyptischen Spätzeit: Ihre geistesgeschichtliche und literarische Bedeutung*, PdÄ 2 (Leiden, 1954), p. 144.
8. P. Leiden I 350 VI 9–10; *ÄHG*, no. 142.
9. G. Lefebvre, *Les Inscriptions*, vol. 2 of *Le Tombeau de Pétosiris* (Cairo, 1923), p. 83, no. 116; idem, *ASAE* 21 (1921): 158–159.
10. On this motif see G. Posener, "La complainte de l'échanson Bay," in *Fragen an die altägyptische Literatur*, ed. J. Assmann, E. Feucht, and R. Grieshammer (Wiesbaden, 1977), pp. 385–397; M. Lichtheim, "Praise of Cities in the Literature of the Egyptian New Kingdom"), in *Panhellenica*, ed. S. M. Burstein and L. A. Okin (Festschrift. Truesdell S. Brown) (Lawrence, Kansas, 1980), pp. 15–23.

H. Guksch has been able to show that the motif occurs already in the early New Kingdom; see "'Sehnsucht nach der Heimatstadt': ein ramessidisches Thema?" *MDAIK* 50 (1994): 101–106.

11. P. Anastasi IV, 4.11–5.5; R. A. Caminos, *Late Egyptian Miscellanies*, BES 1 (London, 1954), pp. 150–152; S. Schott, *Ägyptische Liebeslieder, mit Märchen und Liebesgeschichten* (Zurich, 1950), p. 116, no. 57; *ÄHG*, no. 184. This passage, the following one, and other examples of the genre have been treated by Posener, in "La complainte de l'échanson Bay," esp. pp. 390–391.

12. O. Petrie 39 = J. Černý and A. H. Gardiner, *HO* I 8.3 (Oxford, 1957). Posener, "La complainte de l'échanson Bay," p. 391. Same text: O. IFAO, inv. 2683; G. Posener, *Catalogue des ostraca littéraires de Deir el-Médineh*, fasc. 2 (Cairo, 1936), no. 1594.

13. P. Sallier I, 8.2–8.7; A. H. Gardiner, *Late-Egyptian Miscellanies*, BAe 7 (Brussels, 1937), pp. 85–86; Caminos, *Late Egyptian Miscellanies*, p. 321; G. Fecht, *Literarische Zeugnisse zur "Persönlichen Frömmigkeit" in Ägypten*, AHAW, Jahrgang 1965, no. 1 (Heidelberg, 1965), pp. 73 ff.; *ÄHG*, no. 182.

14. O. Gardiner 25; *HO* 38.1, rto. = *ÄHG*, no. 183.

15. Berlin 6768; see H. Grapow, *Wie die alten Ägypter sich anredeten, wie sie sich grüssten und wie sie miteinander sprachen*, APAW, no. 11, fasc. 3 (Berlin, 1941), p. 63.

16. P. Anastasi II, 1.3–5; Caminos, *Late Egyptian Miscellanies*, p. 37 = P. Anastasi IV, 6.3–6.5; Caminos, op. cit., pp. 152–153.

17. BM 581; see K. Sethe, *Ägyptische Lesestücke zum Gebrauch im akademischen Unterricht: Texte der Mittleren Reiches* (Leipzig, 1928; reprint Hildesheim, 1959), p. 80.

18. Louvre E 3336; see P. Pierret, *Recueil d'inscriptions inédites du . . . Louvre*, vol. 2, Études Égyptol. 8 (Paris, 1878), p. 89.

19. K. Sethe, *Urk.* IV (Leipzig, 1927–1930), p. 364.

20. *Urk.* IV, p. 164.

21. Graffito of Osorkon; see G. Daressy, *RdT* 18 (1896): 182, ll. 18–20.

22. O. Leiden I 350 II, 10–15; see G. Fecht, *ZÄS* 91 (1964): 39–40.

23. E. Drioton, *ASAE* 44 (1944): 135–136.

24. G. Posener, "L'Anachoresis dans l'Égypte pharaonique," in *Le monde grec: Hommages à Claire Préaux*, ed. J. Bingen et al. (Brussels, n.d.), pp. 663–669.

25. G. Posener, *L'Enseignement loyaliste: Sagesse égyptienne du Moyen Empire* (Geneva, 1976), pp. 115–116, §11.9–12.

26. Ibid., pp. 115–116, §11.9 and 12.

27. P. Insinger 28.4; see M. Lichtheim, *The Late Period*, vol. 3 of *Ancient Egyptian Literature* (Berkeley, 1980), p. 207; idem, *Late Egyptian Wisdom Literature in the International Context: A Study of Demotic Instructions*, OBO 52 (Freiburg and Göttingen, 1983), pp. 162–163.

28. P. Leiden I 350 III, 6–14 = *ÄHG*, no. 134; see G. Fecht, *ZÄS* 91 (1964): 46–51; similarly, *STG*, no. 113 (k).

29. *ÄHG*, no. 115, ll. 11–18; P. Chester Beatty IX, rto. 13 = P. Cairo 58030, XIV; P. Berlin 3056, VII: J. Assmann, *LL* (Berlin, 1969), pp. 248–249.

30. *ÄHG*, no. 118, ll. 13–16; P. Chester Beatty IX, rto. 14, 3–8 = P. Berlin 3055, X.6–XI.1.

31. N. de G. Davies, *The Decoration*, vol. 3 of *The Temple of Hibis in El-Khargeh Oasis* (New York, 1953), pl. 31.3; see *LL*, p. 254; for many similar formulae, see ibid., pp. 253–257.

32. *Urk.* VIII, p. 42; see *LL*, p. 254, n. 44.

33. On this passage and a number of similar usages, see H. Brunner, in *Archäologie und Altes Testament: Festschrift für Kurt Galling*, ed. A. Kuschkeu and E. Kutsch (Tübingen, 1970), pp. 27–34.

34. A. M. Blackman and H. W. Fairman, in *Miscellanea Gregoriana: Racolta di scritti pubblicati nel centenario della fondazione del Pont. Museo egizio (1839–1939)* (Vatican, 1941), pp. 397–428, text E, I–II; F (subsidiary deities); G, I (parts of the body, aspects), II (parts of the body and insignia), III (city and temple).

35. Asclepius 24, *Corpus Hermeticum*, p. 326.

36. Blackman and Fairman, *Miscellanea Gregoriana*, p. 401, fig. 3, etc.
37. J. Dümichen, *Ägyptische Tempelinschriften in den Jahren 1863–1865 an Ort und Stelle gesammelt und herausg. von Johannes Duemichen*, vol. 2 (Leipzig, 1867), T 24; see S. Morenz, *Egyptian Religion* (Ithaca, 1973), p. 318, n. 59.
38. (a): A. Mariette, *Dendérah: Description générale du grand temple de cette ville*, vol. 1 (Paris, 1870), p. 87 a; (b): ibid., p. 29 c; see Morenz, *Egyptian Religion*, p. 318, nn. 60–61.
39. H. Junker, *Die Stundenwachen in den Osiris-Mysterien* (Vienna, 1910), p. 6; see Morenz, *Egyptian Religion*, p. 318, n. 56.
40. Esna 284.5; S. Sauneron, *Les Fêtes religieuses d'Esna aux dernier siècles du paganisme*, vol. 5 of *Le Temple d'Esna* (Cairo, 1962), p. 128.
41. Mariette, *Dendérah*, vol. 2 (Paris, 1872), p. 73 c.
42. Ibid., p. 45 c.
43. *Urk.* IV, p. 1526 (written as though the text said "on the leaves of the *mnw*-trees").
44. P. BM 10112, ll. 14–15; see L. V. Žabkar, *A Study of the Ba Concept in Ancient Egyptian Texts* , SAOC 34 (Chicago, 1968), p. 133, n. 48, with a number of similar text passages regarding the "alighting" of the *ba* on the corpse.
45. Ani, P. Boulaq 4, VII, 15–16; see A. Volten, *Studien zum Weisheitsbuch des Anii* (1937–1938), pp. 111–116.
46. J. Assmann, *MDAIK* 28 (1973): 126–127.
47. Memphite Theology, ll. 59–60; see Morenz, *Egyptian Religion*, p. 163–166.
48. W. Helck, ed., *Der Text der Lehre für Merikare*, pp. 77–79; G. Posener, ACF 66 (1966–67): 342–343. The contrast between hiddenness (*imn*) and the visibility of the deity materialized in the cult statue corresponds on the human level to the contrast between ethics (directed toward the hidden deity) and cultic worship (directed toward the visible deity).
49. W. Barta, *LÄ*, vol. 3, ed. W. Helck and E. Otto (Wiesbaden, 1979), cols. 839–848, gives a summary of the various sources from the New Kingdom, especially P. Berlin 3055 (A. Moret, *Le Rituel du culte journalier en Égypte* [Paris, 1902; reprint, Geneva 1988]), Karnak (H. Nelson, *JNES* 8 [1949]: 201–232 and 310–345), and Abydos (R. Davis, *A Guide to Religious Ritual at Abydos* [rev. ed., Warminster, 1981]).
50. Nelson, *JNES* 8 (1949): 208–209, fig. 5, ep. 4.
51. Ibid., p. 209, ep. 5.
52. Ibid., p. 221, fig. 17, ep. 18.
53. Ibid., p. 315, fig. 27, ep. 35.
54. Ibid., p. 323, fig. 31, ep. 39.
55. Pyr. 95c; see J. Assmann, *GM* 25 (1977): 19.
56. P. Berlin 3055.

Chapter 3. The Cosmos

1. G. Michaelides, *BIFAO* 49 (1949): 23.
2. E. Edel, *Zu den Inschriften auf den Jahreszeitenreliefs der "Weltkammer" aus dem Sonnenheiligtum des Niuserre*, vol. 1, NAWG 1961/8 (Göttingen, 1961), pp. 211–218 with fig. 3.
3. Ibid., pp. 239–243.
4. Instruction for Merikare, P 130–138; see J. Assmann, *Re und Amun: Die Krise des polytheistischen Weltbilds im Ägypten der 18.–20. Dynastie*, OBO 51 (Freiburg and Göttingen, 1983), pp. 168–169.
5. P. Cairo 58038 (Boulaq 17); see J. Assmann, *ÄHG* (Zurich, 1975), no. 87E, and Assmann, *Re und Amun*, pp. 173–174.
6. M. Sandman, *Texts from the Time of Akhenaten*, Bibl. Aeg. 8 (Brussels, 1938), p. 95, ll. 12–13; see *ÄHG*, no. 92, ll. 115–117; G. Fecht, *ZÄS* 94 (1976): 33 with n. 7; Assmann, *Re und Amun*, pp. 116 and 217.

7. Sandman, *Texts*, p. 15.1-9; see *ÄHG*, no. 91, 53-56; Assmann, *Re und Amun*, pp. 115 and 217; J. Assmann, *STG, Theben* 1 (Mainz, 1983), text 253.
8. *ÄHG*, no. 92, ll. 105-109.
9. P. Ramesseum 9; see G. Posener, *RdeE* 28 (1976): 147-148; sim. W. Pleyte and F. Rossi, *Papyrus de Turin*, vol. 2 (Leiden, 1876), 133.9 = P. Chester Beatty XI, rto. 3.5.
10. W. Barta. *ZÄS* 109 (1982): 81-86.
11. O. Neugebauer and R. A. Parker, *The Early Decans*, vol. 1 of *Egyptian Astronomical Texts*, BES 3 (London, 1960), plate 50, text Dd.
12. Ibid., text Ff.
13. Ibid., text Ee; on the Egyptian "theory" of the migratory birds, see Edel, *Zu den Inschriften auf den Jahreszeitenreliefs*, vol. 2, NAWG 1963/4 (Göttingen, 1963).
14. Assmann, *Re und Amun*, pp. 29-30 with n. 36.
15. P. Chester Beatty IV, rto.; see *ÄHW*, no. 195, ll. 275-278; A. de Buck, *De godsdienstige opvatting van den slaap, inzonderheid in det oude Egypte*, MEOL (Leiden, 1939).
16. J. Assmann, *Der König als Sonnenpriester: Ein kosmographischer Begleittext zur kultischen Sonnenhymnik in thebanischen Tempeln und Gräbern*, ADAIK 7 (Glückstadt, 1970); see also *ÄHG*, no. 20; Assmann, *Re umd Amun*, pp. 24-25, with further literature in nn. 3-11.
17. Amduat; see E. Hornung, *Ägyptische Unterweltsbücher*, 2d ed. (Zurich, 1984), p. 59.
18. Hornung, *Ägyptische Unterweltsbücher*, p. 74.
19. Ibid., p. 76.
20. Ibid., p. 78.
21. Ibid., p. 81.
22. Ibid., p. 85.
23. Ibid., p. 152.
24. Ibid., p. 140.
25. Ibid., p. 118.
26. Ibid., p. 134, and sim. pp. 136-139, passim.
27. Ibid., p. 161.
28. Ibid., p. 194.
29. A. de Buck, *CT*, vol. 7, (Chicago, 1961), 262.
30. *CT*, vol. 7, 282-283.
31. Hornung, *Ägyptische Unterweltsbücher*, p. 129.
32. BD, chapter 100.
33. E. F. Wente, *JNES* 41 (1982): 161-179 interpreted this motif and the pertinent passages in the Amduat and other Books of the Netherworld as expressions of mysticism, aiming at an "*unio mystica*" of god and man. The idea is, however, not about a union of god and man, but, rather, about a union of the officiant and a that-worldly group of adorers; see J. Assmann, "Unio liturgica: Die kultische Einstimmung in götterweltlichen Lobpreis als Grundmotiv 'esoterischer' Überlieferung im alten Ägypten," in *Secrecy and Concealment: Studies in the History of Mediterranean and Near Eastern Religions*, ed. H. G. Kippenberg and G. Stroumsa (Leiden, 1995), pp. 37-60.
34. The Epigraphic Survey, *Medinet Habu*, vol. 6, OIP 84 (Chicago, 1963), pp. 422-423.
35. P. Brooklyn 47.218.50, II, 10; J.-C. Goyon, *La Confirmation du pouvoir royal au Nouvel An*, Bibl. d'Ét. 52 (Cairo, 1972), p. 58.
36. A. Klasens, *A Magical Statue Base (Socle Behague) in the Museum of Antiquities at Leiden*, OMRO, n.s., 33 (Leiden, 1952), pp. 31-32, 57, 96; cf. J. Assmann, "Königsdogma und Heilserwartung: Politische und kultische Chaosbeschreibungen in ägyptischen Texten," in *Apocalypticism in the Mediterranean World and the Near East: Proceedings of the International Colloquium on Apocalypticism, Upssala, August 12-17, 1979*, ed. D. Hellholm (Tübingen, 1983), pp. 345-377.
37. P. Derchain, *Le Papyrus Salt 825 (B.M. 10051): Rituel pour la conservation de la vie en Égypte*, Académie Royale de Belgique, Classe des lettres et des sciences morales et politiques, Mémoires, 2d. ser., 8 (Brussels, 1965), I 1; Assmann, "Königsdogma," p. 370.

38. Pyr. 1120.
39. Pyr. 393.
40. Pyr. 1443a; on this topic, see J. Assmann, *Liturgische Lieder an den Sonnengott: Untersuchungen zur altägyptischen Hymnik*, MÄS 19 (Berlin, 1969), pp. 257–258.
41. P. Leiden I 350 II, 2–10; see *ÄHG*, no. 132.
42. C. de Wit, *Les Inscriptions du temple d'Opet, à Karnak*, vol. 1, Bibl. Aeg. 11 (Brussels, 1958), p. 186.
43. Marriage Stela of Ramesses II; K. A. Kitchen, *Ramesside Inscriptions: Historical and Biographical*, vol. 2 (Oxford, 1979), pp. 236–237.
44. P. Derchain, *Le Papyrus Salt 825 (B.M.10051)*; cf. also idem, "Le rôle du roi d'Égypte dans le maintien de l'ordre cosmique," in *Le pouvoir et le sacré* (Brussels, 1961).
45. Prophecies of Neferti 24–25; W. Helck, *Die Prophezeiung des Nfr.tj* (Wiesbaden, 1970), pp. 21–25.
46. Prophecies of Neferti 51–53; Helck, *Die Prophezeiung*, pp. 42–43; Assmann, "Königsdogma," p. 358.
47. L. Koenen, "Die Prophezeiungen des Töpfers," *ZPE* 2 (1968): 178–209.
48. Asclepius 25–26, *Corpus Hermeticum*, vol. 2, 5th ed., ed. A. D. Nock, trans. A. J. Festugière (Paris, 1992). Coptic version in Nag Hammadi Codex VI 73.12–22; see M. Krause and P. Labib, eds., *Gnostische und hermetische Schriften aus Codex II und Codex VI*, ADAIK, kopt. Reihe 2 (Glückstadt, 1971), pp. 198–199. See J. Assmann, "Königsdogma," p. 373.
49. On this and similar passages, see J. Assmann, *Zeit und Ewigkeit im alten Ägypten: Ein Beitrag zur Geschichte der Ewigkeit*, AHAW 1975/1 (Heidelberg, 1975), p. 44 with n. 155.
50. Derchain, *Le Papyrus Salt 825*, 18, 1–2; see J. Assmann, *Liturgische Lieder*, pp. 101–105, and Assmann, *Re und Amun*, pp. 89–90.

Chapter 4. The Verbal or Mythic Dimension

1. Pyr. 1478.
2. Pyr. 577c–d.
3. Pyr. 580.
4. Pyr. 614.
5. Pyr. 616.
6. Pyr. 620.
7. PT spell 366.
8. Pyr. 249.
9. Pyr. 614.
10. Ramesseum Dramatic Papyrus, ll. 101–103; K. Sethe, ed., *Dramatische Texte zu altägyptischen Mysterienspielen*, UGAAe 10 (Leipzig, 1928); see J. Assmann, *GM* 25 (1977): 16–18.
11. PT spell 373.
12. BD chapter 15 B III; *ÄHG* 41; J. Assmann, *LL* (Berlin, 1969), text I 2.
13. Ramesseum Dramatic Papyrus, 48.
14. Ibid., 49.
15. PT spell 539.
16. BD chapter 99, Ibi version, after K. Sethe, "Die älteste Fassung der Einleitung des Totenbuch Kapitel 99," *Miscellanea Academica Berolinensia: Gesammelte Abhandlungen zur Feier des 250jährigen Bestehens der Deutschen Akademie der Wissenschaften zu Berlin* (Berlin, 1950), pp. 77–96; K. Sethe, *Ägyptologische Studien (Hermann Grapow zum 70. Geburtstag gewidmet)*, VDAW 29 (Berlin, 1955), 176–185; D. Bidoli, *Die Sprüche der Fangnetze in den altägyptischen Sargtexten*, ADAIK 9 (Glückstadt, 1976), pp. 26–35.
17. A. de Buck, *CT*, vol. 5 (Chicago, 1954), 9d–13d, 15d–e; Bidoli, *Sprüche der Fangnetze*, pp. 83–91.
18. See J. Assmann, *GM* 25 (1977): 7–43.

19. Pyr. 2128.
20. Pyr. 95c.
21. Ramesseum Dramatic Papyrus; see note 10 above.
22. Stela from year 6 of Taharqa, published by M. F. L. Macadam, *The Temples of Kawa: Oxford University Excavations in Nubia* (London, 1949), plate X.
23. S. Schott, *Der Denkstein Sethos' I. für die Kapelle Ramses' I. in Abydos,* NAWG Jahrgang 1964 (Göttingen, 1964), p. 81.
24. PT spell 422.
25. J. Assmann, *ÄHG* (Zurich, 1975), no. 22A, ll. 28–32.
26. J. Assmann, *STG, Theben* 1 (Mainz am Rhein, 1983), text A = *LL,* text III 1.
27. *STG,* text C.
28. After E. Hornung, *Ägyptische Unterweltsbücher,* 2d ed. (Zurich, 1984), pp. 489–492.
29. After ibid., p. 493.
30. Isis and Re, W. Pleyte and F. Rossi, *Papyrus de Turin* (Leiden, 1876), 133.10 = P. Chester Beatty XI, rto. 3.6; *LÄ,* vol. 1, ed. W. Helck and E. Otto (Weisbaden, 1975), col. 939, no. 29.
31. *CT,* vol. 1 (1935), 191c; cf. *RdT* 32 (1912): 87.
32. BD spell 15 B; see note 12 above.
33. *ÄHG,* no. 22B, ll. 4–6.
34. Book of Caverns, Hornung, *Ägyptische Unterweltsbücher,* p. 317.
35. BD spell 100.

Chapter 5. Myth

1. E. Hornung, *Der ägyptische Mythos von der Himmelskuh: Eine Ätiologie des Unvollkommenen,* OBO 46 (Freiburg and Göttingen, 1982), pp. 1 (text) and 37 (translation).
2. Ibid., pp. 5 and 38 (verse 49).
3. Ibid., pp. 10 and 40 (verse 105).
4. Ibid., pp. 12 and 41 (verse 139).
5. Ibid., pp. 29 and 48 (verses 315–320).
6. H. Brunner, *Die Geburt des Gottkönigs: Studien zur Überlieferung eines altägyptischen Mythos,* Äg. Abh. 10 (Wiesbaden, 1964), p. 43; J. Assmann, "Die Zeugung des Sohnes: Bild, Spiel, Erzählung und das Problem des ägyptischen Mythos," in *Funktionen und Leistungen des Mythos: Drei altorientalische Beispiele,* ed. J. Assmann, W. Burkert, and F. Stolz, OBO 48 (Freiburg and Göttingen, 1982), p. 27. For the text, see K. Sethe, *Urk.* IV (Leipzig, 1927–1930), p. 221.
7. PT spell 600; see E. Otto, *Studi in memoria di Ippolito Rosellini nel primo centenario della morte (4 giugno 1843),* vol. 2 (Pisa, 1955), pp. 223–237.
8. Pyr. §1466.
9. Pyr. §1040; on similar statements, see H. Grapow, *ZÄS* 67 (1931): 34–38, and E. Hornung, *Conceptions of God in Ancient Egypt: The One and the Many,* trans. J. Baines (Ithaca, 1982), pp. 174–176.
10. A. de Buck, *CT,* vol. 4 (Chicago, 1952), 193d–e; see E. Hornung, *Saeculum* 22 (1971): 53.
11. PT spell 532.
12. Pyr. §§1280–1282.
13. Pyr. §972.
14. PT spell 477.
15. *CT* spell 148, vol. 2 (Chicago, 1938).
16. Medical Papyrus. London XIV, 8–14; see J. Assmann, *GM* 25 (1977): 24–27.
17. A. Klasens, *A Magical Statue Base (Socle Behague) in the Museum of Antiquities at Leiden,* OMRO, n.s., 33 (Leiden, 1952), pp. 22–34, 54–58, and 81–98, text IV; J. F. Borghouts, *Ancient Egyptian Magical Texts,* Nisaba 9 (Leiden, 1978), no. 91.
18. *Urk.* IV, pp. 239–240; see J. Assmann, "Die Zeugung des Sohnes," p. 37.
19. *CT* spells 7–9, vol. 1 (Chicago, 1935).

20. J. Assmann, *MDAIK* 28 (1972): 54–55 and 65–66.
21. H. Junker, *Die politische Lehre von Memphis*, APAW, Jahrgang 1941, no. 6 (Berlin, 1941), pp. 23–36.
22. A. H. Gardiner, *Late-Egyptian Stories*, Bibl. Aeg. 1 (Brussels, 1932), p. 8. See also J. Spiegel, *Die Erzählung vom Streite des Horus und Seth im Pap. Chester Beatty I als Literaturwerk*, LÄS 9 (Glückstadt, 1937).
23. J. Assmann, *ÄHG* (Zurich, 1975), nr. 241.
24. P. Chester Beatty I, 16.5–8; Gardiner, *Late-Egyptian Stories*, p. 60.
25. Philae I 257.
26. R. Anthes, in *Fs zum 150jährigen Bestehen des Berliner Ägyptischen Museums*, SMBMÄS 8 (Berlin, 1974), p. 41.
27. E. Chassinat, *Le Temple d'Edfou*, vol. 6, MMIFAO 23 (Cairo, 1931), p. 88s; J. Assmann, *LL* (Berlin, 1969), p. 105, n. 81.
28. *ÄHG*, nr. 215, ll. 9–19.
29. *ÄHG*, nr. 216, ll. 27–33.
30. *ÄHG*, nr. 214, ll. 39–55 (BD spell 183).
31. *ÄHG*, nr. 213, ll. 87–153.

Chapter 6. On the Meaning of the Three Dimensions: Concluding Remarks

1. See E. F. Wente, *JNES* 41 (1982): 161–179.

Chapter 7. The Unity of Discourse

1. K. Bühler, *Theory of Language: The Representational Function of Language*, trans. D. F. Goodwin, Foundations of Semiotics 25 (Amsterdam, 1990); originally published as *Sprachtheorie: Die Darstellungsfunktion der Sprache* (Jena, 1934).
2. Instruction for Merikare, P 32; see A. Volten, *Zwei Altägyptische politische Schriften: Die Lehre für König Merikarê (Pap. Carsberg VI) und die Lehre des Königs Amenemhet*, An. Aeg. 4 (Copenhagen, 1945), p. 13.

Chapter 8. Theodicy and Theology in the Middle Kingdom

1. See J. Assmann, "Weisheit, Schrift und Literatur im alten Ägypten," in *Weisheit*, ed. A. Assmann (Munich, 1991), pp. 475–500; M. Lichtheim, "Didactic Literature," in *Ancient Egyptian Literature: History and Forms*, ed. A. Loprieno (Leiden, 1996), pp. 243–262.
2. But see J. Assmann, "Cultural and Literary Texts," in *Definitely: Egyptian Literature*, Studia monographica 2 of *Lingua Aegyptia* (Göttingen, 1999), pp. 1–15.
3. Cf. G. Posener, "Sur le monothéisme dans l'ancienne Égypte," in *Mélanges bibliques et orientaux en l'honneur de M. Henri Cazelles*, AOAT 212 (Neukirchen, 1981), pp. 347–351.
4. Cf. E. Blumenthal, "Die literarische Verarbeitung der Übergangszeit zwischen Altem und Mittlerem Reich," in *Ancient Egyptian Literature*, ed. Loprieno, pp. 105–136.
5. For an English translation, see M. Lichtheim, *The Old and Middle Kingdoms*, vol. 1 of *Ancient Egyptian Literature: A Book of Readings* (Berkeley, 1973), pp. 149–163.
6. Ibid., pp. 159–160.
7. Ibid., pp. 97–109.
8. Ibid., pp. 106–107.

9. Instruction for Merikare P 67; P 130; J. Assmann, *LÄ*, vol. 1, ed. W. Helck and E. Otto (Weisbaden, 1975), col. 1089, n. 13; idem, *Re und Amun: Die Krise des polytheistischen Weltbilds im Ägypten der 18.–20. Dynastie*, OBO 51 (Freiburg and Göttingen, 1983), pp. 159–160.

10. Lichtheim, *Old and Middle Kingdoms*, pp. 131–133.

11. A. de Buck, *CT*, vol. 7 (Chicago, 1961) 461c–464f.

12. *CT*, vol. 7, 4663e–467d.

13. J. Assmann, *Der König als Sonnenpriester: Ein kosmographischer Begleittext zur kultischen Sonnenhymnik in thebanischen Tempeln und Gräbern*, ADAIK 7 (Glückstadt, 1970), pp. 19, 22, 35, 60–65.

14. Lichtheim, *Old and Middle Kingdoms*, p. 101.

15. *CT*, vol. 7, 464g–465a.

16. For a recent and in many points different interpretation of spell 80 and the group of Shu-texts, see H. Willems, *The Coffin of Heqata (Cairo JdE 36418)* (Leuven, 1996), pp. 273–324.

17. *CT*, vol. 2 (Chicago, 1952), 28e–31as; cf. *CT*, vol. 4 (Chicago, 1952), 240h–i.

18. *CT*, vol. 2, 32b–33a.

19. *CT*, vol. 2, 33e–34f.

20. *CT*, vol. 2, 34h–35a.

21. *CT*, vol. 2, 32b–33a.

22. *CT*, vol. 2, 4g–h.

23. *CT*, vol. 2, 3f–40a; vol. 1, 344c.

24. *CT*, vol. 1, 356a–b.

25. *CT*, vol. 2, 3h–4a.

26. *CT*, vol. 1, 336–339.

27. *CT*, vol. 2, 35j, 36a, 44b.

28. *CT*, vol. 2, 42b–43h. See S. Morenz, *Wiener Zeitschrift für die Kunde des Morgenlandes*, 54 (1957): 119–129.

29. BM 581; K. Sethe, *Aegyptische Lesestücke zum gebrauch im akademischen Unterricht* (Leipzig 1924), p. 80.

30. On the religious significance of Abydos in the Middle Kingdom, see J. Spiegel, *Die Götter von Abydos: Studien zum ägyptischen Synkretismus*, GOF 1 (Wiesbaden, 1973).

31. J. Assmann, *ÄHG* (Zurich, 1975), no. 204; Louvre C 30 and variants.

Chapter 9. The New Gods

1. For details, see J. Assmann, *Egyptian Solar Religion in the New Kingdom* (London 1995), pp. 102–111.

2. J. Assmann, *STG* (Mainz am Rhein, 1983), no. 68 = J. Assmann, *ÄHG* (Zurich, 1975), no. 76.

3. K. Sethe, *Urk.* IV (Leipzig, 1927–1930), p. 518.

4. *Urk.* IV, p. 111.

5. P. Lacau and H. Chevrier, *Une Chapelle d'Hatchepsout à Karnak*, vol. 1 (Cairo, 1977), pp. 97–101.

6. Ibid., p. 99, ll. 15–16.

7. Cairo Journal d'entrée 11509; see *Re und Amun*, p. 180.

8. See J. Assmann, *Egyptian Solar Religion*, pp. 120–125.

9. *ÄHG*, no. 87C; *Re und Amun*, pp. 176–177.

10. Instruction for Merikare, P 134–135.

11. *STG*, no. 165 = *ÄHG*, no. 75, ll. 23–24.

12. *ÄHG*, no. 72, ll. 5–7.

13. *ÄHG*, no. 83, ll. 6–7.

14. W. M. F. Petrie, *Sedment*, vol. 2, BASE 35 (London, 1924), p. 49; *Re und Amun*, p. 184.

15. *STG*, no. 67; cf. *Re und Amun*, p. 184, n. 133.
16. O. Cairo 12189; see G. Posener, *RdeE* 27 (1975): 209.
17. The most important text of this tradition is the long hymn to Amun published by J. Zandee, *Der Amunhymnus des Pap. Leiden I 344 verso*, 3 vols. (Leiden, 1992). For an interpretation of this hymn along the lines of the "New Solar Theology" see J. Assmann, *ÄHG*, 2d. ed. (Fribourg and Göttingen, 1999), pp. 558–562.
18. *ÄHG*, no. 90, l. 7.
19. *STG*, no. 253.
20. *STG*, no. 54.
21. BM 706; see K. A. Kitchen, *Ramesside Inscriptions: Historical and Biographical*, vol. 1 (Oxford, 1975), p. 330.
22. P. Berlin 3048 = *ÄHG*, no. 143, ll. 206–208; see also *Re und Amun*, pp. 101–102, with a number of further examples.
23. *STG*, no. 83, ll. 8–11.
24. N. de G. Davies, *The Temple of Hibis in El Khargeh Oasis*, vol. 3 (New York, 1953), plate 16; cf. *Re und Amun*, p. 105, no. 37.
25. J. E. Quibell, *1908–10*, vol. 4 of *Excavations at Saqqara* (Cairo, 1912), pl. 7.3 = P. Berlin 3048 and *ÄHG*, no. 143, l. 17.
26. Davies, *Temple of Hibis*, vol. 3, pl. 32, ll. 4–5 = *ÄHG*, no. 129, ll. 20–21; see *Re und Amun*, pp. 104–106 for a number of other attestations.
27. P. Berlin 3050 = J. Assmann, *LL* (Berflin, 1969) 206 (32), with many other attestations of this topos.
28. P. Leiden I 350 II, 19.
29. P. Chester Beatty IV, rto. 3, 7 = *ÄHG*, no. 195, l. 8; see *Re und Amun*, pp. 108–110, with many further attestations.
30. *STG*, no. 151, l. 15, and cf. p. 196 (k).
31. Quibell, *1908–10*, pl. 70.
32. Sobk-Re, P. Strasbourg IV, 21–22 = *ÄHG*, no. 144C, l. 75; Neskhons 18 = *ÄHG*, no. 131, l. 47.
33. Stela of Ramesses IV; see W. Helck, *ZÄS* 82 (1958), pl. 5.14.
34. J. Assmann, *MDAIK* 27 (1971): 4–5.
35. *STG*, no. 76, l. 14; cf. Assmann, *MDAIK* 27 (1971): 8–11, with many further attestations of this topic.
36. *STG*, no. 151, l. 26.
37. Cairo Catalogue général 42208 = *ÄHG*, no. 200, l. 13; see *Re und Amun*, pp. 110–111, n. 87a.
38. *STG*, no. 156, l. 15 = *ÄHG*, no. 108, l. 15.
39. P. Chester Beatty IV, rto. = *ÄHG*, no. 195, l. 237; cf. M. Sandman, *Texts from the Time of Akhenaten*, Bibl. Aeg. 8 (Brussels, 1938), p. 23, l. 5.
40. Stela from Deir el-Bahari, see J. Lipínska, *ASAE* 60 (1968): 167, pls. 11–12, figs. 17, 19.
41. *STG*, nos. 161 and 253, and cf. p. 355 (u).
42. BM 170; see I. E. S. Edwards, *Hieroglyphic Texts from Egyptian Stelae, etc.*, vol. 8 (London, 1939), pl. 34; see *ÄHG*, p. 57, with p. 513, n. 39, and *STG*, pp. 90–91, for further attestations.
43. Instruction for Merikare, P 134.
44. *STG*, no. 54, ll. 7–8 = *ÄHG*, no. 96; see also J. Assmann, *Zeit und Ewigkeit im alten Ägypten: Ein Beitrag zur Geschichte der Ewigkeit*, AHAW 1975/1 (Heidelberg, 1975), pp. 49–50, n. 1, with further attestations.
45. Assmann, *MDAIK* 27 (1971): 4–5 and 12–15.
46. P. Leiden I 350 II, 17; see J. Assmann, *Zeit und Ewigkeit*, p. 49.
47. *STG*, no. 113, l. 11 and p. 155 (g) = *ÄHG*, no. 102, l. 11; see J. Assmann, *Zeit und Ewigkeit*, p. 44 with n. 155.
48. N. de G. Davies, *TheTomb of Nefer-hotep, at Thebes*, PMMA 9 (New York, 1933), pls. 58–59; cf. Assmann, *Zeit und Ewigkeit*, p. 62.
49. Sandman, *Akhenaten*, pp. 9–10 = *ÄHG*, no. 95, ll. 52–54.
50. P. Leiden I 350 II, 15.

51. Assmann, *MDAIK* 27 (1971): 13–14 = *ÄHG*, no. 89, ll. 21–22.
52. *ÄHG*, no. 50, ll. 8–9; see J. Assmann, *Zeit und Ewigkeit*, p. 51.
53. *ÄHG*, no. 89, l. 40; see *Re und Amun*, p. 119.
54. *ÄHG*, no. 87, l. 115.
55. Sandman, *Akhenaten*, p. 7, l. 7.
56. *Urk.* IV, p. 1971, l. 15.
57. *ÄHG*, no. 92, l. 25.
58. *ÄHG*, no. 92, l. 55.
59. Sandman, *Akhenaten*, p. 89, ll. 14–15.
60. *ÄHG*, no. 92, l. 26.
61. Sandman, *Akhenaten*, p. 21, l. 3; see *STG*, no. 188, l. 7 and p. 166 (c).
62. *ÄHG*, no. 91, ll. 21–22.
63. *ÄHG*, no. 91, ll. 55–56; see *Re und Amun*, pp. 115 and 217; *STG*, no. 253 and pp. 354–355 (s).
64. *ÄHG*, no. 91, ll. 53–54 and no. 92, ll. 110–111.
65. *Urk.* IV, p. 1971.
66. *ÄHG*, no. 95, ll. 52–54.
67. *ÄHG*, no. 92, ll. 85–86.
68. *ÄHG*, no. 92, ll. 125–128.
69. *Urk.* IV, p. 1971, l. 13; see *STG*, no. 113 and p. 155 (f).
70. *ÄHG*, no. 87, ll. 121–122.
71. *ÄHG*, no. 92, ll. 76–78.
72. *ÄHG*, no. 92, l. 100.
73. *ÄHG*, no. 92, ll. 27–34.
74. *ÄHG*, no. 92, ll. 126–127.
75. *Re und Amun*, p. 142 with n. 199a. In his new translation of the Amarna Letters, *Les Lettres d'El-Amarns* (Paris, 1987), p. 8, W. L. Moran renders the passage as "qui accorde la vie par son doux souffle et revient avec son vent du nord," basing his translation on an article by C. Grave, "Northwest Semitic *sapanu* in a Break-up of an Egyptian Stereotype Phrase in EA 147," *Orientalia*, n.s., 51 (1982): 161–182. The rendering of *i-ZA-HAR* as "revient" is a mere guess. Albright had read *i-sa-hir* "who diminishes," (scilicet life), which makes better sense if the passage relates to the sun god, whereas Grave's translation seems preferable if the reference is to the king. But with or without this mediation via Tyre, it seems evident to me that the idea of intermittent divine introjection of life into the world is common to both the psalm and the Egyptian hymn. The "sweet breath" (*sehu*), which appears in the Bible as *ruchakha*, is a common Egyptian metaphor both for time and light. "The sight of your rays," we read in the Shorter Hymn, "is breath of life in their noses"; see Sandman, *Akhenaten*, p. 15, ll. 6–9. See also C. Uehlinger, "Leviathan und die Schiffe in Ps. 104, 25–26," *Biblica* 71 (1990): 499–526.
76. C. Grave, "Northwest Semitic *sapanu*": 161–182.
77. Moran, *Les lettres d'El-Amarna*, p. 378.
78. Sandman, *Akhenaten*, p. 15, ll. 6–9.
79. *ÄHG*, no. 91, l. 56; see *STG*, p. 189 (c).
80. *ÄHG*, no. 92, ll. 115–117.
81. *ÄHG*, no. 92, l. 128.
82. *ÄHG*, no. 91, l. 20.
83. *ÄHG*, no. 92, ll. 130–137.
84. *ÄHG*, no. 92, ll. 22–24.
85. *ÄHG*, no. 92, ll. 125–127.
86. Sandman, *Akhenaten*, p. 75, ll. 16–18.
87. For example, *ÄHG*, no. 92, ll. 1–14; for further examples, see J. Assmann, *JNES* 31 (1972): 152, n. 60.
88. *ÄHG*, no. 91, ll. 50–51.
89. *ÄHG*, no. 92, ll 120–123.

90. *ÄHG*, no. 92, l. 124.
91. *ÄHG*, no. 87.
92. *STG*, no. 165, ll. 23–24 = *ÄHG*, no. 75; see *Re und Amun*, p. 166.
93. *ÄHG*, no. 91, ll. 21–22.
94. *STG*, no. 225, ll. 23–24; for further attestations, see *Re und Amun*, p. 120.
95. *ÄHG*, no. 147.
96. *ÄHG*, no. 148B, ll. 1–24.
97. Ibid., ll. 37–38.
98. Ibid., ll. 39–40.
99. Ibid., ll. 46–47; the same formula is also to be found in B. Bruyère, *Rapport sur les fouilles de Deir el Médineh (1945–47)*, FIFAO 21 (Cairo, 1952), pl. 8.
100. *ÄHG*, no. 150B, ll. 5–10.
101. *ÄHG*, no. 152, ll. 5–6, and no. 153, ll. 11–12.
102. *ÄHG*, no. 190, ll. 20–25.
103. *ÄHG*, no. 182, ll. 19–24.
104. *ÄHG*, no. 169, ll. 1–3.
105. *Urk.* IV, p. 2027; H. A. Schlögl, *Echnaton-Tutanchamun: Fakten und Texte* (Wiesbaden, 1983), p. 86.
106. Inscription in the rock temple of Aya at es-Salamuni.
107. P. Chester Beatty IV, rto. 7.11–8.7 = *ÄHG*, no. 195, ll. 132–150; see *Re und Amun*, pp. 269–271.
108. A.-P. Zivie, *La Tombe de Pached à Deir el-Médineh [no. 3]*, MIFAO 99 (Cairo, 1979), p. 36 and pl. 19.
109. *ÄHG*, no. 196, l. 12; for the passages that follow, see ll. 57–61 and 65–66.
110. Block statue of a Ramose, in private hands; kind communication of P. Vernus and F. Herbin.
111. *ÄHG*, no. 148, ll. 48–52.
112. Banishment Stela; J. von Beckerath, *RdeE* 20 (1968): 7–36, and see *ÄHG*, pp. 70–71.
113. *STG*, no. 156.
114. P. Leiden I 350 V, 19–20; see *ÄHG*, no. 141.
115. *ÄHG*, no. 196, ll. 19–28; further attestations in *Re und Amun*, pp. 250–258.
116. O. Boston MFA 11.1498; see J. Černý, *JEA* 44 (1958): 23 and pl. 10.
117. Neskhons 23–24 = *ÄHG*, no. 131, ll. 58–59.
118. P. Berlin 3049, VIII.4 = *ÄHG*, no. 127B, ll. 34–35; see *Re und Amun*, p. 273, n. 318, for further attestations.
119. *STG*, no. 88, ll. 12–15.
120. *ÄHG*, no. 130, ll. 205–206; see *Re und Amun*, p. 246.
121. *ÄHG*, no. 127B, ll. 81–82.
122. Ibid., ll. 96–97.
123. Assmann, *Zeit und Ewigkeit*, p. 66, n. 88.
124. Ibid., p. 66, with n. 90; see also M. Lichtheim, *Late Egyptian Wisdom Literature in the International Context: A Study of Demotic Instructions*, OBO 52 (Freiburg and Göttingen, 1983), pp. 7–8.
125. Instruction of Amenemope VI.18–VII.10; see J. Assmann, *Zeit und Ewigkeit*, pp. 66–67.
126. P. Leiden I 350, IV, 12–21 = *ÄHG*, no. 138; see *Re und Amun*, pp. 200–203.
127. P. Leiden I 350, IV, 21–22 = *ÄHG*, no. 139, ll. 1–5.
128. *ÄHG*, no. 196, ll. 13–14.
129. *"Livre que mon nom fleurisse"*; see *Re und Amun*, p. 215.
130. *STG*, no. 17 = no. 186, see p. 22 (6); Assmann, *Zeit und Ewigkeit*, p. 69, and *Re und Amun*, pp. 269 and 283–286.
131. P. Mag. Harris III.10–IV.8; see *ÄHG*, no. 129.
132. K. Preisendanz, *Papyri Magicae Graecae: Die griechischen Zauberpapyri* (Leipzig, 1928–1931), XII, ll. 242–244; XIII, ll. 767–769; XXI, ll. 4–6; see J. Assmann, "Primat und Tranzendenz: Struktur und Genese der ägyptischen Vorstellung

eines 'Höchsten Wesens,'" in *Aspekte der spätägyptischen Religion*, ed. W. Westendorf, GOF 9 (Wiesbaden, 1979), p. 7.

133. S. Sauneron, *Le Papyrus magique illustré de Brooklyn: Brooklyn Museum 47.218.156* (New York, 1970), p. 23 and pls. 4 and 4a; see J. Assmann, "Primat und Transzendenz", pp. 12–13.

Bibliography

Chapter 1

General Treatments of Egyptian Religion

Assmann, J. *Ma'at: Gerechtigkeit und Unsterblichkeit im alten Ägypten*. 2d ed. Munich, 1995.
Bonnet, H. *Reallexikon der ägyptischen Religionsgeschichte*. Berlin, 1952.
Brunner, H. *Grundzüge der altägyptischen Religion*. Darmstadt, 1983.
Daumas, F. *Les Dieux de l'Égypte*. Que sais-je 1194. Paris, 1965.
Derchain, P. "Divinité selon l'Égypte ancienne." In *Dictionnaire des mythologies et des religions des sociétés traditionelles et du monde antique*, ed. Y. Bonnefoy. Paris, 1981.
Dunand, F., and C. Zivie-Coche. *Dieux et hommes en Égypte 3000 av. J.C.–395 apr. J.C.* Paris, 1991.
Erman, A. *Die Religion der Ägypter: Ihr Werden und Vergehen in vier Jahrtausenden*. Berlin and Leipzig, 1934.
Frankfort, H. *Egyptian Religion: An Interpretation*. New York, 1948.
———. *Kingship and the Gods: A Study of Ancient Near Eastern Religion as the Integration of Society and Nature*. Chicago, 1948.
Hornung, E. *Conceptions of God: The One and the Many*. Trans. J. Baines. Ithaca, 1982.
Junker, H. *Pyramidenzeit: Das Wesen der altägyptischen Religion*. Einsiedeln, 1948.
Kees, H. *Der Götterglaube im alten Ägypten*. Leipzig, 1941.
Koch, K. *Geschichte der ägyptischen Religion*. Stuttgart, 1993.
Meeks, D. and C. Favard-Meeks. *Daily Life of the Egyptian Gods*. Trans. G. M. Goshgarian. Ithaca, 1996.
Morenz, S. *Egyptian Religion*. Trans. Ann E. Keep. Ithaca, 1973.
———. *Gott und Mensch im alten Ägypten*. Leipzig, 1965.
Otto, E. *Die Religion der alten Ägypter*. HdO, Section 1, Vol. 8.1. Leiden, 1964.
Quirke, S. *Ancient Egyptian Religion*. London, 1992.
Schafer, B. A., ed. *Religion in Ancient Egypt*. Ithaca, 1991.
Traunecker, C. *Les Dieux de l'Égypte*. Que sais-je 1194. Paris, 1992.

The Monotheism Problem

Assmann, J. *Monotheismus und Kosmotheismus: Altägyptische Formen eines "Denkens des Einen" und ihre europäische Rezeptionsgeschichte*. SHAW 1993/2. Heidelberg, 1993.
Brunner, H. "Monotheismus." In *LÄ*, ed. W. Helck and E. Otto. Vol. 4. Wiesbaden, 1980, cols. 198–200.
Hornung, E. *Conceptions of God: The One and the Many*. Trans. J. Baines. Ithaca, 1982.

———. "Die Anfänge von Monotheismus und Trinität in Ägypten." In *Der eine Gott und der dreieine Gott*, ed. Karl Rahner. Zurich, 1983, pp. 48–66.
———. "Monotheismus im pharaonischen Ägypten." In *Monotheismus im alten Israel und seiner Umwelt*, ed. O. Keel. Bibl. Beitr. 14. Fribourg, 1980, pp. 83–97.
Morenz, S. *Die Heraufkunft des transzendenten Gottes in Ägypten*. SSAW 109.2. Berlin, 1964.
Otto, E. "Altägyptischer Polytheismus: Eine Beschreibung." *Saeculum* 14 (1963): 249–285.
———. "Monotheistische Tendenzen in der ägyptischen Religion." *WdO* 2 (1955): 99–110.
Posener, G. "Sur le monothéisme dans l'ancienne Égypte." In *Mélanges bibliques et orientaux en l'honneur de M. Henri Cazelles*. AOAT 212. Neukirchen, 1981, pp. 347–351.

Hermetism

Daumas, F. "Le Fonds égyptien de l'Hermétisme." In *Gnosticisme et Monde hellénistique:Actes du colloque de Louvain-la-Neuve (11–14 mars 1980)*, ed. J. Riess, Y. Janssens, and J.-M. Sevrin. Louvain-la-Neuve, 1982, pp. 1–25.

Chapter 2

The Egyptian State

Assmann, J. *Herrschaft und Heil: Politische Theologie in Altägypten, Israel und Europa*. Munich, 2000.
———. "State and Religion in the New Kingdom." In *Religion and Philosophy in Ancient Egypt*, ed. W. K. Simpson. YES 3. New Haven, 1989, pp. 55–88.
Bonheme, M. A., and A. Foreau. *Pharaon: Les Secrets du pouvoir*. Paris, 1988.
Butzer, K. W. "Siedlungsgeographie." In *LÄ*, ed. W. Helck and E. Otto. Vol. 5. Wiesbaden, 1984, cols. 924–933.
Hammond, M. *The City in the Ancient World*. Cambridge, Mass. 1972, esp. pp. 65–76.
Kemp, B. J. *Ancient Egypt: Anatomy of a Civilization*. London, 1989.
———. "The City of el-Amarnah as a Source for the Study of Urban Society in Ancient Egypt." *WA* 9 (1977): 123–139.
———. "The Early Development of Towns in Egypt." *Antiquity* 51 (1977): 185–200.
———. "Temple and Town in Ancient Egypt." In *Man, Settlement and Urbanism: Proceedings of a Meeting of the Research Center in Archaeology and Related Subjects Held at the Institute of Archaeology, London University*, ed. P. J. Ucko, R. Tringham, and G. W. Dimbleby. London, 1972, pp. 657–680.
O'Connor, D. "Cities and Towns." In *Egypt's Golden Age: The Art of Living in the New Kingdom*. Boston, 1982, pp. 17–24.
———. "The Geography of Settlement in Ancient Egypt." In *Man, Settlement and Urbanism*, ed. P. J. Ucko, R. Tringham, and G. W. Dimbleby. London, 1972, pp. 681–698.
O'Connor, D., and D. Silverman, eds. *Ancient Egyptian Kingship: New Investigations*. Prob. Äg. 9. Leiden, 1995.
Schemeil, Y. *La Politique dans l'ancient Orient*. Paris, 1999.
Valbelle, D. *Histoire de l'état pharaonique*. Paris, 1998.
Vernus, P., and J. Yoyotte. *Les Pharaons*. Paris, 1988.

Temples
AS ECONOMIC ENTERPRISES

Helck, W. *Materialien zur Wirtschaftsgeschichte des Neuen Reichs*. 4 vols. Mainz, 1960–1969.
———. *Wirtschaftsgeschichte des Alten Ägypten*. HdO, 1. Abt. Vol. 1.5. Leiden, 1975.
Janssen, J. J. "The Role of the Temple in the Egyptian Economy during the New Kingdom." In *State and Temple Economy in the Ancient Near East: Proceedings of the International Conference organized by the Katholieke Universiteit Leuven from the 10th to the 14th of April, 1978*, OLA 5–6, ed. E. Lipinski. Leuven, 1979, pp. 505–515.
Pierce, R. H. "Land Use, Social Organization and Temple Economy." *Royal Anthropological Institute Newsletter (RAIN)* 15 (August 1976): 15–17.
Quaegebeur, J. "Documents égyptiens et rôle économique du clergé en Égypte hellénistique." In *State and Temple Economy in the Ancient Near East*, ed. E. Lipinski. Leuven, 1979, pp. 707–729.

AS ARCHITECTURAL CONCEPT

Arnold, D. *Wandrelief und Raumfunktion in ägyptischen Tempeln des Neuen Reiches*. MÄS 3 Berlin, 1962.
Baines, J. "Temple Symbolism." *Royal Anthropological Institute Newsletter (RAIN)* 15 (August 1976): 10–15.
Bonnet, H. "Tempel." In *Reallexikon der ägyptischen Religionsgeschichte*. Berlin, 1952, pp. 778–788.
Finnestad, R. B. *Image of the World and Symbol of the Creator*. SOR 10. Wiesbaden, 1985.
Kurth, D. "Eine Welt aus Stein, Bild und Wort: Gedanken zur ägyptischen Tempeldekoration." In *5000 Jahre Ägypten: Genese und Permanenz pharaonischer Kunst*, ed. J. Assmann and G. Burkard. Nussloch, 1983, pp. 89–101.
Otto, E. In *Ägyptische Kunst*, by M. Hirmer and E. Otto. Munich, 1971, pp. 13–43.
Shafer, B. E., ed. *Temples of Ancient Egypt*. Ithaca, 1997.
Teichmann, F. *Der Mensch und sein Tempel: Ägypten*. Stuttgart, 1978.
van de Walle, B. "Le Temple égyptien d'après Strabon." In *Hommages à Waldemar Deonna*. CL 28. Brussels, 1957, pp. 480–508.
Winter, E. *Untersuchungen zu den ägyptischen Tempelreliefs der griechisch-römischen Zeit*. DÖAW Wien 98. Vienna, 1968.

Cult Statues

Hornung, E. "Der Mensch als 'Bild Gottes' in Ägypten." In *Die Gottebenbildlichkeit des Menschen*, ed. O. Loretz. Munich, 1967, pp. 123–156.
Morenz, S. *Egyptian Religion*. Trans. Ann E. Keep. Ithaca, 1973, pp. 150–156.

Egyptian Cult

Alliot, M. *Le Culte d'Horus à Edfou*. Bibl. d'Ét. 20. 2 vols. Cairo, 1949 and 1954.
Altenmüller, H. "Feste." In *LÄ*. Vol. 2. Wiesbaden, 1976, cols. 171–191.
Altenmüller-Kesting, B. "Reinigungsriten im ägyptischen Kult." Ph.D. diss., Hamburg University, 1968.
Assmann, J. "Das ägyptische Prozessionsfest." In *Das Fest und das Heilige: Religiöse Kontrapunkte zur Alltagswelt*, ed. J. Assmann and T. Sundermeier. SVR 1. Gütersloh, 1991, pp. 105–122.
Barta, W. "Kult." In *LÄ*. Vol. 2. Wiesbaden, 1976, cols. 839–848.
David, R. *A Guide to Religious Ritual at Abydos*. 2d ed. Warminster, 1981.

Dunand, F., and C. Zivie-Coche. *Dieux et hommes en Égypte 3000 av. J.C.–395 apr. J.C.*. Paris, 1991, pp. 80–112.

Fairman, H. W. "Worship and Festivals in an Egyptian Temple." *BJRL* 37 (1954): 165–203.

Meeks, D., and C. Favard-Meeks. *Daily Life of the Egyptian Gods*. Trans. G. M. Gosgarian. Ithaca, 1996, pp. 187–198.

Moret, A. *Le Rituel du culte divin journalier en Égypte d'après les papyrus de Berlin et les textes du temple de Séti Ier à Abydos*. Annales du Musée Guimet BE 14. Paris, 1902. Reprint, Geneva, 1988.

Nelson, H. H. "Certain Reliefs at Karnak and Medinet Habu and the Ritual of Amenophis I." *JNES* 8 (1949): 201–232 and 310–345.

Otto, E. *Das ägyptische Mundöffnungsritual*. 2 vols. Äg. Abh. 3. Wiesbaden, 1960.

Roeder, G. *Kulte, Orakel und Naturverehrung im alten Ägypten. Die ägyptische Religion in Texten und Bildern*. Vol. 3. Zurich, 1960.

S. Abd el Azim el-Adly. "Das Gründungs- und Weihritual des ägyptischen Tempels von der frühgeschichtlichen Zeit bis zum Ende des NR." Ph.D. diss., Tübingen University, 1981.

Sauneron, S. *Les Fêtes religieuses d'Esna aux dernier siècles du paganisme. Le Temple d'Esna*. Vol. 5. Cairo, 1962.

———. *The Priests of Ancient Egypt*. Trans. D. Lorton. Ithaca, 2000.

Chapter 3

Cosmography of Visible Reality

Edel, E. *Zu den Inschriften auf den Jahreszeitenreliefs der "Weltkammer" aus dem Sonnenheiligtum des Niuserre*. Vol. 1. NAWG 1961/8. Göttingen, 1961; Vol. 2. NAWG 1963/4. Göttingen, 1963; Vol. 3. NAWG 1963/5. Göttingen, 1963.

Cosmography of Invisible Reality

Assmann, J. *Der König als Sonnenpriester: Ein kosmographischer Begleittext zur kultischen Sonnenhymnik in thebanischen Tempeln und Gräbern*. ADAIK 7. Glückstadt, 1970.

Hornung, E. *Ägyptische Unterweltsbücher*. 2d ed. Zurich, 1984.

———. *The Ancient Egyptian Books of the Afterlife*. Trans. D. Lorton. Ithaca, 1999.

———. *Die Nachtfahrt der Sonne: Eine altägyptische Beschreibung des Jenseits*. Zurich, 1991.

———. *Liturgische Lieder an den Sonnengott: Untersuchungen zur altägyptischen Hymnik*. MÄS 19. Berlin, 1969.

———. *Re und Amun: Die Krise des polytheistischen Weltbilds im Ägypten der 18.–20. Dynastie*. OBO 51. Freiburg and Göttingen, 1983, ch. 1.

Neugebauer, O. and R. A. Parker. *Egyptian Astronomical Texts*. Vol. 1, *The Early Decans*. BES 3. London, 1960.

Wente, E. F. "Mysticism in Pharaonic Egypt?" *JNES* 41 (1982): 161–179.

Natura Loquitur

Assmann, J. "Königsdogma und Heilserwartung: Politische und kultische Chaosbeschreibungen in ägyptischen Texten." In *Apocalypticism in the Mediterranean World and the Near East: Proceedings of the International Colloquium on Apocalypticism, Upssala, August 12–17, 1979*, ed. D. Hellholm. Tübingen, 1983, pp. 345–377.

———. "Solar Discourse: Ancient Egyptian Ways of World-Reading." *DVLG* 68 (1994): 107–122.

Derchain, P. *Le Papyrus Salt 825 (B.M. 10051): Rituel pour la conservation de la vie en Égypte.* Brussels, 1965.

———. "Le Rôle du roi d'Égypte dans le maintien de l'ordre cosmique." In *Le Pouvoir et le sacré.* Brussels, 1961.

———. "Perpetuum Mobile." *OLA* 6/7 (1975/76): 153–154.

Hornung, E. "Verfall und Regeneration der Schöpfung." *Eranos* 47 (1977): 411–449.

Cosmos and Time

Assmann, J. "Das Doppelgesicht der Zeit im altägyptischen Denken." In *Die Zeit*, ed. A. Peisl and A. Mohler. Munich, 1983, pp. 189–223.

———. *Zeit und Ewigkeit im alten Ägypten: Ein Beitrag zur Geschichte der Ewigkeit.* AHAW 1975/1. Heidelberg, 1975.

Hornung, E. "Zeitliches Jenseits im alten Ägypten." *Eranos* 47 (1978): 269–307.

Chapter 4

The "Name Formula"

Altenmüller, H. *MDAIK* 22 (1967): 9–18.

Brunner, H. "Name, Namen und Namenlosigkeit Gottes im alten Ägypten." In *Der Name Gottes*, ed. H. v. Stietencron. Düsseldorf, 1975, pp. 33–49.

Schott, S. *Mythe und Mythenbildung im alten Ägypten.* UGAÄ 15. Leipzig, 1945, esp. pp. 30–32.

Sacred Word and Sacred Knowledge

Assmann, J. *ÄHG.* Zurich, 1975, pp. 26–54.

———. "Death and Initiation in the Funerary Religion of Ancient Egypt." In *Religion and Philosophy in Ancient Egypt*, ed. W. K. Simpson. YES 3. New Haven, 1989, pp. 135–139.

———. *LL.* Berlin, 1969, pp. 363–372.

———. *Re und Amun.* Chapter 2.

Zandee, J. "Das Schöpferwort im alten Ägypten." In *Verbum: Essays on Some Aspects of the Religious Function of Words, Dedicated to Dr. H. W. Obbink, Professor in the History of Religions and Egyptology, University of Utrecht, on November 14th, 1964*, ed. van Baaren, Th. P., et al. Utrecht, 1964, pp. 33–66.

Ritual and Myth

Otto, E. *Das Verhältnis von Rite und Mythos im alten Ägypten.* SHAW 1958. Heidelberg, 1958.

Language and Personality

Assmann, J. *LL.* Berlin, 1969. pp. 333–359.

———. "Persönlichkeitsbegriff und -bewusstsein." In *LÄ*, ed. W. Helck and E. Otto. Vol. 4. Wiesbaden, 1980, cols. 963–978.

———. *Re und Amun.* Chapter 2.

Chapter 5

General Treatments of the Problem of Myth in Ancient Egypt

Assmann, J. "Die Verborgenheit des Mythos in Ägypten." *GM* 25 (1977): 7–43.
———. "Die Zeugung des Sohnes: Bild, Spiel, Erzählung und das Problem des ägyptischen Mythos." In *Funktionen und Leistungen des Mythos: Drei altorientalische Beispiele*, ed. J. Assmann, W. Burkert, and F. Stolz. OBO 49. Freiburg and Göttingen, 1982, pp. 13–61.
Brunner-Traut, E. *Gelebte Mythen: Beiträge zum altägyptischen Mythos.* Darmstadt, 1981.
———. "Mythos." In *LÄ*, ed. W. Helck and E. Otto. Vol. 4. Wiesbaden, 1980, cols. 277–286.
Schott, S. *Mythe und Mythenbildung im alten Ägypten.* UGAAe 15. Leipzig, 1945.

The Pictorial Nature ("Iconicity") of Egyptian Myths

Assmann, J. "Die Zeugung des Sohnes: Bild, Spiel, Erzählung und das Problem des ägyptischen Mythos. In *Funktionen und Leistungen des Mythos: Drei altorientalische Beispiele*, ed. J. Assmann, W. Burkert, and F. Stolz. OBO 49. Freiburg and Göttingen, 1982, pp. 13–61.
——— *Re und Amun* Chapter 2.
Hornung, E. "Die Tragweite der Bilder." *Eranos* 48 (1979): 183–237.

The Myth of the Heavenly Cow

Hornung, E. *Der ägyptische Mythos von der Himmelskuh: Eine Ätiologie des Unvollkommenen.* OBO 46. Freiburg and Göttingen, 1982.

The Myth of the Divine Birth of the King

Assmann, J. "Die Zeugung des Sohnes: Bild, Spiel, Erzählung und das Problem des ägyptischen Mythos." In *Funktionen und Leistungen des Mythos: Drei altorientalische Beispiele*, ed. J. Assmann, W. Burkert, and F. Stolz. OBO 49. Freiburg and Göttingen, 1982, pp. 13–61.
Brunner, H. *Die Geburt des Gottkönigs: Studien zur Überlieferung eines altägyptischen Mythos.* Äg. Abh. 10. Wiesbaden, 1964.

Cosmogony

Assmann, J. "Schöpfung." In *LÄ*, ed. W. Helck and E. Otto. Vol. 5. Wiesbaden, 1984, cols. 677–690.
Sauneron, S., and J. Yoyotte, "La Naissance du monde selon l'Égypte ancienne." In *La Naissance du monde: Égypte ancienne, Sumer, Akkad, Hourrites et Hittites, Canaan, Israel, Islam, Turcs et Mongols, Iran préislamique, Inde, Siam, Laos, Tibet, Chine.* SO 1. Paris, 1959, pp. 17–91.

The Myth of Osiris

Assmann, J. "Das Bild des Vaters im alten Ägypten." In *Das Vaterbild in Mythos und Geschichte: Ägypten, Griechenland, Altes Testament, Neues Testament*, ed. H. Tellenbach. Stuttgart, 1976, pp. 29–49.
Griffiths, J. G. *The Origins of Osiris and His Cult.* SHR 40. Leiden, 1980.

Münster, M. *Untersuchungen zur Göttin Isis vom Alten Reich bis zum Ende des Neuen Reiches*. MÄS 11. Berlin, 1968.

Chapter 6

Albrektson, B. *History and the Gods: An Essay on the Idea of Historical Events as Divine Manifestations in the Ancient Near East and in Israel*. CB 1. Lund, 1967.

Assmann, J. "Königsdogma und Heilserwartung: Politische und kultische Chaosbeschreibungen in altägyptischen Texten." In *Apocalypticism in the Mediterranean World and in the Near East: Proceedings of the International Colloquium on Apocalypticism, Uppsala, August 12–17, 1979*, ed. D. Hellholm. Tübingen, 1983, pp. 336–359.

——. "Krieg und Frieden im alten Ägypten: Ramses II. und die Schlacht bei Kadesch." *MF* 83/84 (1983): 175–230.

——. "Tod und Initiation im altägyptischen Totenglauben." In *Sehnsucht nach dem Ursprung: Zu Mircea Eliade*, ed. H. P. Duerr. Frankfurt am Main, 1983, pp. 336–359.

——. "Weisheit, Loyalismus und Frömmigkeit." In *Studien zu altägyptischen Lebenslehren*, ed. E. Hornung and O. Keel. OBO 28. Freiburg and Göttingen, 1979, pp. 11–72.

Borghouts, J. F. *Ancient Egyptian Magical Texts*. NISABA 9. Leiden, 1978.

Cancik, H., ed. *Rausch, Ekstase, Mystik: Grenzformen religiöser Erfahrung*. Düsseldorf, 1978.

Hornung, E. *Geschichte als Fest*. Darmstadt, 1966.

von Känel, F. *Les Prêtres-ouab de Sekhmet et les conjurateurs de Serqet*. BEHE 87. Paris, 1984.

Wente, E. F. "Mysticism in Pharaonic Egypt?" *JNES* 41 (1982): 161–179.

Chapter 8

General (on Intellectual History from the End of the Old Kingdom to the Middle Kingdom)

Assmann, J. "Schrift, Tod und Identität: Das Grab als Vorschule der Literatur im alten Ägypten." In *Schrift und Gedächtnis: Beiträge zur Archäologie der literarischen Kommunikation*, ed. A. Assmann, J. Assmann, and C. Hardmeier. Munich, 1983, pp. 64–93.

Breasted, J. H. *Development of Religion and Thought in Ancient Egypt: Lectures Delivered on the Morse Foundation at Union Theological Seminary*. New York, 1912, pp. 165–311.

Posener, G. *Littérature et politique dans l'Égypte de la XIIe dynastie*. BEHE 307. Paris, 1956.

The "Reproach of God"

Fecht, G. *Der Vorwurf an Gott in den "Mahnworten des Ipu-wer": Zum geistigen Krise der Ersten Zwischenzeit und ihrer Bewältigung*. AHAW 1972. Berlin, 1972.

Gardiner, A. H. *The Admonitions of an Egyptian Sage from a Hieratic Papyrus in Leiden (Pap. Leiden 344 recto)*. Leipzig, 1909.

Otto, E. *Der Vorwurf an Gott: Zur Entstehung der ägyptischen Auseinandersetzungsliteratur*. Hildesheim, 1951.

The Instruction for Merikare

Blumenthal, E. "Die Lehre für König Merikare." *ZÄS* 107 (1980): 5–41.
Helck, W. *Die Lehre für König Merikare.* Wiesbaden, 1977.
Volten, A. *Zwei altägyptische politische Schriften: Die Lehre für König Merikarê (Pap. Carlsberg VI) und die Lehre des Königs Amenemhet.* An. Aeg. 4. Copenhagen, 1945.
Quack, J. F. *Studien zur Lehre für Merikare.* GOF 23. Wiesbaden, 1992.

Coffin Texts Spell 1130

Fecht, G. *Der Vorwurf an Gott in den "Mahnworten des Ipu-wer": Zum geistigen Krise der Ersten Zwischenzeit und ihrer Bewältigung.* AHAW 1972. Berlin, 1972, pp. 120–127.
Otto, E. "Zur Komposition von Coffin Texts 1130." In *Fragen an die altägyptische Literatur: Studien zum Gedenken an Eberhard Otto,* ed. J. Assmann, E. Feucht, and R. Grieshammer. Wiesbaden, 1977, pp. 1–18.
Schenkel, W. "Soziale Gleichheit und soziale Ungleichheit und die ägyptische Religion." In *"Vor Gott sind alle gleich": Soziale Gleichheit, soziale Ungleichheit, und die Religionen,* ed. G. Kehrer. Dusseldorf, 1983, pp. 26–41.

Coffin Texts Spell 80

Allen, J. P. *Genesis in Egypt: The Philosophy of Ancient Egyptian Creation Accounts.* YES 2. New Haven, 1988, pp. 21–27.
de Buck, A. *Plaats en betekenis van Sjoe in de egyptische theologie.* MKAW 10/9. Amsterdam, 1947.
Zandee, J. "Sargtext Spruch 80." *ZÄS* 101 (1974): 62–79.

Chapter 9

Amun-Re Theology of Dynasty 18

Assmann, J. *Egyptian Solar Religion in the New Kingdom.* Trans. A. Alcock. London, 1995, pp. 102–132.

Amarna Religion and the "New Solar Theology"

Assmann, J. "Akhanyati's Theology of Light and Time." *Proceedings of the Israel Academy of Sciences and Humanities,* VII 4. Jerusalem, 1992, pp. 143–176.
———. "Aton, Atonheiligtümer." In *LÄ.* Vol. 1. Wiesbaden, 1975, cols. 526–549.
———. *Der eine Gott und der dreieine Gott : Das Gottesverständnis bei Christen, Juden und Muslimen,* ed. K. Rahner. Freiburg, 1983, pp. 48–66.
———. "Die 'Häresie' des Echnaton von Amarna: Aspekte der Amarna-Religion." *Saeculum* 22 (1972): 109–126.
———. "Die 'Loyalistische Lehre Echnatons.'" *SAK* 8 (1980): 1–32.
———. *Egyptian Solar Religion in the New Kingdom,* pp. 67–101.
Hornung, E. *Akhenaten and the Religion of Light.* Trans. D. Lorton. Ithaca, 1999.
———. *Conceptions of God in Ancient Egypt: The One and the Many.* Trans. J. Baines. Ithaca, 1996, pp. 244–250.
———. *Monotheismus im alten Israel und seiner Umwelt,* ed. O. Keel. Bibl. Beitr. 14. Freiburg, 1980, pp. 83–97.
———. *Re und Amun,* pp. 96–143.
Redford, D. B. *Akhenaten the Heretic King.* Princeton, 1984.

Schlögl, H. A. *Echnaton-Tutanchamun: Fakten und Texte*. Wiesbaden, 1983, pp. 71–88.

Ramesside Religion

Assmann, J. *ÄHG*, Zurich, 1975, pp. 66–77.
———. *Egyptian Solar Religion in the New Kingdom*, pp. 133–210.
———. *Moses the Egyptian: The Memory of Egypt in Western Monotheism.*
Cambridge, 1997, pp. 23–44 and 168–192.
———. "Primat und Transzendenz: Struktur und Genese der ägyptischen
Vorstellung eines 'Höchsten Wesens.'" In *Aspekte der spätägyptischen Religion*,
ed. W. Westendorf. GOF 9. Wiesbaden, 1979, pp. 7–40.
———. "Weisheit, Loyalismus und Frömmigkeit." In *Studien zu altägyptischen
Lebenslehren*, ed. E. Hornung and O. Keel. OBO 28. Freiburg and Göttingen,
1979, pp. 11–72.
———. *Zeit und Ewigkeit im alten Ägypten: Ein Beitrag zur Geschichte der
Ewigkeit*. AHAW 1975/1. Heidelberg, 1975, pp. 49–71.
Baines, J. "Society, Morality, and Religious Practice." In *Religion in Ancient
Egypt: Gods, Myths, and Personal Practice*, ed. B. E. Shafer. Ithaca, 1991, pp.
123–200.
Borghouts, J. F. "Divine Intervention in Ancient Egypt and Its Manifestations
(*b3w*)." In *Gleanings from Deir el Medîna*, ed. R. J. Demarée and J. J. Janssen.
EU 1. Leiden, 1982, pp. 1–70.
Breasted, J. H. *Development of Religion and Thought in Ancient Egypt: Lectures
Delivered on the Morse Foundation at Untion Theological Seminary.* New York,
1912, pp. 344–370.
Brunner, H. "Der freie Wille Gottes in der ägyptischen Weisheit." *Les Sagesses
du Proche Orient ancien: Colloque de Strasbourg, 17–19 mai, 1962.* Paris, 1963,
pp. 103–117.
———. "Persönliche Frömmigkeit." In *LÄ*, ed. W. Helck and E. Otto. Vol. 4.
Wiesbaden, 1980, cols. 951–963.
———. *Grundzüge der ägyptischen Religion.* Darmstadt, 1983, pp. 103–121.
Junge, F. "Isis und die ägyptischen Mysterien." In *Aspekte der spätägyptischen
Religion*, ed. W. Westendorf. GOF 9. Wiesbaden, 1979, pp. 93–115.
———. "Wirklichkeit und Abbild: Zum innerägyptischen Synkretismus und
zur Weltsicht der Hymnen des Neuen Reichs." In *Synkretismusforschung,
Theorie und Praxis*, ed. G. Wiessner. Göttinger Orientforschungen, Reihe
Grundlagen und Ergebnisse 1 Wiesbaden, 1978, pp. 87–108.

Index

Note: Page numbers followed by *f* indicate figures.

DATE DUE